"I came that they may have life and life to the full."
—The Gospel of John

Bernardin: Life to the Full

Bernardin: Life to the Full

Eugene Kennedy

Bonus Books, Inc., Chicago

01   00   99   98   97   5   4   3   2

Library of Congress Catalog Card Number: 96-80273

International Standard Book Number: 1-56625-082-X

Bonus Books, Inc.
160 East Illinois Street
Chicago, Illinois 60611

Expanded from the hardcover edition titled *Cardinal Bernardin*

Composition by Point West, Inc., Carol Stream, IL

Printed in the United States of America

For Reggie Ho

Preface

This book is intended, not as an exhaustive biography, but as a psychological portrait of America's most influential cardinal-archbishop, Joseph Louis Bernardin. In a way, this is also a portrait of the kind of men who reach such high positions in the Roman Catholic Church. While the long gallery of their likenesses reveals great individual differences in the Americans who have become ecclesiastical princes, they share striking similarities as well. In learning about Joseph Bernardin we learn something about all of them and of the church that called them to their high rank and expects unquestioned loyalty and dedication from them.

All have been "churchmen" as that term is employed in this account of Bernardin's life and career. Men of varied faults and virtues—if we have had kindly pastors we have had pompous tyrants, too—their personalities have been marked by dutifulness, by an intense readiness if not a need, to carry out whatever the church asks of them. There is no doubt that these ecclesiastical leaders—"overseers" as the Greek for bishop puts it—have often paid an internal price for their institutional dedication but they pay it nonetheless. The word Cardinal comes from the Latin word for "hinge." These men of the scarlet cloth are meant to hold things together, to maintain the organizational integrity and unity of teaching and tradition of the church. They are fundamentally men of the church, and of the faith as the church teaches it, men committed to husband the institution and its eternal claims in the unforgiving field of time.

This portrait of Bernardin is painted against the background of his generation's experience of both Catholicism and America. He has lived in and been a part of an interesting epoch and his story and the cluster of human stories that surround it reveal twentieth century American Catholicism as no charts or percentage points ever can.

Cardinal Bernardin recapitulates in his own life a narrative classic to America and to his faith. The son of Italian immigrants, he was born in the same year that Al Smith went down in a humiliating defeat in a presidential campaign lighted by clansmen's torches. The raging anti-Catholic propaganda raised the spectre of the pope's coming to the White House. Just too young for World War II, Bernardin entered the seminary in the last great swell of vocations that provided record breaking ordination classes in the fifties and seemed a guarantee of a culture that was entering a gilded age of success in the United States.

As a young priest, he witnessed the election of the first Catholic president and, as a relatively young archbishop, the arrival of Pope John Paul II, in ironic and unexpected fulfillment of every hateful prophecy of the 1928 election, in front of a Baptist president's White House. Achieving the dream of every well-scrubbed seminarian of his time in becoming the cardinal-archbishop of America's most powerful archdiocese, Bernardin has confronted ironies of his own. He has been called to give leadership to a church and its encompassing national culture radically different from that in which he and his classmates first aspired to the priesthood.

The golden age that Catholicism had seemed to be entering in the early sixties turned out to be the last act of the glorious period of its enormous immigrant growth and establishment. The Catholic culture in America did not, however, as many gloomy observers contend, collapse because the supporting arches of faith were eaten away by the infections of Vatican Council II. It outgrew itself, changed because it had succeeded so remarkably in educating its young and becoming a part of what is known as mainstream America. The events through which Bernardin has lived and served were shaped by the colorful, panoramic parade of that culture. If he became a priest and then a bishop in the twilight of the influence of an Irish dominated hierarchy, he was called to administer the church through those tumultuous decades when their power—and their style—waned in Catholicism.

As it might be said that Mario Cuomo was the first Italian-American to achieve national political eminence, so Bernardin was the first Italian-American to become a prince of the church. His Mediterranean soul has been an enormous asset in mediating the conflicts of post-conciliar Catholicism. Many Irish hierarchs seemed to enjoy a good fight, but Bernardin has always sought for human compromises that avoid clashes while honoring the integrity of the disputing parties. His central commitment has been to the development of structures that would properly institutionalize the processes of collegial reflection and discussion mandated by Vatican II.

Bernardin's calmness and self-containment have sustained him through an extraordinary range of experiences. Sometimes the incidents in which he has been involved, such as those surrounding Cardinal Cody's last sad and embattled years, possessed the surreal quality that invests life when empires are tottering and the rules of a previous order lose their force. The notion that a cardinal-archbishop might be investigated by the federal government was unthinkable during the great years of Catholic ascendancy; that it happened signalled the advanced state of inner decay of old-fashioned, pre-conciliar style institutional authority. Bernardin's task was to refurbish that authority by casting it into a new non-imperious collegial form.

Other developments, such as Bernardin's overseeing the composition of a pastoral letter that challenged Reagan administration policy on nuclear arms, were signs that the new Catholicism—reflective, socially involved, collegially organized—was being successfully implemented. At the core of almost every major event of post-conciliar American Catholicism Bernardin stands as the mediating leader. He has always proceeded with an appreciation of the fallen condition of human beings, which makes him the forgiving and realistic pastor, and with hopes that room will be made for the consistent and steady growth of a continually changing church, which makes him a patient and idealistic churchman.

Perhaps that word *churchman* describes Bernardin better than any other. It captures the essential qualities that bishops are expected to possess and one that is the source of enormous structural, or bureaucratic, strength for the church as an organization. The leaders mentioned in this book, including such figures as John Cardinal O'Connor of New York, and Archbishop Rembert Weakland of Milwaukee, are, like Bernardin, churchmen in this sense. Prelates such as these provide cohesion and stability for the great organizational life of Catholicism, for the visible bureaucratic church that seems to sit immovably as Buddha in the world's imagination.

Bernardin does this, not so much through dramatic or charismatic gestures whose effects sometimes quickly dissipate, but through establishing organizational changes that will outlast the present and still bear the weight of the future. He is, in a real sense, a prince of bureaucrats, an obsessive worker whose personal life is one with his public life. There is nothing hidden about this remarkable man who, with dedication that, like a grindstone that can outlast any sword, takes on successive ecclesiastical challenges with practiced consistency. His greatest strength lies in his personality even though, as a prime strategy in his introducing practical collegiality into the church, he has attempted to submerge himself beneath the collaborative processes that are its foundation.

The truth, however, is that Bernardin the man—quiet, diligent, undramatic—is not easily separated from the processes to whose institutionalization he has devoted so much energy. He breathes a spirit into these procedures that transforms them from potentially dull administrative routines into vehicles for cooperation and progress. Under his guidance they become politically viable theological pathways, wide enough for all sides to walk on. While he has consistently placed the emphasis on policy that will last rather than personality that will fade, Bernardin has, to a large extent, been the reason that, in so many crises, collegial procedures have proven effective.

This psychological rendering reveals, then, a master administrator whose faith, intelligence and human sensitivity have prepared him well for his role as a contemporary church leader, for being a churchman in the classical sense. He understands his vocation to preserve the church as a visible organized vehicle that will continue to house and give religious identity to Catholics. This is not easy in an age in which many Catholics acknowledge but no longer bow automatically to church structures.

This portrait resembles Gilbert Stuart's of George Washington. It is necessarily unfinished and leaves a satisfying aura of mystery, a suggestion of unknowability, a hint of tales yet to be told, of a destiny not yet fulfilled. This book will help the reader appreciate the manner in which Bernardin, with his brother bishops, works through the already evident challenges to the institutional wholeness of American Catholicism. For if Catholics, and other believers, seek a deeper spirituality as the new century and the space age fully dawn, they also question whether familiar religious institutions, such as highly organized Roman Catholicism, can provide it for them. Bernardin's story is far from over but, perhaps more than that of any of his colleagues, his will continue to parallel and to reflect the larger narrative of American Catholicism.

Eugene Kennedy
June 1989

I

L
ike G.K. Chesterton's Father Brown, Joseph L.
Bernardin, archbishop of Chicago for just five
months, did not often look at himself in the mirror.
But on this glowing Roman winter morning in 1983 as he shaved in
the bathroom of his plain, motel-like suite in the Villa Stritch, a residence for priests set among umbrella pines near the Pamphili Park
away from the center of the eternal city, he half-smiled at his reflection. He could not help but think of the pilgrimage, unlikely in itself
and unlike that of most other Americans who had risen to powerful
positions in the Roman Catholic Church, that had brought him to this
moment. A long journey, he mused silently, for a little first generation Italian-American boy who grew up during the Depression in a
Protestant neighborhood in Columbia, South Carolina, to find himself
about to receive the red hat of a cardinal from the hands of the pope.

He placed the Braun electric razor back into its case. The interval between his becoming Chicago's archbishop and his being named
a cardinal had been hardly more than a hundred days and was without parallel in American Catholic history. The ceremony of his installation had taken place only the previous August 25, the feast of St.
Louis . . .

Archbishop Pio Laghi, the Vatican Nuncio to the United States, had
presided and had read the official rescript of Bernardin's appointment, signalling its significance in the tone of his voice. Laghi, the
trained diplomat whose measured gestures were ordinarily as unre-
vealing as those of an ambassador who had not yet examined the

treaty terms, had paused almost imperceptibly, raised his brown eyes that twinkled in the summer light that floated through Holy Name Cathedral. *"Maxima,"* he said, subtly inflecting the adjective that described the archdiocese of Chicago. *Maxima,* the largest.

Laghi took delight in the word as a sommelier did in a sip of the finest vintage. He glanced at the power structure of American bishops gathered in the sanctuary, compressing into its utterance the fullest nuance of the historical, territorial, and ecclesiastical prominence of the see whose burdens and glories were in that hour being transferred to the 54-year-old Joseph Louis Bernardin. That the silken, silver haired Laghi unmistakably expressed a sense of relief that he was in place surprised nobody who had followed the dramatic and troubling events of the previous year. These incidents had brought shock, grief, and scandal to Catholic Chicago and had almost destroyed the career of Bernardin, then an innocent bystander as the archbishop of Cincinnati.

John Cardinal Cody had served as archbishop of Chicago since 1965, the year of the last session of Vatican Council II. He had arrived, fittingly enough, by train, as if out of the past, to a city that was to become a fierce example of the whole country's shattering collision with the future. Having previously served as archbishop of New Orleans and Kansas City, John Patrick Cody had longed to become archbishop of Chicago to place a scarlet seal on the career he had pursued single-mindedly since his Roman ordination on Dec. 8, 1931. If most American boys of Cody's era dreamed of becoming president of the United States, Catholic youths with an interest in the priesthood imagined themselves as crimson clad princes of their church. This mixture of Horatio Alger and earnest Catholic aspiration was sentimentally idealized, appropriately enough, at mid-century, near the high-point of the American immigrant church's greatest flowering, in Henry Morton Robinson's hugely successful novel, *The Cardinal*. This apex of the pre-Vatican II American Catholic culture found it a respectable, achieving presence, expressed in universities, churches, schools, and in the great numbers of priests and religious men and women who supervised and staffed them. All of these accomplishments were the fruits of the sacrifices of the immigrant peoples who had given not only their hard earned money to build the church but also their sons and daughters to serve it.

The apple-cheeked and amiable Cody was, in fact, a classic example of the bright ecclesiastic who rode the tide of Catholic assimilation that flowed to a bishop's mitre and beyond. The son of a St. Louis fireman, Cody had played at saying Mass as a child, cutting vestments out of the newspapers. Because of his intelligence and drive he was chosen to complete his seminary theological training in Rome, a move then considered the first essential step for youths who would later be selected for influential positions in the church. The young Cody loved the Tiber more than the Mississippi, understanding well that the friendships his geniality helped him to forge with other men studying in the shadow of St. Peter's would serve him well later.

Cody's career followed the pattern of many other able and ambitious young American priests for whom the church was not only a theological mystery but also a rich and magical world as wonderful as a treasure cave out of Aladdin. In his authorized biography, Francis Cardinal Spellman, archbishop of New York from 1939 to 1967, describes candidly the way young seminarians attached themselves to Roman cardinalatial patrons, mastering the rules of ecclesiastical advancement even before they were ordained priests. Americans might speak of "having a vocation" to the priesthood but Romans spoke of "making a career" in the church. Cody grasped the significance of combining an ideal of service with an ambitious plan for his future.

Cody's Irish ancestry was another attribute that suited him for advancement in the American church. The Irish, perhaps because they already spoke English and settled in large metropolitan areas, also took over Police Departments and City Halls as well as the management of the church. Irish Catholics still predominate in the American hierarchy and, in fact, Bernardin's appointment was the first of an Italian-American to a large American archdiocese. Cody, blessed by Gaelic lineage and Roman training, on his return to St. Louis quickly involved himself in the administration of the diocese, becoming a trusted aide and chancellor to Archbishop John Glennon. He accompanied Glennon to Rome when the latter was made a cardinal in the first post World War II consistory in 1946.

Glennon was his mentor and when the latter fell ill in Ireland returning from Rome, Cody chose to stay at his deathbed even though his own mother was gravely ill back at home. This was the kind of sacrificial loyalty that the institutional church did not overlook. He was named an auxiliary bishop in the next year. Cody went on to prove his devotion to Mother Church many times after that and, it was said, had successfully promoted his own selection as archbishop of Chicago through employing the network of his old Roman acquaintances, including Pope Paul VI, after the quiet, scholarly Albert Cardinal Meyer died of a brain tumor in April 1965.

Cody arrived, however, just as the regal phase of Catholic life in which he had grown up was changing drastically. His manner might have been suitable for the Chicago of 1935 when the then Cardinal, George Mundelein, was driven throughout the archdiocese by a leather-legginged chauffeur in a limousine with crimson strutted wheels. But Cody's imperial style, the product of his training and experience, was to prove disastrous in the era in which authoritarianism would be savagely challenged in both church and state. Through 17 years of conflict and recrimination with many of his priests as well as members of religious orders and large numbers of laity, Cody, an obsessive worker supremely confident that he was preserving church authority, continued to be the unreconstructed, arbitrary leader from an earlier page of history.

On Sept. 10, 1981, the *Chicago Sun Times* published a sensational front page story revealing that Cody was under federal investigation for the possible misappropriation of church funds and detailing a somewhat ambiguous lifelong close relationship with a woman cousin, Helen Wilson. The last year of Cody's life was grimly counterpointed by recurrent hospitalizations for congestive heart failure, sensational media coverage, and a melancholy gathering of the nation's bishops to celebrate the fiftieth anniversary of his ordination as a priest on Dec. 8, 1981. With the cloud of charges against him undispersed, he died in his sleep on Apr. 25, 1982, in the many chimneyed Northside brick residence in which he had lived reclusively, its splendid old rooms cut up into office space with runners of phosphorescent lighting buzzing above them. Outside, the lawns came to resemble worn Astroturf and the untended gardens became overgrown as the obsessive Cody worked, often through the night on minor tasks, so deep inside his dark wooded pyramid that rumors mounted that he didn't live there at all.

The accusations against Cody, which he interpreted as indirect ways of attacking the church, compounded by the publication of excerpts from Father Andrew Greeley's Roman diary, attracted international press coverage and, like a car out of control, sideswiped Bernardin three hundred miles away in Cincinnati. The latter's name was erroneously associated with an alleged plot, comic opera to the core, to overthrow Cody and to replace him with Bernardin. Chicago, although a city familiar with scandal and an archdiocese accustomed to sin, had been badly shaken by the incident. Its aftershocks were felt throughout the last months of Cody's incumbency.

There had never been anything like the furor over the federal investigation of Cody and the subplots of bubbling clerical mutiny. In an ironic symbolization of the problem, after his death and funeral, Cody's massive coffin would not fit into the silver lined mausoleum crypt prepared for it and the final entombment had to be delayed until corrective measures could be taken. Was Cody's uneasy spirit, that of a man who came to authority out of due time, resisting graceful burial? Or was it just another grim footnote to his anachronistic career? Was it also mirrored in the amazed reactions of the prelates who gathered for his funeral at learning that Cody, having been denied the traditional cardinalatial flat red hat by ceremonial changes after Vatican II, ordered one to be made for himself anyway? Still, this inferior and unauthorized reproduction, the boy's dream Cody would not deny himself, hangs next to the more splendid headgear of his predecessors, catching the Chicago light brilliantly high above the main altar of Holy Name Cathedral.

The Vatican would need to select as a replacement for the embattled Cody an extraordinary bishop of unimpeachable integrity and ability, a peacemaker who could restore the church's reputation and also confer some measure of rest and dignity on Cody's memory. He would also be called on to generate a fresh image of ecclesial authority in the city that might be considered second in the nation but was recognized as first in position and influence in the American Catholic Church. For the Chicago archdiocese, like a crest set on the nation, had long been recognized as a dynamic, progressive center to which other dioceses looked for leadership and direction.

Donning his clerical attire, Bernardin's face betrayed no hint that he recalled the reckless episode that had whirled through his life like a tornado near the end of September 1981, when excerpts were published from journal-like tapes made by Greeley, a Chicago priest, during the late seventies as Greeley was researching a proposed book on the election of the next pope. Afterward, Greeley described the bizarre contents as late night fantasies and wine inspired musings about the possibility of overthrowing Cody and installing Joseph L. Bernardin as his successor, all for the apparent purpose of turning Bernardin into an "inside" conclave source about the forthcoming papal election.

Bernardin had long before put out of his mind those low point weeks during which it seemed possible that his chances of ever becoming archbishop of Chicago had been grievously and permanently damaged by the sensational publicity falsely implying that he had been a party to Greeley's fantastic scenario. Up until that difficult time, most informed church observers had considered Bernardin the best available choice to take on the formidable challenge of healing the wounds that the Chicago church had suffered. Many had worried that he would innocently inherit the lonely destiny of remaining in Cincinnati for the rest of his days. Bernardin liked Cincinnati and would have accepted a permanent assignment there as a sign of God's will. But he would also have borne a reputation that had been unfairly sullied by the outlandish affair. The clerical grapevine would have crackled with stories of how Bernardin had been denied Chicago, and the American church his seasoned leadership, by what amounted to a freak accident.

Raconteurs of priestly stories had often mentioned one of his predecessors in that Ohio River city, Archbishop John McNicholas who had, in fact, found his own career radically altered by an accident of history a little more than forty years before. Patrick Cardinal Hayes of New York had died in the fall of 1938 and the then pope, Pius XI, had decided on McNicholas as the successor to that important post. But before the appointment could be made official, Pius XI died and was succeeded by his secretary of state, Eugenio Cardinal Pacelli, whose friendship had been cultivated by Francis Spellman during the long years he had spent in Rome before becoming an auxiliary bishop of Boston. Spellman was made archbishop of New York by the new Pope Pius XII and McNicholas died many years later, his opportunity for great influence in the American church destroyed by this unexpected turn of events.

A similar hazardous situation had been created by Greeley, a controversial figure who was now, as a Chicago priest, under Bernardin's ecclesiastical jurisdiction. During the few months he had been in Chicago, Bernardin had suffered no lack of advice on how to deal with this priest whose internationally publicized monologue had almost imperiled Bernardin's reputation and sentenced him to live, as McNicholas had, with what Ralph Waldo Emerson called "the sound of things that almost happen" forever in his ears. Bernardin listened noncommittally to all the counsel about what to do with Greeley. He would deal with him as he had with the reporters clamoring for information about Cody's finances after he arrived in Chicago—in his own way and in his own time.

———————————

Bernardin walked slowly down the staircase to the ground floor. He glanced nervously at his watch, a gesture as characteristic and revealing of him as plucking at the sleeve of his coat, the car seat covering, or the table cloth when he felt the pressure of an impending, important engagement. Promptness and exactitude were not only the virtues extolled in the thirties public school classrooms of his childhood, but they were also aspects of the sense of obligation that was seeded deep in the consciousness of all Catholics, especially Americans. The latter's obsessive attitudes toward church rules were thought, in the popular ecclesiastical mythology of the day, to differentiate them sharply from their European counterparts, especially the Italians, who were considered far more casual in their approach to church regulations.

Bernardin's parents, Maria and Joseph, had been dutiful, practical people from the small town of Tonadico in the valley of Primiero. Its simple, chalk white cottages stood out against the vastness of the Dolomite Mountains of Northern Italy. Their common sense piety and hardworking example shaped his perception of duty, whose overriding religious value may be understood by the title of a spiritual book, *The Sacrament of Duty,* popular during Bernardin's seminary years. But this man who within a few hours would be made a cardinal had also been influenced by the Old South whose spirit still strongly pervaded the state of South Carolina during his formative years. His voice, it had once been said, sounded like a softly rustling Confederate flag. As Bernardin moved north in his various assignments, the southern tones had grown fainter and by the time he had arrived in Chicago, they were barely audible.

Now, waiting for the three priest aides who had accompanied him to Rome, he stood tall and rangy, having rigorously dieted off during his years in Cincinnati the weight he had gained during his crowded early years in the priesthood. Beneath his prominent brow his brown eyes looked gently through large lensed glasses. He was, in many ways, not only a worthy prospective prince of the church but also a classic southern gentleman. His reserved, mannered presence—warm but by no means intimate, self-contained as behooved a trusted keeper of hard truths and harder secrets—recapitulated in himself the ante-bellum traditions of courtliness and human sensitivity that respected social customs and gracefully and vigilantly avoided hurt or embarrassment to others.

He looked down at his watch again. It would be a long day packed with several ceremonies that had previously been spread across three days. Studying him closely, one could observe the slight tightening of his jaw muscles and the small quick movements that, like an uncoiling rope behind a harpoon, trailed the contained but intense thrust of his concentration into any approaching field of obligation. He smiled at the three Chicago priests who, in their own way, reflected the history of northern urban Catholicism that was so sharply different from the thinly manned picket lines of the church in the Old South.

Their names—Roache, Keating, and Lyne—were as Irish as their Pat O'Brien faces and their experience had been that of northern big city Catholicism. Each was a good symbol of the handsome fine student that the nuns had cooed over in grammar school and who, from their middle class backgrounds, had entered the seminary system in their first year of high school. There they discovered an extraordinary universe of educational opportunity, something like a yellow brick road that included a major seminary of matched Georgian buildings, a gym and a golf course. This 900-acre world an hour's drive northwest of Chicago, like a fabulous Hollywood backset, also included a museum, a stately reproduction of a New England church, and a brick replica of Washington's home at Mt. Vernon in which the archbishop could take his ease. The seminarians would spend their summers in an exclusive villa four hundred miles north on the trembling waters of a northern lake. They were to be trained as gentleman priests who would lead a life of service and privilege in the thickly Catholic stretches of the archdiocese.

This esteem for the clergy, common in all large northern cities, had been earned for them in previous generations by the priests who had guided, served, and fought for the rights of the arriving immigrant Catholics. The parish priest had often been the only educated man in the clustering immigrant communities and had not only helped fill out his people's citizenship papers and been their intermediary in a hundred challenges of adjustment, but had also campaigned vigorously, especially in organizing the union movement, to secure their economic rights. Generations before priests joined the 1965 civil rights marches in Selma, Alabama, for example, they had marched in behalf of the stockyard workers' strike in Chicago.

Priests such as these high ranking diocesan officials who accompanied Bernardin to Rome, had been in abundant supply until the century's silently forming social, cultural, and religious transformations manifested themselves in Vatican II and in the other wrenching and reordering events of the sixties. Now these priests, well into middle age, two of them to become bishops within the year, were reminders of an older rapidly fragmenting tradition of American Catholic life. These trusted associates reminded Bernardin not only of Chicago's powerful past in the American Catholic Church but of its currently diminishing ranks of clergy and religious, of once flourishing parishes and schools now unsupported and largely empty, of the new waves of Hispanic, Haitian, and Oriental immigrant Catholics far different from the Irish, Polish, and Germans who had been the mainstays of the church in the past.

As Bernardin climbed with his priest associates into the dark Fiat sedan that would take them to the Vatican, he was well aware that the Chicago archdiocese that he had come to lead had enormous new problems. Now that its primary immigrant period had ended, the church was regrouping as a well-educated, professionally oriented, theologically sophisticated people who looked on their church—and on their cardinal—with expectations very different from those of their parents. They did not depend heavily on the church for social acceptance and support. Careers other than religious callings had opened mainstream American life for them. They took seriously their own obligations in conscience and did not automatically fall in line when bishops spoke. Strangely, as their wealth increased, their support for the church had leveled off.

After this day of splendor had drawn to a close, Bernardin would understand the dizzying magnitude of the challenge that waited for him not only in Chicago but in the national church as well. That he was chairman of a committee of American Catholic bishops charged by their colleagues with drawing up a pastoral letter on the morality of nuclear war was not only a sharp indication of how much once unquestioningly patriotic American Catholicism had changed but a responsibility that had involved Bernardin in the tense world of geopolitical maneuver. The ongoing development of the letter had not only disturbed the Reagan administration but it had also raised questions among some curial officials. Bernardin had journeyed to Rome just two weeks before this day to explain the progress of the pastoral letter. The new Chicago archbishop was not naive about the pressing need to do more than just recall American Catholicism's glorious past. If American Catholicism had changed considerably already, it would need collegial rather than authoritarian shepherding to preserve its faith and to prepare it for organic and healthy growth into the twenty-first century.

Still, Bernardin could not look out at the familiar coffee colored buildings of Rome streaming past the car window without thinking of the history and progress of the American church. On this unseasonably warm February 2, the Candlemas feast that brought the liturgical season of Christmas to a close, he was the sole American among the eighteen who would shortly be invested as princes of the Church. No American had been named a cardinal since William Baum, then archbishop of Washington, D.C., in 1976. It was significant that Bernardin had been chosen but strange that the United States, with over fifty million Catholics and a history of faith and generosity unparallelled in Roman Catholicism, had not been given greater recognition in recent years.

Perhaps this was one further indication of the inquiring if not skeptical attitude he had experienced in his sessions with curial officials about the nuclear pastoral letter only a few weeks before. They reflected a more generalized European attitude toward the new world. Some Roman authorities, as the clerical gossips said, viewed American Catholicism as a "superpower church in a superpower country." If John Patrick Cody, delighting in the prerogatives of being the cardinal archbishop of Chicago, had assumed that position in the last sunset glow of a splendid, clergy dominated era, Bernardin experienced the full weight of a church and world greatly changed for both Catholics and cardinals. He also understood that the sun already rode high in the morning sky of this new age.

As the car passed through the gates just off St. Peter's Square and turned toward the Hall of the Nervi where the ceremonies would be held, Bernardin recalled the costly and elegant celebrations that had surrounded the appointments of the cardinal archbishops in that now closed golden era. When Cody had been appointed a cardinal in 1967, two chartered jets were soon filled with pilgrims eager to be present when their archbishop became a cardinal but did not receive the *galero*, a flat, tasseled medieval piece of headgear that, along with long silk trains, had been done away with in reforms of Pope Paul VI after Vatican II.

Cody's action in causing an imitation *galero* to be fabricated was an authentic reflection of his sense of himself as a cardinal of the old school, of his long held ambition from that time in which princes of the church gave vicarious pride to Catholics by living and acting regally, by being as important as the mayor, and living in a house as imposing as the governor's. It seemed natural to Cody, on arriving in Rome to become a cardinal, to settle, with his large party, into a suite at the deluxe Cavalieri Hilton Hotel that looked down on Rome from Monte Mario. Hundreds of Chicagoans, including then Mayor Richard J. Daley and his wife, had journeyed with him to Rome for that moment filled with the echoes of the Catholicism in which they had grown up. The occasion was an illustrious period piece, as glittering and expensive as such triumphant affairs were supposed to be, and additional brilliant parties and receptions were repeated when the entourage returned to Chicago. On the same day that Cody had settled in, Karol Wojtyla, the 47-year-old archbishop of Crakow, arrived quietly from behind the Iron Curtain to become a cardinal. In 1978 he would be elected Pope John Paul II.

As Bernardin vested for the first time in the crimson cassock he would wear for the ceremony, he wondered if his own decision to discourage chartered flights and gala festivities would set a precedent for the future. Bernardin's approach differed from that of his brother cardinal designate, Carlo Maria Martini of Milan, who, for example, had brought 2000 pilgrims with him. Instead, Bernardin had asked that a special collection for the poor be taken up in place of chartering planes and holding expensive Roman fetes.

Having designated half the $120,000 thus raised for good works in Chicago, he had brought the rest as a gift to the pope for his charities. He had booked passage for himself and his priest assistants, along with his closest relatives, on a regular TWA flight from Chicago. Although he was surprised by a small delegation of friends from South Carolina who joined the flight in New York, he had purposely tried to simplify, if not to demythologize, the events surrounding his becoming a cardinal. The southern gentleman had combined with the modest, practical pastor in him: He wanted everything to be correct, dignified, and unassuming. In short, and although he did not advert to it, just like himself.

The cardinals lined up to enter Paul VI Hall, named after the pope who had commissioned it. Designed by the architect Nervi who had also produced the Olympic Palace of Sport, it spoke in a fresh language of expressive construction to the silent majesty of the ancient pillars and towers of the Vatican. It was another example of the way in which Pope Paul VI, who had served from 1963 to 1978, had written his distinctive signature in the very heart of Roman Catholicism. Pope Paul VI had succeeded the charismatic Pope John XXIII and was faced with the enormous task of seeing Vatican Council II through to its conclusion of implementing its reforms. He had a profound appreciation of symbols and gestures and, in the turbulent era of transforming the customs and practices of the church, he understood that emblematic changes, like myths, contained a message and a sense of direction within themselves.

The 18 new cardinals slowly proceeded into the canted hall whose wall was shaped like a huge half eye with a glittering elliptical stained glass pupil. Although they were vested in brilliant red, the woolen garments were far plainer and simpler than the spectacular watered silk of that earlier period, termed "triumphal" by many observers, in which the monarchical model had been central to the church's human understanding and expression of itself. It was no accident, then, that Paul VI had trimmed away so many of the royal incidentals of the College of Cardinals. That was part of his plan to break its Italian dominance and to refurbish and revitalize the college as a more adequate symbol of the universal church. The title cardinal was 1500 years old. It had been derived from the Latin *cardo,* "hinge of a gate," suggesting the seven gates to the wall of ancient Rome. Dominated by Italian prelates it had grown musty, its numbers limited to seventy until Pope John XXIII shattered that tradition shortly after his election in 1958, raising its number to 90 within a year. They were meant to be the pope's closest advisers and in a press conference only the day before Bernardin had noted that Pope John Paul II was, in fact, already calling more often on these special counselors.

If Pope Paul VI had gone on to make the college less a gathering of local princes and more an expression of the many races and pigments of Catholicism, he also knew that he was authoring a change that would have greater effects than a hundred quickly forgotten decrees. In addition, he had begun the process of doing away with the triple papal crown, known as the tiara, for he was thus phasing out the image of the pope as a royal figure, and accenting him as a servant rather than a ruler. Paul had also resisted demands for closing the Vatican Museum in order to sell its treasures. Instead, he had installed a wing of modern art close to the Sistine Chapel, observing at its dedication that the voice of the artist should always be heard in the center of the Catholic Church.

So the Nervi Hall, with room for 7,000, a gracefully curved auditorium, free of pillars, anchored by great struts of concrete, was not an accidental structure. Paul VI had designated it as the site for papal audiences, thus insuring that future popes would be seen in a contemporary setting, as men of the modern world as well as of the ancient traditions so powerfully evoked by the buildings of the Vatican itself. The subtlety of Paul VI was not lost on Bernardin who, in his own rooms, as far back as his friends could remember, had always displayed tasteful modern art along with more familiar religious pictures and statues.

The new archbishop of Chicago also shared with Pope Paul VI, the pontiff who had appointed him a bishop in 1966, an understanding of the achingly difficult task of moving a two thousand-year-old church into a totally new age. No conscientious and loyal churchmen could make sensational transformations overnight. Many good Catholics, after all, had been disturbed by even some of the minor changes that flowed from Vatican II. The ecclesiastical leader who wanted the church to flourish in the twentieth century had to respect its traditions while making sure that it had adequate room in which to grow, as Bernardin often noted, in an "organic" manner toward a new fullness. Like his friend and father figure, John Cardinal Dearden, Bernardin was never the man for the showy, dramatic gesture but rather the thoughtful, careful planner who always looked beyond the moment in his work and decisions. If that disappointed some who wished for more immediate theatrical actions, it worked, as Paul VI's symbols did, toward more gradual, stable, and trustworthy growth.

The new cardinals, just moving into their places in the front row, had not been present at the earlier ceremony of the morning, the so-called "secret consistory" in which the pope met with the men who were already cardinals and who were now seated opposite the Sistine Choir on one side of the great stage-like space. That space was dominated by a swirling, state of the art modern sculpture from which a majestic Christ broke free in resurrection. This convoluted reredos sat like a coral reef through whose porous structure one could see the scarlet fish of ceremonial aides darting in the background. Bernardin took the fourth chair from the center aisle on the right. Directly behind him sat Father James Roache, Chicago's vicar-general or second in command, in a white surplice. Bernardin, along with his brother princes-to-be and almost everybody else in the hall, seemed solemn but happy, like choir members who had just finished a thundering *Gloria* at Christmas eve mass. He thought of the advice that his mother had given him before his ordination to the bishopric seventeen years before. "Walk straight," Maria Bernardin had advised her son, "and try not to look too pleased with yourself."

Bernardin, among the tallest of the new cardinals, glanced quickly down the row of extraordinary men that spread out on either side of him. Among them were 54-year-old Josef Glemp, the archbishop of Warsaw, the short, sloe-eyed prelate to whom the Polish pope had entrusted the leadership of his homeland church. Needing a little help in rising and sitting was the oldest candidate, the 87-year-old Julijans Vaivods of Riga, Latvia, who would be the first cardinal to live in the Soviet Union.

Not far away was the 75-year-old, spade bearded Antoine Pierre Khoraiche from war sundered Lebanon. There was also Alexandre Do Nascimento of Lubango, Angola, who along with four nuns and two missionaries, had been, within the previous year, kidnapped and held captive by guerilla forces in his homeland. Half way across the section on the other side of the aisle sat Parisian archbishop Jean Marie Lustiger whose Jewish mother had died in the death camp at Auschwitz. Also present was a man who was not an archbishop of a great diocese but a French Jesuit theologian, 86-year-old Henri de Lubac, who had been condemned by Rome in the fifties for his views. His being named a cardinal had been a popular move, hailed everywhere as a salute not only to the beloved de Lubac but to the vocation of theologians in the church. He symbolized something unusual in Vatican life, a scholar rehabilitated in his own lifetime.

In all, there were 10 new cardinals from Europe, two from Africa, two each from Asia and the Middle East, and one from New Zealand. They constituted the fulfillment of Pope Paul VI's dream for a reinvigorated college of cardinals. Seventy-one of the now 138 cardinals would be European but the representative character of the body had been radically and forever changed. Fifty years before, only seven countries had been represented. Now, 56 were, and, while in 1960, there had been only one black prince of the church, there would now be 12.

Bernardin's thoughts drifted momentarily away from his brother candidates, new and old, some ramrod straight, some bent with age or illness, as they waited for Augustino Cardinal Casaroli, papal secretary of state. He would shortly appear on the bulge of the stage apron to summon and hand each his *biglietto,* or official letter informing him of his nomination and acceptance into the College of Cardinals. The voices of the Sistine Choir softened the electric state of excitement that was now building in the auditorium, providing a background for personal thoughts. In the few moments that remained before he received the ceremonial notification of his new office, Bernardin drifted back in memory to his childhood during that aching, spartan decade of the thirties.

Six of the Bernardin brothers had been stonecutters who had mastered their trade in Italy. His father Joseph, known as Bepi, had journeyed with his brothers, first to Barre, Vermont, and then to South Carolina early in the twenties, attracted by the abundant quarries and the need, in those still boom times, for skilled artisans. Three of the brothers moved to other cities. Joseph remained with two others, establishing themselves well near Columbia, the capitol city that, set at the very center of the off-angle wedge shaped state, bound together the large, slash-like lakes that dominated the Piedmont plain on either side of it. The smell of Civil War battles still permeated Columbia's imagination. Fully a fourth of that city had been consumed in flames on the night of the day that Union General William Tecumseh Sherman had marched into it some sixty years before.

The first ordinance of secession had been passed just down the river in Charleston in 1860 and across the waters of that Atlantic port the first shell of the war between the states had whistled into the northern harbor installation of Fort Sumter. Joseph and Severino would a few years later marry sisters, Maria and Lina Simion, and bring them to this city thick with Confederate memory and Protestant faith. Catholics were few and many of the priests who served their small congregations had come from Ireland, ''on the mission'' as they described it, in the United States. Even Catholic churches remained segregated, as so many institutions did in post World War I America. The veterans of the Civil War were closer in time to the blood darkened fields of Gettysburg and Manassas than, at the moment of this cardinalatial rite, World War I veterans were to Verdun and Chateau Thierry.

The twenties had swelled with prosperity and the Bernardin brothers had done well enough to return to Italy to be married to the Simion sisters who, like many other immigrant wives, had patiently waited behind until their future husbands established themselves in the new world. As Cardinal Casaroli walked slowly out onto the stage Bernardin thought of his father and mother and of the four hundred-year-old Church of San Sebastian in the hamlet of Tonadico in which they were married in 1927. His mother was already pregnant with him when she and his father embarked on the long, slow sea voyage to America. Bernardin felt their presence as he ascended the curved flight of steps to receive his *biglietto.* He then joined the procession of the newly named cardinals as they went to add the last vestment, the crimson, mantle-like mozetta and ceremonial cross, that would complete their attire for the final part of the ritual.

It was shortly after 11:30 a.m. as the cardinals-designate again took their places in the chairs spread below the curved main platform. Behind them those in attendance included white tied diplomats, uniformed men wearing bold sashes and elaborate decorations, as well as simple, half-curious, half awe-struck pilgrims. They alternately chatted good-naturedly and peered to the left side where a Swiss Guard, clad in his yellow and red striped uniform, stood at attention, staff in hand, waiting for the pope to enter. The Chicago cardinal thought of his 78-year-old mother, Maria, who had not been able to make this triumphant return to her homeland with her only son. Too ill for travel, she resided at the Little Sisters of the Poor Center for the Aging not far from Bernardin's residence on the North Side of Chicago.

———

Maria Simion Bernardin had always been a determined, practical woman, the Chicago prelate thought as the colorful sounds and sights of the benevolently tense hall blurred and faded for a moment. His mother's face rose in his imagination. Next to hers was that of his father. But it was shadowed and he could not get it into sharp focus. As a young couple they had settled in the same house on Wayne Street with their companion newlyweds, his brother and her sister, classic examples of industrious newcomers determined to make a success of life in America.

Their son Joseph was born on Apr. 2, 1928, the year that would see another son of immigrant Catholics, Governor Alfred E. Smith of New York, lose a presidential election marred by vicious attacks on the Church of Rome. South Carolina had been settled chiefly by Germans, Scotch-Irish, and Welsh and those who came with the Catholic faith often lost it because of the inability of the few priests to reach and care for their people with quite the same regularity as the famous circuit riding Protestant ministers. Those Catholics who persevered in their religion often settled, as they did in other parts of the country, in the larger cities along on the coastal plain, giving the faith an Irish flavor.

In Charleston there stood a famous Hibernian Hall, alternately led by a Catholic and a Protestant, that had hosted the convention that nominated Stephen Douglas for president in 1860. Charleston was also the diocese headed by one of the most remarkable and progressive of nineteenth century Catholic bishops, the Irish born John England. The roots of the Catholic world in which Joseph Bernardin grew up were sunk, therefore, in misty Celtic history rather than in the sunny highlands of Northern Italy. The Bernardins were, in a sense, twice foreign, as Catholics and Italians, in a state in which in 1928 anti-Catholic feeling ran deep as staunch Democrats, frightened by fantastic projections of a pope in the White House, voted overwhelmingly for Republican Herbert Hoover.

The stock market crash occurred when Bernardin was a year and a half old, ending the roaring twenties and opening the terrible road to the Great Depression. South Carolina, in ruinous condition after the Civil War, occupied by federal troops until 1877, had staggered toward recovery for decades. The economic collapse of the thirties plunged the state back into harsh economic times. Bernardin later recalled that the vicar general of the diocese, Monsignor James J. May, liked to evoke the thirties by saying, "We were so poor we didn't even know there was a Depression."

Bernardin remembered that long stretch of his boyhood years as shadowed not only by the spectre of the Great Depression but by what, for a little boy, was the at first surprising, then intermittent, and finally regular visitations at home of the phantom of illness and death. Bepi Bernardin was originally diagnosed as having cancer before his marriage. He had undergone surgery in Italy and had insisted that his bride-to-be talk to his doctor before they went ahead with their plans. The doctor had reassured them that all was well but five years later when his son Joseph was barely four years old and shortly before his daughter Elaine was to be born, the cancer reoccurred. The part of the house they shared was filled with the alternate bustle and quiet that go with long illnesses, with happy periods of hope and anxious spells of uncertainty.

Bernardin glanced down at his new crimson cassock, fresh from one of the master ecclesiastical tailors of Rome. His mother, a skilled seamstress, had carried on in her characteristically quiet, determined, and eminently practical way after his father grew ill. She cared for the children and tended to her slowly dying husband who was in and out of hospitals several times before he died in 1934. Bernardin, sitting in plain but fine cardinalatial red half a century later, could summon up an image of his father from family photographs but he had no memories of his own distinct enough to recall.

Bernardin recalled the tightly bound atmosphere of America during the Great Depression, Franklin D. Roosevelt's chiseled profile and its domination of the national imagination, the Blue Eagle symbol of the National Recovery Administration on display everywhere, and hamburger at ten cents a pound and still expensive for most families, a season of Lenten fasting that had fallen across the whole land. It had been a constricted world in which travel was mostly for weddings or funerals, new clothes came out at Easter if at all, and the seeds of obligation rather than the right to self-fulfillment were sown in the souls of all the living. Life in the thirties, although romanticized generations afterwards, was as hard and gritty as the streets paved by the federally subsidized laborers of the Works Progress Administration, the famous WPA.

The decade had been capped by the coming of the second World War and, although it brought an end to the Depression it also flooded the nation with new worries and the demand for new sacrifices. Bernardin would still be too young for the service when the war ended in 1945 but he could vividly recall growing up in ·the atmosphere of global conflict, of boys not much older than he fighting and dying in Europe and Asia, and of blue and gold star flags in the front windows of houses throughout the ordinary neighborhoods of Columbia. The city was flooded with soldiers from nearby Fort Jackson, reactivated just before the war began, and bulging, during the conflict, with 100,000 troops.

Bernardin thought again of his mother, the determined and industrious woman who had insisted that the five thousand dollars left by her husband be left untouched. It was a handsome estate in those mean days and she intended to preserve it for later use and to make a living for herself and her two children through her sewing skills. So without complaint she worked for the WPA and took in seamstress jobs in the house that they still shared with her sister and her husband and their two children. As little Joseph, who attended public school for the first four grades, grew, he was often given the responsibility of caring for his sister Elaine while Maria Bernardin worked to keep the roof over their heads. Young Joseph, as his sister recalls, was never a boy for mischief and was well liked by everybody. He often had to prepare dinner so that Maria could finish her work. He had learned to cook Italian dishes such as the Spaghetti Carbonara which became his specialty. Even after he became a bishop, he had enjoyed occasional nights of cooking for friends. There had been no leisure for that since he had arrived in Chicago.

There was a stir in the air and a sudden break in the buzz that filled the hall. All eyes turned toward the white covered, gold trimmed papal chair at the center of the stage, softly lit through the ice-cube tray ceiling. It was 11:40, almost time for Pope John Paul II to arrive to complete the installation of the new cardinals. Many of the men being raised along with him had grown up in the same world that Bernardin had known, some of them, like Lustiger, for example, in far more difficult conditions. The pope himself had grown up in the same world of privation and war. But John Paul, Bernardin reflected, had no memory of his mother, only of the years of siege and occupation in which the Catholic faith had been not only a source of formation but of strength and consolation as well. It was indeed a challenging and bewildering new world they, as the highest leaders of the church, were now about to enter.

Maria Bernardin had, in fact, found steady employment because of the impact of World War II. Life for her small family had only begun to stabilize when she received a civil service position in the quartermaster corps, qualifying, because of her skilled fingers, as a tailor at Fort Jackson. In 1941 she moved with her children into Gonzales Gardens, a garden apartment public housing development. It would not be until 1951, just a year before Bernardin's ordination to the priesthood, that, with the five thousand dollar inheritance Maria had managed to preserve throughout the difficult times following her husband's death, they would at last build their own small house on Edgehill Road in Forest Acres, a suburb on the east side of Columbia.

The auditorium suddenly became still behind the sheer veil of the Sistine Choir voices. It was 11:44 a.m. The pope, characteristically just ahead of time, strode briskly in, hands folded together in front of his chest, escorted by his masters of ceremony. John Paul II wore a broad stole over the crimson mozetta that covered his shoulders. His eyes half closed above the planes of his slavic face, the pope stood lightly clenching his fists as the choir concluded its hymn. For the new cardinals, he was Peter, the binding center of their new responsibilities as well as the center and sign of unity for the Catholic Church that was the consuming calling of their lives. John Paul sang the opening Latin prayer in his strong melodious voice and took his place for the solemn singing by two young priests of the readings from scripture. The pope sat with his hands fluted to his lips, his eyes still half closed, as if abstracted by some intense effort of reflection. The priest sang words from the first letter of St. Peter, "Do not be overbearing..."

No one who had ever known Joseph Bernardin thought that he needed that kind of advice. His manner had been consistently modest and gentle, even as, according to his mother's recollections, she enrolled him in grammar school at age five to allow him a time outside the house during the grueling periods of his father's illness. He had graduated from St. Peter's grammar school when he was thirteen and, therefore, finished the three year public high school as a straight A student when he was only sixteen. In this beating heart of the Roman Church to which he had consecrated his existence, Bernardin recalled that he had not even considered the priesthood as a possible calling until he had entered on scholarship a pre-medical course at the University of South Carolina. He recalled the parish priests whose examples had first given him the idea of following them into the service of the church. There had been Father Charles Sheedy, the associate pastor at St. Peter's, whose friendship and goodness had meant so much to the young Bernardin. And there was Monsignor Martin C. Murphy, the pastor from Ireland who, after Bernardin had made his decision to enter the seminary, had been understanding and supportive. Without those men, Bernardin felt, he might not be seated in scarlet today.

He smiled inwardly as he recalled telling his mother of his change of plans. Maria Bernardin had been taken totally by surprise. Their home, while solidly religious, had never been pietistic. She expressed her concerns about Joseph's leaving the university after only one year. "What will happen," she had asked her son, evincing her ever practical turn of mind, "if you decide you want to leave the seminary? Will you be able to get your scholarship back?"

The pope rose for the gospel, gazed from beneath his softly indented brow, rocking slightly, calmly surveying the 18 men who would soon be cardinals. "Be simple as lambs. . . ." The words from the gospel of Matthew cut like a fine blade across the excitement of the attentive crowd. Red was the color of the occasion, the symbolic red that symbolized faithfulness to the church even unto the shedding of blood. If the college of cardinals had in its long history known worldly princes like Wolsey and Richelieu, it had also boasted many who had suffered for the faith. The mood of the morning was now tinctured by the high expectations that the church would make on the loyalty of these newly chosen princes. That would be the theme of the address that would be given by the patriarch Koraiche of the Maronites on behalf of all the cardinals at the conclusion of the gospel.

As the Latin scripture verses were slowly sung, Joseph Bernardin remembered how he had proposed to enter the seminary just after the conclusion of World War II very much like many of the returning veterans who shared the same hopes. He had never studied Latin, then the universal tongue of the Roman Church. This lack was but another signal of the path he was pursuing to the priesthood. It was certainly not that of the big city Catholic youths who, in Chicago, for example, had to have begun their classical education in the first year of the high school seminary if they were to be accepted in the ranks of the clergy of that archdiocese.

The 17-year-old Bernardin had been sent for a special Latin make-up course at St. Mary's Seminary in Kentucky. He recalled well the teacher, Father Frank Jagelwicz, who had divided the 50 or 60 students into progressive sections, letting the most able, like Bernardin, move at their own pace. Submerging himself in the thirteen hour a week class, Bernardin quickly mastered the language that had been the source of the Italian that he had heard spoken at home. He was soon ready for the regular program of college training at St. Mary's Seminary in Baltimore where he received his A.B., *summa cum laude,* in 1948. For his advanced studies, he was sent to Theological College just across the street from the Catholic University of America in Washington, D.C.

Although the era of closed seminary education was still firmly in place, there was an openness to university life that Bernardin still recalled fondly. He had enjoyed the classes that he had taken with lay students when, in addition to his regular theological studies, he enrolled in extra courses for a master's degree in education. But he had also been called upon to make a decision that could have affected his career, had he been conscious of possibilities that lay before him at the time. He was invited by his bishop, Emmet M. Walsh, to complete his seminary education at the North American College in Rome, the traditional training ground for bishops and other likely candidates for church leadership. Because his mother had been ill, Bernardin turned down the opportunity. Some classmates thought that the bright young man from Columbia, South Carolina, was missing the chance of a lifetime.

The Maronite patriarch concluded his address. The pope bowed his head, pursed his lips tightly, touched his hand to his right temple, and began speaking in Italian into the microphone that rose like a curious silver swan at the side of his chair. "Fratelli," he said in his rich, gentle voice, *my brothers,* welcoming them, switching to various languages to repeat his message, eliciting flag waving and a sprinkling of cheers from the different groups of visitors. He looked down, his expression tinged with sadness, at the cardinals-to-be, sitting as attentively as university students. After the pope concluded his remarks, the cardinals rose in an uncertain wave, some like the theologian de Lubac, needing assistance, and bowed in unsynchronized fashion toward the pope. The new cardinals then recited in unison their profession of faith, their pledge of unity in belief with him, and their oath of loyalty, pledging themselves anew to him and the traditions of the church. There was a second's pause as they looked uncertainly around and then slowly took their seats again.

Pope John Paul recited the prayer of investiture in the plural, beginning with the word *accipite,* receive, before he bestowed the red birettas on the new cardinals. Bernardin, like the others, had entered a priesthood in which obedience to superiors was taken for granted. He was ordained just after his 24th birthday, and had been assigned as curate to St. Joseph's Church in Charleston and also as a teacher at Bishop England High School. All of us here were ordained, Bernardin thought, in a different world. The patriarch from Lebanon stood up, ascended the steps, almost falling, and the pope placed on his head the red biretta and solemnly embraced him.

Thirty-one years ago Bernardin had been told, just a few days before the school year began, that, in addition to his priestly duties, he would be teaching world history, American history, church history, and civics. The next year he was switched with hardly any warning to lead classes in algebra, geometry, and business mathematics. That was the now hard to remember era in which bright young people who gave themselves to the church were expected to take on such responsibilities without question or complaint.

Within two years, Bernardin had been assigned to chancery office work where he soon took on several official and unofficial assignments, holding nearly every position in the office at one time or another. There were periods when he managed four or five overlap-

ping administrative assignments, including superintendant of ceme-
teries. He had served for five years as chaplain at the Citadel, the
military school, and had also served as the director of vocations and
charities, archivist, and secretary to the bishop. But he had loved it,
he remembered, for if the work was hard, the people and his fellow
priests had been good, and if he had been overworked, he had also
been happy. But that was a lost world of cheerful acceptance of
authority in American Catholicism. It was not the kind of church of
which he was now a principal leader.

The moment had come for Maria and Bepi Bernardin's son to
stand and ascend the steps that led to the Holy Father. Bernardin
smiled slightly as he knelt before the pope. John Paul II looked down
at the man he had chosen to become archbishop of Chicago, the
leader responsible for fashioning one of the most sensitive pastoral
letters ever issued in the church, that on peace and nuclear war, the
priest and bishop from whom he confidently expected loyalty to the
shedding of blood. He placed the crimson skullcap on Bernardin's
lowered head, then placed the square, red-winged biretta on top of
that. The pope leaned forward and embraced Bernardin who rose, a
fully vested prince of the church.

As he walked to the group of older cardinals who were ritually
embracing the new members of the college, he thought again of his
parents. When his mother, who lived with him during his last two
years in Cincinnati, had heard rumors that he might be named archbishop of Chicago, she had said, "If they offer it, you must turn it
down." She liked Cincinnati, the ever practical woman had said, and
she had wanted to stay there. But, of course, she had gone to Chicago
with him and now, as he knew, she was watching on television as her
only son became a cardinal. The pope would send back a special rosary for her and there would be great celebrations for the Bernardin
clan. But now, as he took his place, the new cardinal thought of his origins and of the strength that he had gained from his mother and father.
He glanced at his crimson sleeve and heard once more his mother's
voice, "Walk straight and try not to look too pleased with yourself."

II

In 1958, Joseph L. Bernardin, hardworking parish priest and diocesan official in Charleston, South Carolina, turned thirty, too absorbed in his work to think much about that occasion or about events of that year that would profoundly affect the direction of his life and career. For most Americans that placid twilight of the Eisenhower years was crowded with the discharge of responsibilities rather than the search for options in their personal or professional lives. The revolutions of the coming decade had still not invaded the dreams of the country and Bernardin, handling several assignments, enjoyed little time for anything but work. He was the classic, dutiful, unquestioning priest of the period. Years later, sitting in the dark wooded residence in which he lived as archbishop of Chicago, he would recall those times, the half smile shared by those who are not sure progress has been an improvement lighting his face, "You just did what you were supposed to do in those days—go where they sent you, do what they asked of you." The ethos and the conscience of pre-Vatican II American Catholicism revealed in a phrase.

Yet rivulets of energy flowing from widely separated sources during 1958 would ultimately converge into a Mississippi that would cut through the landscape of that Catholicism, transforming it, and Bernardin's life within it, permanently.

In that year, 47-year-old Paul Hallinan, a priest from Cleveland who had served as director of the Newman Club at Case Western Reserve University, was named bishop of Charleston. He wore a Purple Heart from his service as a chaplain in World War II but was a genial, scholarly, pastoral figure who would emerge as one of the great leaders of the Vatican II era in America. He was unique among his episcopal confreres for his commitment to the intellectual life and completed his doctoral dissertation and received his degree after he became a bishop. Bernardin would later recall that Hallinan kept two desks in his study, one for diocesan business, the other for the historical research to which, often late at night, he would turn his attention after he had fulfilled his episcopal responsibilities for the day.

Hallinan brought to non-Catholic Charleston a sense of comfort with the world and with himself. He had no taste for authoritarian assertion, preferring to employ mediation and cooperation in his relationships with both civic and ecclesiastical colleagues. He was, as Catholic historian John Tracy Ellis chose to describe him, a *princeps facile,* a polished leader who valued understanding and collaboration in solving problems and in initiating new programs. "He was a man of great faith and optimism," Bernardin would later say of their years of work together, "no matter how dark or bleak things seemed to be. He believed that if you had faith and worked as hard as you could at a problem, you would resolve it or at least learn to live with it."

Still, Hallinan, the scholar who understood the rhythms of history and the decorated chaplain who had seen men die, was no abstract idealist. Although positive and determined, he had a sure feel for the human condition and its flawed aspirations for nobility. Operating as a Northerner in a South still largely suspicious of Catholicism, Hallinan, as Bernardin would remember, was "always able to be kind to people even in hard situations. While he was totally loyal to the church and its teachings, he was also always sensitive to people and their needs." The future cardinal was serving an apprenticeship under a bishop whose lessons of unswerving devotion to the church and pastoral realism would not be lost on him, would, in fact, inspire him to follow his own healthy instincts to serve the church and its people in the same way.

Bernardin smiled appreciatively many years later as he offered an example of Hallinan's approach. "He was a man of great principle," the Cardinal archbishop of Chicago recalled in the tones of a grown son's savoring of a father's memory, "and on one occasion in Charleston we were faced with a very difficult situation. Bishop Hallinan insisted that we defend the principle involved. 'It's hard, Joe,' he said. 'But stick with it and you'll get this resolved.' And I did. Then, six months later in another part of the diocese, an almost identical problem arose although the circumstances were different. Then Bishop Hallinan wanted to apply a very different solution. 'What about the principle?' I asked. And he looked at me and said, 'Joe, there are times when one must rise above principle.' "

Hallinan was not long in Charleston before he recognized Bernardin's ability. The quiet, reserved young priest, always friendly if not intimate, was not only bright and efficient, in Hallinan's judgment, but he possessed other remarkable qualities. He was, much like Hallinan himself, a gentleman whose good manners did not obscure a healthy and down to earth personality. The young priest knew how to get things done even when he was forced to deal with the most difficult of local personalities. His self-effacing style and his gift for mediation identified Bernardin as a priest with much to contribute to the church.

In October 1958, the 82-year-old Pope Pius XII, who had guided the church through the savage years that encompassed World War II and the aftermath search for peace, took his last labored breath in Rome. In what can now be understood as a signal of the crumbling timbers beneath the deepest crypts of the ancient church, his physician, an oculist named Galeazzi who reveled in his title as a papal count, snapped pictures of Pius' death agonies and sold them to *LIFE* magazine. Galeazzi also bungled the preparation of the unembalmed body for burial and, in a macabre incident, its accumulated gases loudly cracked open the casket cover during the ceremonial journey past the great churches of the eternal city toward St. Peter's. The startling noise was really the sound of a historical period collapsing.

The episodes surrounding Pius XII's passing, accented by Galeazzi's bizarre performance, revealed the dry rot and strange cavities that had developed inside the institution that had, like every other institution, been badly weathered by the war and the harsh years of readjustment and rebuilding afterward. The Roman Catholic Church had not had the time or the inclination to examine its own internal life for many decades. The late pope, celebrated for his intense and singleminded leadership as well as for the many and varied encyclicals he composed on his white portable typewriter, had led the church that, in its somewhat top-heavy structure, had emerged from Vatican Council I. That gathering, which recessed in 1870 as Victor Emmanuel's troops seized the secular kingdom of the papal states and stood at the gates of Rome, had solemnly declared the pope infallible in matters of faith and morals.

But the figure of the pope, greatly enhanced by the aura of infallibility, soon cast a gigantic shadow across the rest of the world's bishops. Indeed, the heads of European governments were impressed and disturbed by the declaration. England's Prime Minister William Gladstone, fearing that Catholics would be more loyal to Rome than to the crown, wrote a critical book, which he termed an "expostulation" on the subject, *The Vatican Decrees in Their Bearing on Civil Allegiance.* John Henry Cardinal Newman, in fact, issued a nuanced response to this work. The decree on papal infallibility was, therefore, a cultural as well as a theological event both inside and outside Catholicism. It gave rise to the closed universe of papally dominated Catholicism that, reinforced especially by Pope Pius X in his brutal and thorough suppression of what was termed "modernism" in the first decade of the new century, was in its fullest flower when Joseph L. Bernardin was born in 1928.

For almost one hundred years after Vatican Council I, the pope totally dominated the imagination of American Catholicism. The inner Catholic world was characterized by unquestioning obedience and unswerving loyalty to Rome and to the pope in all matters. The newfound emphasis on papal infallibilty had strengthened the notion of an essentially centralized church. This enhanced authority was employed in the generation after Vatican I to consolidate Roman control of the church in the United States, which in curial parlance was still technically a "missionary" country, that is, one deemed not mature enough to function on its own.

It was an era in which individual prelates, rather than the national group of bishops, wielded great influence and voiced the ideals and aims of the church. Just as in England the scholar Newman, in his response to Gladstone, spoke for that country's Catholics, so in America, James Cardinal Gibbons of Baltimore, the "primatial" see or primary diocese of the United States, fulfilled a similar role. Other figures, such as Francis Cardinal Spellman at midcentury, would do the same, in effect employing their status and the prominence of their dioceses as entitlements to express the mind and desires of American Catholicism. The progressive bishops of the late nineteenth century were best exemplified by the energetic Archbishop John Ireland of St. Paul. He was a friend and supporter of President Theodore Roosevelt and he thought nothing, for example, of offering himself as a mediator to avert the 1898 war with Spain.

Ireland, along with his fellow bishops, was convinced that the Catholic Church had prospered in the environment of democracy. He not only endorsed the ideals of the republic but defended its institutions, including public schools. A vague charge of an even vaguer heresy termed "Americanism" was made against the United States bishops by Roman officials who remained highly suspicious of freedom and democracy. Although the accusations remained amorphous, Pope Leo XIII, who had strongly reinforced Thomistic philosophy as the sole acceptable system of thought for Catholicism, in 1899 issued a document, *Testem Benevolentiae,* that discouraged adaptation to the modern world. It also distinguished between church authority and governmental authority, reminding Catholics that they owed their allegiance to the infallible pope. "Fanatics," Ireland responded, "conjured up an 'Americanism'—and put such before the pope."

This rebuke was followed shortly by the crackdown on the incipient intellectual revival in American seminaries by the papal condemnation of another protoplasmic heresy, "modernism." This alleged that contemporary means of scholarship were inimical to the church. In a tragic but classical example, Father James Driscoll, the scholar rector of the New York archdiocesan seminary was dismissed, his fledgling theological journal was aborted, and his progressive faculty routed. He was replaced by the chaplain of the Police Department, who had been Navy chaplain on the battleship Maine when it exploded in Santiago harbor, and who, although heroic, had no academic qualifications and little interest in anything but a highly disciplined seminary life. Thus the genetic loading of the priesthood that would endure for half a century—manly, affable, obedient, antiintellectual—was achieved. Throughout the world, priests were required to take an oath against modernism and, in many United States dioceses, committees of vigilance were formed to check on what priests were reading and on their loyalty to the Holy See. A truly dark night of highly controlled, nonintellectual isolation from the world settled over priestly training.

The almost overwhelming centrality of Rome meant that every program and textbook needed Vatican approval to assure its purity and validity. This reservation of all decisions, even about matters far removed from the stylized ecclesiastical milieu of the Vatican, to the pope and his eagerly supportive curial staff, sharply attenuated the claims of individual bishops to the exercise of their own authority within their jurisdictions. For generations, Rome would justify the famous motto *Roma locuta est, causa finita est,* (Rome has spoken, the matter is settled) by pressing the ring of the fisherman, as the symbol of papal authority was known, into the seals of decisions all over the world. Pope Pius XI, the former librarian and energetic mountain climber who served from 1922 until 1939, had at times acted out his sense of being a true monarch by allowing cardinals and other officials to remain on their knees throughout their audiences with him. Nobody was surprised at such regal expressions of papal authority. At that time his installation was known as a coronation and he wore a triple tiered crown called a tiara as a sign of the supreme power of his office.

The new century soon witnessed upheavals and wars so devastating to the continent that poet T.S. Eliot would describe its spiritual landscape as the Waste Land. Although the symbolic eagles of monarchy fell all across Europe, the Roman Catholic Church maintained the regal model as the authentic expression of the nature of the church and of the decisive authority of the pontiff. Fragile and shelllike by the time of Pius XII's death, this ecclesiastical construction rose from the foundation notion that all church authority flowed from Rome, that the pope was not only the first among the world's bishops but also the source of such authority as he chose to delegate to them. This was a reflection of the church's immediate cultural past, of its breathing the air and speaking the language of Western Europe. It was not until Vatican II that the church regained the collegial sense of itself that had marked its founding.

The accumulated inertia of the administrative side of Catholicism in the last years of Pius XII, who had served as his own secretary of state since 1944, had begun, even in the judgment of friendly critics, to weigh it down. Throughout the curial bureaucracy ecclesiastical careerists held their breath, functioning with no temptation to innovation in what they regarded as the last act of a heroic papal reign. A few years meant little, in their judgment, in the eternal life of the church. Things could be let go for awhile longer. As a sign of things unattended, in October 1958, there were only 52 members out of the full complement of 70 in the College of Cardinals.

As the world stood on the cusp of the jet age, one of the three American princes of the church, Edward Mooney, the highly regarded 76-year-old archbishop of Detroit, had entrained in the motor city for New York and there boarded an ocean liner to Rome to vote in the conclave that would choose Pius XII's successor. That mode of travel, born in the nineteenth century, matched well the leaders like Mooney who had risen out of the immigrant church culture that was utterly loyal to the pope and staunchly defensive of every papal prerogative. Mooney, like other men of his times, had completed his studies at Rome's North American College, and had been finely trained to respect the rigid, highly controlled Catholicism of the first half of the twentieth century. Although Mooney held two doctorates from Rome, these were achieved in an era when the academic demands were hardly on a par with those of later years. Many degrees, such as those earned a generation later by John Patrick Cody, were thought, in part at least, to have been purchased as much as earned.

A suspicion of the seemingly souless empiricism that had been spawned by the Enlightenment had made the church uneasy about rational inquiry and intellectual discovery of every kind. This mistrust of science and the free life of the mind flavored the ethos of world Catholicism, rendering it in America, at least, a pragmatic, politicized culture akin to that of business, the military, government, and union organizing, to all of which it was intimately related. The church was run by loyal, practical, highly intelligent men who, while energetic promoters of education, had little taste for theory, creativity, or the intellectual life. By 1958, American Catholicism had become a many layered, colorful and seemingly stable world, well known by the warmhearted Mooney, but as much on the eve of change as the mode of transportation he had chosen to travel to Rome.

Another American cardinal, Francis J. Spellman of New York, perhaps more ruefully aware of the changes taking place and of the possibility that with the death of his mentor and protector, Pius XII, his influence in Rome might suddenly wane, flew directly to Italy. He stopped first, however, to see Giovanni Battista Montini, the new archbishop of Milan who, although not yet a cardinal, was spoken of regularly as a future pope and would, in fact, become Paul VI five years later.

On Oct. 25, 1958, as the opening of the conclave approached, the ailing Cardinal Mooney died suddenly in his quarters at the North American College. That left Spellman and his former New York protege, the hardbitten James Francis Cardinal McIntyre, archbishop of Los Angeles, as the only Americans among the 51 surviving princes of the church. These cardinals, locked according to ancient custom into the area around the Sistine Chapel, elected within three days what some termed a ''compromise'' candidate, 'the 77-year-old patriarch of Venice, Angelo Cardinal Roncalli, who chose to be called John XXIII. He was picked, according to most observers, to provide a papacy, sure to be brief, that would give the church a transitional breathing space after the constricted years of the dominant Pius XII. John, however, made history and became beloved to the world through his own pastoral warmth and by convening, against the opposition of a reluctant curia, Vatican Council II in order to bring *aggiornamento,* or updating, to the church.

But he did other things as well.

In his first appointments in the American church scarcely a

month after becoming pope, John XXIII chose 51-year-old Bishop John Dearden, a Cleveland priest who knew Paul Hallinan well and had served as head of the Pittsburgh diocese for 10 years, to succeed the late Cardinal Mooney as archbishop of Detroit. Known as "Iron John" when he had earlier served as the demanding rector of the Cleveland seminary, the urbane, scholarly Dearden would be transformed by his experience at Vatican II into perhaps the most important leader of the American church in the twentieth century.

Then, in 1962, as the Council was about to hold its first session, the already mortally ill Pope John XXIII appointed Paul Hallinan of Charleston to be the first archbishop of Atlanta, Georgia. Although he was to live only six more years, Hallinan's was a vibrant, enlightened pastoral voice during the period in which the collegial spirit of Vatican II was infused into the American church. In 1966, Hallinan petitioned Rome to appoint Joseph Louis Bernardin, whom he had come to know and esteem in Charleston, as his auxiliary bishop in Atlanta, a city that, like the church, was vigorously awakening itself to a new world after a long sleep.

Bernardin not only served as pastor of Atlanta's Christ the King Cathedral but also as vicar general of the archdiocese. On the day that Hallinan was officially installed as archbishop, Bernardin was struck by the forthright position that this bishop from the North took without hesitation in the first city of the South. "Neither in the North nor in the South," Hallinan said of the church, "can she bear the ugly blemish of prejudice and fear," concluding that "small in numbers but great in loyalty, our Catholic people are . . . [moving] toward the reality of full racial justice—with prudence, with courage, with determination." This was an unambiguous message delivered compassionately to the then only 35,000 Catholics of Atlanta, a tiny island of believers in a vast sea of traditional Protestantism.

Bernardin had previously observed Hallinan's approach—clear but nonconfrontational—in Charleston. During his intimate collaboration with Hallinan in Atlanta, Bernardin witnessed the simple, Christian effectiveness of this kind of leadership that addressed the most sensitive matters with courage, openness, and no desire to shame anyone. This example would serve Bernardin well later when as a Southerner he moved as an archbishop into the North.

Hallinan entered vigorously into the civic life of Atlanta, serving on many committees that dealt with racial, ecumenical, and other problems. In a city uncertain about how to receive the Reverend Martin Luther King, Jr., when he returned from Oslo with the Nobel Prize for peace in December 1964, Hallinan was the prime mover in organizing a huge civic banquet for him. But by that time Hallinan was seriously ill with a hepatitis infection that he had contracted during his attendance at the second session of Vatican II the year before, and was forced to attend the celebration in a wheelchair.

Indeed, Hallinan spent nine months in the hospital in 1964. Although he remained as active as possible, he realized that he was losing his battle to the illness that was scarring and destroying his liver. When he returned from the last session of the council after only four weeks in 1965, the weakened Hallinan understood that the time had come for an auxiliary bishop who would not only discharge the normal obligations of an assistant but who could also work closely with him in carrying out his local and national responsibilities. That man, of course, was Joseph Bernardin. On Apr. 26, 1966, just a few weeks after his 38th birthday, Bernardin was ordained, his mother's advice to walk straight and to try not to look too pleased ringing in his ears, as titular bishop of Ligura and auxiliary bishop of Atlanta.

Prophetic of a challenge that would come to Bernardin almost two decades later was his close partnership with Hallinan in drafting, in 1966 when Vietnam was a burning ember in the folds of the national consciousness, a local pastoral letter on War and Peace that would become the basis for one to be issued by the entire National Conference of Bishops. Bernardin, as a young bishop in the newly established conference, was asked, on the basis of his Atlanta experience, to collaborate with Lawrence Cardinal Sheehan of Baltimore in drafting a letter to represent the convictions of all the American bishops, *Peace in Viet Nam*. It was, as Bernardin later recalled, ''much in the spirit of the Atlanta'' document. This letter, released on Nov. 18, 1966, also anticipated in many ways the major pastoral statement,

The Challenge of Peace, that the American bishops under Bernardin's leadership, would issue in 1983.

In 1966, Hallinan and Bernardin had written:

> As the great debate on war and peace gathers momentum, certain urgent questions demand that we respond:
> 1. What are the demands of true patriotism?
> 2. Is it possible to speak of a just war today as we did in the past?
> 3. On a broader level, should nations try to maintain peace by a balance of terror?
> 4. Does universal disarmament (all sides) differ morally from unilateral disarmament (one side)?
> 5. What are our obligations in contributing toward a genuinely moral consensus regarding American involvement in Viet Nam?

As Bernardin was given this first of many vital assignments on the national level, he was being watched carefully by Archbishop John Dearden, the first president of the newly reorganized conference of bishops. Bernardin and Dearden had not known each other before but Dearden had heard his old friend Hallinan speak of his young assistant and was interested in evaluating him for other developing possibilities. Dearden wanted an able bishop to become the first General Secretary, or operating officer, of the national conference that he was then restructuring along the lines of a plan prepared in 1966, at the bishops' request by the consulting firm of Booz, Hamilton, Allen. Dearden liked what he saw.

Hallinan's health worsened in 1967 and Bernardin had to assume increasing responsibility in running the archdiocese of Atlanta. Hallinan, however, did not want Bernardin to remain only in the local church of the South. Keenly aware that Bernardin was capable of playing a significant role in the American Catholic Church, the ailing prelate wanted Bernardin to get as much national experience and exposure as possible. Realizing that he had only a few months to live, Hallinan repeatedly urged Bernardin to accept Dearden's invitation to move to Washington to manage the conference on a day to day basis. Bernardin, anxious to serve Hallinan fully, twice refused. Finally, the increasingly enfeebled Hallinan told him, "You *have* to take it."

Shortly before Hallinan died in March 1968, Bernardin agreed to accept the appointment as General Secretary of the National Conference of Bishops.

If he did so reluctantly, it was because of his loyalty to Hallinan, an extraordinary man who, aware that he had but a few weeks to live, asked his auxiliary to arrange a party "with caps and favors." When Bernardin asked him why he wanted such a gathering, Hallinan replied cheerfully that it was to be a "going away party." Bernardin would later recall the calmness, courage, and generosity of spirit with which Hallinan, clad in pajamas and bathrobe and unable to eat, welcomed the members of the chancery staff to his residence on Wesley Drive. "He enjoyed himself," Bernardin remembered, "and saw to it that everybody had a good time. He was completely unafraid of death and there was no falseness in his having such a party. It was just the way he was."

These significant events in Bernardin's life occurred against a flaming background of world and national events, some of them omens, others the explosive fulfillment of problems long suppressed. In the last week of July 1967, riots had broken out after Detroit police had raided an after hours drinking club on the city's West Side. President Johnson called in federal troops to restore order during the seven days of violence that left 41 dead and 2,000 injured. If such apocalyptic scenes were typical of the long hot summers of that decade, so too was the arrest of H. Rap Brown, chairman of the Student Nonviolent Coordinating Committee, for inciting a riot by telling a crowd in Cambridge, Maryland, to "burn this city down." Thurgood Marshall became the first black justice of the Supreme Court the next month and in October 35,000 anti-war protesters marched on the Pentagon.

Such events hinted at even greater challenges to the stability of the republic yet to come, while something also occurred in American Catholicism that in many ways symbolized the closing of a period and a style in ecclesiastical influence. On Dec. 9, 1967, Francis Cardinal Spellman, long the dominant figure in the Catholic Church in the United States, was found dead in his residence behind St. Patrick's Cathedral in New York City. In the intervening months, before his hand-picked successor ("the first successful soul transplant," clerical wags would say) Terence Cooke could be installed, not only would Archbishop Hallinan die but the nation also would be racked by painful and unforgettable spasms of change.

The intelligence vessel *Pueblo* would be seized by North Korea in January 1968, the same month in which the North Vietnamese would launch the Tet offensive. Richard M. Nixon would announce his candidacy for the Republican nomination for president the next month and, in March, Senator Eugene McCarthy would win 42 percent of the New Hampshire primary vote, giving a clear signal of the nation's disaffection with President Lyndon B. Johnson. Johnson would announce his refusal to run for re-election on the last day of that same month, the one in which Paul Hallinan died.

Bishop Bernardin would preach at Hallinan's funeral, looking down at the first pew, in which the archly segregationist Governor Lester Maddox and the Reverend Martin Luther King, Jr., sat next to each other. Only a mediator such as Archbishop Hallinan, Bernardin reflected, could have brought these foes together. Bernardin encountered church historian Monsignor John Tracy Ellis outside the cathedral before the funeral. They embraced briefly and wept together at the loss of a man who, along with the archbishop with whom Bernardin would shortly serve, had given so much light and hope to the American church.

The country was rocked by a series of incidents in April. On April 4, the glum President Johnson sat in the front pew of St. Patrick's Cathedral as Terence Cooke became archbishop of New York. That evening, Martin Luther King, Jr., died from an assassin's gunshot on the balcony of a Memphis motel. Rioting and burning raged across the land, Mayor Daley issued a "shoot to kill" order against arsonists in Chicago, and curfews were imposed in great cities across the land. America, in the politics of authority in government and in Catholic life, was experiencing massive and uncertain change.

Bernardin served as administrator of the diocese until the installation of Archbishop Thomas Donnellan, a New Yorker who had, like scores of other prelates around the country, been a protege of the late Francis Cardinal Spellman, on July 17, 1968. In a schedule that offered a classic example of Bernardin's dutiful style, he spent half a week in Atlanta and the other half in Washington, D.C., during that four month interval. He, like the country and the church within it, had landed on the shores of a new and bewildering territory of history.

Bernardin's initial apprenticeship in the everyday tasks of running a diocese were over. His novitiate, traditionally a time of trial as well as learning, in understanding national and international church matters was about to begin. So was his relationship with his new guide, John Francis Dearden.

Years later, in an article in the *Chicago Tribune,* Bernardin recalled his two great mentors, describing Hallinan and Dearden in the reserved style that paid tribute without revealing the depth of his feelings for these two men. It was the classic expression of the gentleman priest, almost from another age, who, like Dearden and Hallinan, consistently emphasized the needs of the church rather than his own. Yet he understood at some level that these men were not only great models and teachers but substitutes in many ways for the father he could barely remember. In return, these archbishops looked on Bernardin as a son who would carry on their work and make them as proud as the most brightly beaming parent in any graduation audience. Having passed his 40th birthday in the trembling Spring of that momentous year, Bernardin was ready for the next phase in his extraordinary ecclesiastical education.

III

Bernardin continued his shuttle flights between Atlanta and Washington, D.C., above a country as bewildered as a man trying to find his true image in a distorting mirror. Arthur Schlesinger, Jr., wrote later that the dreams of the nation seemed to be borne on the same funeral train that, on June 8, carried Robert Kennedy's body from New York to Washington for burial. In a surrealistic footnote, the capture in London of James Earl Ray, slayer of the Reverend Martin Luther King, Jr., had been announced as the funeral mass for the murdered senator was being offered in St. Patrick's Cathedral. Richard Cardinal Cushing, the archbishop of Boston whose face and voice held the grittiness and sparkle of New England granite, stepped off the mournful train in Washington's Union Station that sweltering evening wearing a hard straw hat.

Cushing looked as if he had just emerged from "Old Southie," his section of Boston where many immigrant Irish had first settled despite the notices in classified advertising and in shop windows that "No Irish Need Apply." The raspy voiced Cushing recapitulated in himself the Catholic experience of the century for if he remembered the darkest days of Brahmin prejudice against Catholics he had also presided at the latter's greatest symbolic triumph, the inauguration of the first Roman Catholic president, John Fitzgerald Kennedy, one of the Kennedys of Boston, on Jan. 20, 1961. Arriving in Washington where Bernardin would shortly take up permanent residence in the staff house of the United States Catholic Conference, Cushing was, through links of memory and his own rough hewn presence, one of the last great dominant individual bishops of the American church.

Cushing had served under and, in 1944, succeeded, William Cardinal O'Connell, who had proved his loyalty to Rome during the Modernist period at the turn of the century in his post as rector of the North American College. Enamored of Roman ways, he had arrived at his first American episcopal appointment in Portland, Maine, in 1901, with an entourage that included a valet and a concertmaster. O'Connell, like secular counterparts such as publisher William Randolph Hearst, imported European manners, art work, and life style on a lavish scale. He even went so far, according to John Tracy Ellis, as to reinvent his own origins in a volume of predated letters, constructing an idyllic childhood far different from his poor beginnings in Lowell, Massachusetts. All copies of this fated gilt edged book were ultimately burned in the furnace of his residence, a victim, as O'Connell was to be, of its own presumptions.

Nonetheless, O'Connell, in reflection of the *arriviste* mentality of newly ascendant Americans at the century's turn, bespoke the longings and the ambition of American Catholics to succeed and prosper in the new world. They also wanted to stand on equal ground with their Protestant neighbors who, having revolted against monarchy, were suspicious of the loyalties of European immigrants. After O'Connell became archbishop of Boston at the age of 47 in 1906, he vied with Boston's Wasp aristocrats in the display of lordly assumptions. He lived on a par with them as a prince of the church, traveling by steamer to Nassau so regularly that his nickname among his priests became "Gangplank Bill."

Until his Roman patron, Rafael Cardinal Merry del Val, fell from influence on the election of Pope Benedict XIV in 1914, O'Connell confidently inhabited a role that expressed the reality of power in American Catholicism. Although he himself progressively lost national influence after Merry del Val's star set permanently, O'Connell typified the strong ecclesiastical personalities that, in the country's most important dioceses, would lead uncomplaining Catholics for nearly half a century. The significant dioceses were, in the

Roman imagination, the major cities of the original colonies plus a thousand mile arc across the upper midwest to include the heavily Catholic industrial centers of Detroit and Chicago.

There would be no cardinal on the west coast until after midcentury; there is, in 1989, still only one city west of the Mississippi in which a cardinal's hat is a certainty, Los Angeles. American Catholicism, on the basis of a progressively out of date curial map, has always been defined in terms of powerful places and powerful people. On the day of Bernardin's installation as archbishop of Chicago in 1982, John Cardinal Dearden, the champion of collegiality, paid tribute to this tradition by telling a friend outside Holy Name Cathedral, "I always wanted to see Joe in a big midwestern diocese like Chicago."

Until well into this century, aside from periodic regional and plenary councils, the American bishops, each prelate the supreme authority within the boundaries of his own diocese, constituted, in effect, a loose confederation with no stable organization through which they could address together their common problems. As the pope dominated the universal church, so cardinal archbishops like O'Connell in Boston, James Gibbons in Baltimore, George Mundelein in Chicago, and Dennis Dougherty in Philadelphia, cast overlapping shadows across American Catholicism. They set the general tone, spoke out on public issues—as O'Connell did, expressing a fine Brahmin sensibility, as he battled with Boston's populist Catholic mayor, Frank Curley—and decided the general course of ecclesiastical policies and appointments.

The resolution of the Modernist crisis through strategies that emphasized the centrality of Vatican control over the training and discipline of priests severely tested the obedience and loyalty of the American bishops. The princes of the church in the main cities along the eastern seaboard implemented Vatican wishes without hesitation. This willing acceptance of Roman authority tempered the initiative and independence of thought that had been expressed previously by such figures as St. Paul's Archbishop John Ireland. The American bishops before World War I engaged, according to historian Joseph McShane in "masterful inactivity." (*Sufficiently Radical: Catholi-*

cism, Progressivism and the Bishops' Program of 1919, Catholic University Press, 1988.)

The bishops were timid, according to McShane, because "any stance was sure to anger some group; if [the church] condemned unions, she would run afoul of the immigrants; if she condoned them, she was sure to offend Rome and the Nativists [both fearful of socialism]; if she attacked laissez faire capitalism, she would appear completely radical.... If she ever wished to become a partner in effective reform activity, she would have to overcome the problems of ethnic and hierarchical fragmentation, intellectual shallowness, and fear of Nativism that had marred—indeed stunted—her social activity in the 19th century."

This interval of passivity came to an end, however, through the establishment, during the war, of the organizational ancestor of the conference of bishops of which Bernardin would become general secretary half a century later. This National Catholic War Council was established after America entered the war in April 1917, to coordinate Catholic efforts in response to the national emergency. This council, renamed the National Catholic Welfare Council in 1919, would not only be the framework for the bishops' organization that flowed from Vatican II, but would also be the instrument of the bishops' enunciation of a radical social policy. It was described by Catholic historian Francis L. Broderick as "perhaps the most forward looking social document ever to have come from an official Catholic agency in the United States."

This extraordinary transformation of the bishops from an acceptant, Rome-oriented group into the spokesmen for policies that would influence Franklin D. Roosevelt's New Deal fourteen years later was the outcome of the bishops' functioning, loosely yet effectively, through a novel structure. For the first time, it gave them an opportunity to speak with one voice that, while still softer than those of the great personalities of that era, allowed the bishops to address issues in a very different way than they ever had before. Indeed, the major figures in the great dioceses supported this liberal social program. Like the rest of the bishops, they were conservative on matters of dogma and church discipline but generally progressive in their convictions on social questions. This has characterized the American hierarchy throughout the century.

The Program on Social Reconstruction adopted by the bishops in 1919 was, in fact, based on the unedited notes of an undelivered speech of Father John A. Ryan, a priest of St. Paul, Minnesota, who had reconciled, according to McShane, the reform proposals of the Progressives, who were mostly middle-class Protestants, with the natural law principles found in Pope Leo XIII's pioneer social encyclical of 1891, *Rerum Novarum*. The program, its radical nature seemingly so at odds with the bishops' ordinary conservatism, called for a minimum wage, child labor laws, the right of labor to organize, old age and unemployment insurance, collective bargaining, public housing, vocational training, and control of monopolies.

Although the president of the National Association of Manufacturers complained to Cardinal Gibbons that the program was partisan, pro-labor union, socialist propaganda, the utopian writer Upton Sinclair hailed it as the "Catholic miracle," and Raymond Gram Swing wrote in *The Nation* of the social vision of the institution that "rightly or wrongly, has been reputed to be the most conservative." The groundwork had been laid not only for future consistent interventions of the Catholic bishops into public policy but for the post Vatican II organization of bishops whose emphasis on process would bring the great age of personality to a close in American Catholic ecclesiastical life. It would also be the organization to which Bernardin would give his complete energies and through which, submerging his own personality to its process and its goals, he would function for the rest of his career.

The conference of bishops called for by Vatican II was essentially different in many ways from the embryonic vehicle established during the First World War. The latter was not an official grouping of bishops to implement the principle of collegiality but a voluntary gathering with no binding jurisdiction on individual bishops that served as an instrument of service and policy development. When Archbishop Dearden was chosen in 1966 as the first president of the National Conference of Catholic Bishops after the conclusion of Vatican II, he faced an enormous and complex challenge. As he himself described his primary task at the time, "I want to develop this into a conference in which the bishops will learn to work together, I want it to be a sound and effective expression of collegiality."

This seemingly undramatic bureaucratic objective was, as Dearden well knew, to be a tense, demanding administrative adventure. First of all, Dearden had to draw the bishops into practical collaboration, something to which they were not at all accustomed; secondly, he had to vindicate the loyalty of the fledgling conference to Roman authorities who, despite Vatican II, were wary of any groupings of bishops who might, even unintentionally, seem to be challenging Roman control of their thinking and actions. Dearden also understood that, although many progressive American Catholics would pressure him to proceed in a charismatic, attention riveting manner, that the task could only be accomplished with subtlety, diligence, and a strong commitment to deepening rather than accentuating American loyalty to the pope and the Holy See. This would demand a hidden life on the part of those working out the new conference, one in which they would be called to submerge themselves into the project at hand. It was to assist in implementing this transformation of the mode of episcopal functioning that Joseph Bernardin had journeyed to Washington in the star-crossed summer of 1968.

Despite the washline slackness of its structures, the prior aggregation of bishops, the National Catholic Welfare Council, had been suspected of being almost subversive of Roman authority when it was first established. It had, in fact, been strongly criticized by two of the warrior kings of that golden ecclesiastical age, O'Connell of Boston and Dougherty of Philadelphia, sons of immigrant Irish who argued, with the fervor of the landlords who had driven their own forebears out of Ireland, that any collaborative venture of the bishops might overshadow or imperil the customary, individual way in which bishops did business with Rome. This argument would be revived fifty years later when national episcopal conferences were under fire once again. In the early twenties, such critiques, made by such powerful figures, led to dramatic consequences.

On Feb. 25, 1922, the Consistorial Congregation, that Roman department responsible for the world's bishops, speaking of the gatherings of the National Catholic Welfare Council, decreed that "such meetings are not to be held anymore." This decision was re-negotiated with Rome by a group of American bishops but for months their organization seemed as fated to disintegration as a dead cardinal's ceremonial hat in the vault of his cathedral. One of the negotiators, Bishop Joseph Schrembs, was American in his direct evaluation of the situation. "They," he said, referring to Roman officials, "are always talking about the autonomy of the single bishop. It's a smoke screen. What they mean is that it is easier to deal with one bishop than with a hierarchy." His statement captured what many considered the essence of the political reality that would reassert itself strongly when the as yet unborn Bernardin was a major factor in American Catholicism. Rome, having reinforced its control of universal church authority after Vatican I and through its stern resolution of the Modernist crisis, would remain skeptical of any developments that might even seem to challenge that control.

Dearden, choosing the path of undramatic implementation of the decrees of Vatican II on national conferences of bishops, felt that a solid foundation would be far more important than engaging in some highly publicized effort to democratize the American church. Such an approach would have gone against his nature, his vision, and his confidence that the task could be managed, respecting curial rights as well as those of the bishops, through patient and determined negotiation, much of it behind the scenes. He understood that the old world of great ecclesiastical figures was waning. The collegial age would require leaders who would forego the splendid isolation of bishops such as the late Thomas Molloy of Brooklyn who, secure in his island kingdom, refused ever to attend bishops' meetings. The new generation of bishops would, on the other hand, grow up attending meetings and working together as a matter of course.

Richard Cardinal Cushing, who had ridden the funeral train to Washington that June night in 1968, returned to a final few years in Boston, his health failing, his mood uncertain about the changing church and country. He would retire in 1970, depressed, among other things, by the fact that he, a great commoner among hierarchs, was faced by the strike of his own seminarians at the once fortress-like

St. John's Seminary of his own archdiocese. The seminarian spokesman during that strike was Bryan Hehir, who, as a priest, would a decade later, figure prominently as a source of intellectual energy in the United States Catholic Conference, the policy making counterpart of the National Catholic Conference of Bishops.

Cushing, weary from years of battling cancer and asthma, felt out of step and longed, he said, to spend his last years as a confessor for priests in a missionary setting in Peru. The vibrant colors had faded from his battle flag when his successor, Bishop Humberto Medeiros of Brownsville, Texas, was announced early in September. Medeiros, a native of the Azores, as a further footnote to change, would be the first archbishop of Boston who was not of Irish descent. Cushing's era seemed to die with him on the somber holy day of All Souls, Nov. 2, 1970. Medeiros soon discovered the challenge that would preoccupy him for most of his tenure as archbishop, paying off the enormous debts and straightening out the tangled organizational problems that had been hidden by the larger than life qualities of Cushing's personality.

The future was to be worked out by a generation of bishops with a very different orientation to their pastoral responsibilities. Joseph L. Bernardin, unpacking in Washington in that hot summer of discontent, would have a major, often unpublicized role, in developing a conference of bishops that would house these new collaborative, collegially minded bishops and be completely loyal to the pope and the Holy See at the same time. John Dearden was very pleased that summer that his old friend Paul Hallinan had urged Bernardin to accept the appointment for which his training, experience, and disposition fit him so well.

IV

Americans moved numbly through 1968's incandescent summer. Not only did they witness the assassinations of the Reverend Martin Luther King, Jr., and Senator Robert F. Kennedy, but they also saw the skies turned the apocalyptic color of blood by the arsonists' fires that accompanied rioting in the nation's largest cities. They were dizzied by the intermingled evening news clips of the Vietnam battlefields and the flag and draft card burning protests across the land. Public authority was at risk. By midyear, 221 demonstrations had taken place on 100 college or university campuses.

President Lyndon B. Johnson's nomination on June 26, 1968, of Associate Justice Abe Fortas to succeed Earl Warren as Chief Justice of the United States was greeted at first skeptically, then with hostility by Congress. Johnson would be forced to withdraw it by the beginning of October. In between, the August Democratic Convention in Chicago became the target and trophy of protestors who understood, under the wild, shadowed moon of that season, that civic authorities could be successfully baited into disastrous overreactions to their street theater.

The Catholic Church rocked with its own parallel convulsions. The period of reform ushered in by Vatican II had removed many of the restraints of the formerly dominant models of life for priests, religious men and women, and parishioners everywhere. The tools of theological and biblical scholarship were being applied in an effort to understand freshly the notions of authority in the New Testament and the early church. Catholics were taking up again the questions that had been suppressed when Modernism, with its spirit of free inquiry and intellectual curiosity, had been crushed more than a half a century before.

Archbishop Dearden, anxious that the enthusiasm for change be channeled in healthy and scholarly directions, understood that the priesthood in America required a careful and respectful assessment in terms of its history, sociology, psychology, theology, and ecumenical relationships. In 1967, he had given leadership to the bishops' funding a multidisciplinary study of the American clergy. Among the chairpersons chosen for the various specialties of the study were Monsignor, later Cardinal, William Baum, Monsignor John Tracy Ellis, Father Andrew Greeley, and the author of this biography. Investigate the priesthood, Archbishop Dearden felt, and the church would better understand itself and the great transformation through which it was passing. Everywhere, American Catholics were abuzz with the excitement of self-examination and self-determination. American Catholicism, like the land in which it was set, was in ferment when Bernardin settled for good into the NCCB staff house in Northeast Washington on July 18, 1968.

Bishop Bernardin was to take over his office at the bishops' headquarters building at 1312 Massachusetts Avenue still dealing with the questions and unresolved feelings with which some of the staff members had greeted his appointment. Many of the priests had functioned for years in the very different and more loosely structured predecessor organization and were adjusting uneasily to the prospect of recasting it along collegial lines. Most of the staff had expected Monsignor Francis Hurley, a highly talented and widely respected California priest who had been working the conference administration for some years, to receive the appointment as its first General Secretary, and were disappointed when the choice went to a man they considered an outsider. There was, therefore, a mixture of skepticism and resentment on the part of many of Hurley's friends and associates that was to test Bernardin's authority as well as his diplomacy as soon as he arrived.

Archbishop Dearden had selected Bernardin, he was later to say, because he needed "a man who was already a bishop," that is, someone who already possessed the episcopal credentials that facilitated his dealing with other bishops and with the varied offices of the Holy See. Hurley, a man of deep experience, could, in the minds of many, have been made a bishop to satisfy this requirement. But Dearden also wanted a fresh face at the conference, a General Secretary who had not been previously involved with the long time staff members, a person free of friendships or other commitments that might hamper his freedom in overseeing change. Whatever the reasoning, an admirable and qualified figure was passed over in favor of this stranger from South Carolina, and one of Bernardin's first tasks was to visit Hurley, whose disappointment he recognized, and to tell him, "Frank, I know you were the logical choice for this job. I turned it down twice and certainly did not want it at the price of your being hurt."

Hurley responded magnanimously, Bernardin later recalled, and was "always a gentleman" during the period that he remained at the conference before he was named a bishop in Alaska, later becoming the archbishop of Anchorage. Hurley's graciousness matched Bernardin's sensitivity to the Californian. The new General Secretary, judged at first to be ambitious, was soon recognized by other staff members for his gentle understanding and appreciation of their positions, and for his determination, even as he changed the world with which they were familiar, never to hurt their feelings. Bernardin approached this first strain in a manner that was soon identified both with him and with Archbishop Dearden: a nonauthoritarian readiness to be collegial themselves as they dealt with the problems of establishing an organizational structure to house the collegial church that had emerged from Vatican II.

In many ways, the Catholic Church's collegial emphasis in Vatican II, effectively shifting it away from its historically acquired monarchical character to a far more collaborative model based on the early church relationship between Christ and the apostles, was remarkably well suited to the times. The Catholic Church, pursuing the *aggiornamento* first proposed in 1959 by Pope John XXIII, was restoring a balance between the pope and the world's bishops that had, in the judgment of many, been temporarily set askew by the singular underscoring of papal authority in the truncated Vatican I. The doctrine of papal infallibility had contributed to the centralization of all authority in Rome, reducing that of the world's bishops so that their authority seemed to be delegated to them by the pope. Vatican II had refurbished the basic theological principle that acknowledged the primacy of the pope but also recognized that bishops possessed, in virtue of their ordination, authority of their own that was not doled out by the Holy Father. The bishops were to function not just in splendid isolation but in relationship to the pope and to each other, much as the college of the first apostles did at the beginnings of the church.

Bernardin's primary challenge was to oversee the day to day transformation of the conference that had grown in two generations from a wartime service vehicle to a combination clearinghouse and center for Catholic social and educational activities as well as information bureau into something almost startlingly different. Vatican II had not only reemphasized the individual authority of bishops but had established a theological basis for the existence of conferences of bishops within each of the world's nations. The structures that had been so vigorously attacked as destructive of church authority by Cardinals Dougherty and O'Connell more than forty years before were now rooted in *Lumen Gentium,* the conciliar document that undergirded collegiality as the authentic blood stream and nervous system of the church. The right of national conferences to exist and to reflect on cultural and moral problems would again be challenged vigorously more than a decade later. Joseph L. Bernardin, by then the cardinal archbishop of Chicago, would be called upon to defend and preserve the very structure whose table of organization he was beginning to supervise in 1968.

As soon as Dearden became first president of the new but as yet undeveloped conference in 1966, he had commissioned the consulting firm of Booz, Hamilton, and Allen to draw up plans for an organization built on Vatican II's collegial theological principles. The consultants were to apply their American organizational techniques, which Dearden had grown to admire in Detroit's auto industry, specifically to the *archtypon,* the framework for constitutions of episcopal conferences developed by the Holy See after the council was concluded. The firm's two volume report constituted Bernardin's blueprints in his new position. Bernardin, his own authority having survived its first testing by the staff, was to manage the practical recasting of church authority just as authority in general was being hammered on the anvil of that fierce and unforgiving summer.

The bitter late winter and early spring had seen Paul Hallinan die and Martin Luther King, Jr., gunned down on a motel balcony in Montgomery, Alabama. Despite the loss of its leader, the Poor People's March, a caravan of black people seeking to dramatize the still aching need for racial justice and a better national grasp of the problem of poverty, rolled its wagons up from the South to the great mall that spread down from the nation's capitol building to the Lincoln monument. On either side of the glittering reflecting pool, the poor pitched their tents in the churned mud and grass under the leadership of King's successor, Dr. Ralph Abernathy. Bernardin, keenly aware of racial problems from his own South Carolina upbringing and his work with Hallinan in supporting the black cause in Atlanta, was, along with most of the other bishops, anxious to provide something more concrete than just moral support and good wishes to the impoverished citizens of the country.

At the same time, he was responsible for responding sensibly and prudently should, as it was rumored, the demonstrators attempt to occupy the bishops' headquarters as other protestors had the offices of the National Council of Churches in New York City. To be sympathetic to the cause of the poor and of racial justice, to which the Catholic Church was pledged, and to deal with activists in a diplomatic and respectful manner were Siamese twin goals for Bernardin as he continued his commuting between Atlanta and Washington, D.C. Bernardin had to anticipate the possibility of an invasion and occupation of the Massachusetts Avenue offices while helping to plan longer range, formal, practical charitable responses to the poor on the part of the National Conference of Catholic Bishops.

The young bishop prepared to act in a manner as characteristic of him as his knowing acceptance of the Catholic doctrine of original sin. He understood that human beings were sinners, that things could go wrong almost infinitely even in the noblest human activities. But he also believed in dealing with an inherently disordered world methodically. In short, the two faces of Joseph L. Bernardin were here revealed—the forgiving pastor and the dedicated bureaucrat—aspects of himself that intermingled, supporting and tempering each other constantly as the creative source of his administrative style and strength.

No attempt to seize the bishops' offices ever took place but a program, the Campaign for Human Development, did grow under Bernardin's guidance, to provide monetary grants for deserving projects aimed at alleviating poverty. The body of bishops voted overwhelmingly for the campaign and for its funding. That left its administration to Bernardin who soon learned that distributing money had problems even more complicated than the task of raising it. Non-Catholic as well as Catholic organizations were eligible for the awards; this created the additional problem for Bernardin of making sure that the bishops' money did not go to support actions, such as abortion, to which the bishops were opposed.

Bernardin worked closely with John Cardinal Krol, archbishop of Philadelphia, in formulating a policy that would safeguard the church's doctrinal commitments while still granting funds to secular agencies and institutions. Bernardin found Krol an exceptionally shrewd and able executive as they forged an understanding that funds could be sent to any organization as long as its basic thrust was not contrary to church teaching. If one element of its operations could be segregated for support, the campaign would approve the grant. Good judgment was the element crucial to the success of the undertaking. Such prudence was considered a principal virtue in the writings of St. Thomas Aquinas and, on the practical level, was, and remains, a central feature of Bernardin's mode of combining his roles as a pastor and a manager.

Bernardin, on the cusp of early middle age, found in the 57-year-old Krol, who had been made a cardinal the year before, a man who was very different, and yet in some ways very like, himself. They were both extremely intelligent and, in one sense, they were both outsiders to the hierarchy which for generations had been controlled by Irish, and to a lesser extent, German-American bishops. Krol was as staunchly pre-conciliar in his views of the church as Bernardin was post-conciliar; Krol was direct, aggressive, aware of his personal authority while Bernardin was open, diplomatic, more attuned to collegial process than the unexamined exercise of episcopal authority.

On the other hand, they had, along with Hallinan and Dearden, sprung from the same root of ecclesiastical influence in the American church, one whose origins and meaning must be appreciated to understand them and the Catholicism they served. Until Pope Pius XII died in 1958, Francis Cardinal Spellman had been without peer in selecting and deploying new bishops in the United States. When Pope John XXIII succeeded to the throne of Peter, he did not wait long to make significant appointments in the Roman bureaucracy. One of his initial moves was to recall to the Vatican the 75-year-old Archbishop Amleto Cicognani, who had served as apostolic delegate in Washington, D.C., for a quarter of a century. John XXIII made him a cardinal and head of the Oriental Congregation, raising him to secretary of state in 1961.

During his time in the United States, Cicognani had become a close friend of Edward Hoban, five years his senior, a Chicago priest who had become the bishop of Cleveland in 1945. He had entertained Cicognani frequently over the years, often at such places as the villa run by the Chicago archdiocese for its seminarians in northern Wisconsin. As soon as Cicognani returned to the Eternal City, Hoban's counsel became prized among the officials who reviewed the candidacy of potential bishops and with the pope who finally appointed them. "Archbishop Hoban," according to John Tracy Ellis, "became *ex aequo* with Cardinal Spellman in his influence on the choosing of new bishops."

Among the many men from the Cleveland region who soon gained prominence in the American church were John Dearden, Paul Hallinan, and John Krol, who had gone to Philadelphia in 1961. Bernardin, chosen by Hallinan to be a bishop, and selected by Dearden to become first General Secretary of the new bishops' conference, shared, therefore, the same hierarchical bloodlines as Krol.

They represented an infusion of midwestern tradition into the politics of an American Catholicism whose major decisions had long been made on the east coast of the country. Although from separate generations, Krol and Bernardin symbolized a shift in emphasis, outlook, and national and career origins in the Catholic Church in the United States. The young bishop and the new cardinal would have a great deal to do with each other in the years ahead.

Bernardin's early close working relationship with John Cardinal Krol, along with so many other events and persons with whom he came into contact were seeds borne on 1968's raging winds that would flower very differently in the years ahead. Archbishop Dearden felt that Bernardin should come to know the leaders of the various Roman departments with whom he would be dealing on routine business as General Secretary. He asked John Cardinal Cody of Chicago to accompany and introduce Bernardin to the curial officials who headed what were technically called the dicasteries of the Roman Catholic Church. Cody, who loved Rome in its promise as well as its intrigues and visited there more than a hundred times during his life, was happy to carry out the task. Genial, confident that he could still handle the Chicago archdiocese whose priests had already rebelled at his imperious ways, Cody was an affable and helpful companion to the man who, 14 years later, would succeed him as archbishop of that city.

Cody's troubles with his priests had started almost as soon as he had stepped off the Panama Limited from his former see of New Orleans to be greeted by Mayor Richard J. Daley and other dignitaries as Chicago's new archbishop in 1965. Cody, whose experience and penchant for absolute control had not prepared him for collegiality as a style of administration, chose to ignore his priests' understandable post-Vatican II interest in greater participation in the decision-making that affected their lives and work. Rebuffed by Cody, who also let his incoming mail pile up in cardboard boxes strewn throughout his residence because he insisted on reading and answering it personally, his priests began, within six months of his arrival, to meet in small groups to discuss their relationships with their new archbishop. They soon organized the Association of Chicago Priests, a nonofficial yet very real structure for expressing the grievances and wishes of the clergy.

By the summer of 1966, 1300 Chicago priests convened for a plenary session at McCormick Place, the slab-like lakefront convention hall. Cody, who had resisted even acknowledging the reality of this movement, recognized the power in the numbers and attended, speaking vague but encouraging words to the assembled priests. The meeting was historical as it foreshadowed the development of similar associations in dioceses throughout the country. A movement similar to this in its democratic aspirations, it should be noted, had taken place among American priests almost 80 years before and had been snuffed out by an unyielding stance toward it on the part of American bishops and Roman authorities. Bishops unsympathetic to extra-canonical structures, such as Philadelphia's Krol, would often refer to the unsuccessful nineteenth century movement in their comments on these grass-roots clerical reactions in the sixties.

In May of 1968, however, priest delegates from around the nation met in Chicago for a constitutional convention to establish the National Federation of Priests' Councils, electing Chicagoan Father Patrick O'Malley as its first president. Patrick Cardinal O'Boyle of Washington, D.C., forbade any of his priests to attend the meeting. The plates were clearly shifting beneath the surface of Catholicism's new world culture. And as the earth heaved and settled, the landscape would be filled with faces with which Bernardin would become very familiar.

One belonged to a priest who was deeply disappointed not to be elected by his fellow clergymen as a member of the first board of the Association of Chicago Priests, or to any role in the national federation whose aims he had encouraged, Father Andrew Greeley. Like Bernardin, he had also celebrated his 40th birthday earlier in that fateful year, throwing himself a lavish party in the tower of the Chicago Hilton. In Rome, Monsignor Giovanni Benelli, a man of the same generation who, just the year before, had been made *sostituto* in the secretariat of state, virtually running that powerful Vatican office, decided that Bishop Joseph Bernardin, whom he had met only recently, was a man whose opinions, along with those of such figures as Notre Dame's Father Theodore Hesburgh, could be trusted. Bernardin had the added grace of being an Italian-American and so needed no education in the subtleties and nuances of Vatican communication. Benelli might not always follow Bernardin's advice but he knew that he would always get a balanced and sensible appraisal from the new General Secretary of the American bishops.

Nine days after Bernardin finally settled full time in Washington, Pope Paul VI issued his encyclical letter *Humanae Vitae* on birth control. The Catholic Church had, in the years of perfervid self-examination immediately after the council, come to resemble a hall stacked with combustible materials. In 1968, this document proved to be the spark that ignited them. Joseph L. Bernardin, reading the text of the encyclical on July 29 of that ill-starred summer, was keenly aware of the rocky history of the document's development and of how, little more than a year before, controversy over the church's traditional prohibition of birth control had spread like an oil slick across the campus of the nearby Catholic University of America.

The Catholic world, and the world in general, had long anticipated a papal statement about the issue of birth control. The church had consistently condemned as intrinsically sinful any attempt to interfere with conception, insisting that the primary end of marriage, according to its traditional teaching, was "procreation and the education of children." In 1951, Pope Pius XII had acknowledged the complexities of the population problem and had, for the first time, approved of the use of the rhythm method of birth regulation for Catholics. Although birth control was not on the agenda of Vatican II, the conflicted subject was in the air. From all corners of the world, bishops, well aware of their flock's dissatisfaction with the church's generally legalistic attitude toward marriage, came to Rome with serious pastoral questions about the issue.

A Catholic physician, John Rock, had developed the birth control pill and, in the spring of 1963, had put into words the doubts and worries that had formed in Catholic consciences everywhere. In *The Time Has Come: A Catholic Doctor's Proposals to End the Battle over*

Birth Control, Rock, a Harvard professor, urged the Catholic Church to reevaluate its position, stating what many already believed, that the pill was a "morally permissible variant of the rhythm method." Rock received enormous criticism from many Catholic sources but his archbishop, Richard Cardinal Cushing, resisted pressures to excommunicate him, and, in Rome, Pope John XXIII had already appointed a six member commission to advise him on the question of birth control. John XXIII died in June 1963, but his successor, Pope Paul VI, expanded the advisory commission on issues of population and fertility control.

This commission, which included not only theologians and bishops but such distinguished laypersons as Mr. and Mrs. Patrick Crowley of Chicago, pioneers of the Cana Conferences that reinforced Catholic marriages, made an exhaustive study of the historical, doctrinal, and cultural dimensions of the problem. The majority of the commission recommended a change in the church's absolute prohibition of birth control as well as a recognition of the nourishment of the love of spouses as a purpose of marriage on the same level with that of procreation.

In mid-April 1967, the *National Catholic Reporter* published the text of the opinion proposed by the majority of the commission, recommending altering the church's position on birth control. This sensational development, which seemed to express the already well formed consensus of Catholics in many countries, highlighted not only the possibility of transformation in the church but of the traditional primacy of conscience for Catholics in their moral decisions. Pope Paul VI, according to his secretary of state, Amleto Cardinal Cicognani, in a letter to bishop members of the commission, "has grieved most heavily over the publication of the documents." In the same week that the premature publication of the majority views so grieved the pope, a 33-year-old professor of moral theology at Catholic University, Father Charles Curran, was told by Monsignor William J. MacDonald, the university rector, that he was being fired because of his dissent from church teachings on birth control. The already sorrowful pope was soon more deeply troubled by reports that a faculty and student strike had erupted in defense of Curran after the papally chartered university's board of trustees refused to rescind MacDonald's decision. Apocalypse, with its jumbled stars and convulsing world, seemed to have arrived in the normally stable Roman Catholic Church.

After several days of picketing and negotiation, the archbishop of Washington, Patrick Cardinal O'Boyle, a staunch defender of traditional teachings and almost aggressively loyal to the pope, stood on the steps of the university library and read a statement. "The board of trustees," he intoned solemnly, "has voted to abrogate its decision." After the shouts died away, the unsmiling O'Boyle continued, "This decision in no way derogates from the teachings of the church by the popes and bishops on birth control." O'Boyle would not forget this bitter moment. His Irish features were set with fierce determination as he turned away. He would not flinch the next time the pope's teaching authority was challenged within the boundaries of his diocese.

The Washington archbishop had grown up in the diamond hard coalfield landscape near Scranton, Pennsylvania. He had known poverty, the death of his father, the enormous sacrifices of his mother, the support of the Catholic Church. John L. Lewis had sounded to the young O'Boyle like Moses when he called the poor, grimestained miners out of their desolation into the protection of the union. Later, as a young priest, he studied social work at Columbia University and headed Catholic War Relief at its New York headquarters. He had seen what the organizations of great institutions could do to alleviate suffering and improve life. No man, as he saw it, could forget that only absolute loyalty kept these institutions strong and vigorous. He grieved inwardly at having to confront his brother priests, but he had no doubt that duty called him to do exactly that.

Pope Paul VI, a deeply sensitive person whose agonies of decision making had earned him a reputation as a Hamlet in the Vatican, had struggled for months before issuing the encyclical. He had, many observers felt, telegraphed his intentions clearly in his address to the United Nations on his one day visit to New York in 1965 when he urged its members to find food for all rather than limit the number of those who sat at the world's table. Still, the advice of a distinguished panel could not be ignored. The head of the Holy Office, Alfredo Cardinal Ottaviani, according to Robert Blair Kaiser in his brilliant book, *The Politics of Sex and Religion,* (Leaven Press, 1985) had orchestrated a second, highly secret commission whose members wrote the draft of the encyclical that would restate the familiar position. While the majority of the first commission's members cited instances in which the church had changed its mind about its moral judgments, the very idea of the church's admitting that it might have erred on a matter of such significance as birth control was the overpowering problem for Ottaviani and, subsequently, for the pope.

It was one thing for the church to have foregone its once absolute condemnation of usury and so give rise to Christian capitalism; it was perhaps admissible that Vatican II had repudiated Pius IX's nineteenth century encyclical, *Quantum Cura,* that had described religious liberty as a "delirium"; it was impossible to admit a change in the matter of birth control without imperilling the teaching authority, or magisterium, of the papacy itself. In the ten years remaining in his pontificate, Paul VI would never write another encyclical after he signed his name to *Humanae Vitae.*

The central argument of this document was stated succinctly in paragraph 11: "It is necessary that each and every marriage act must remain open to the transmission of life." Paragraph 14 repeated the church's traditional position: ". . . Every action which either in anticipation of the conjugal act, or in its accomplishment, or in the development of its natural consequences, proposes, whether as an end or as a means, to render procreation impossible" must be excluded as an acceptable means of regulating birth.

While Bernardin was conferring with Archbishop Dearden to draft a statement of reaction to be checked out by perhaps the first collegial consultation by phone with the American bishops, the ecclesiastical weathervane was sent spinning by the winds of reaction. In Washington, D.C., just two days after the issuance of the encyclical, the Association of Washington Priests, echoing the bishops of Belgium, produced a statement that touched on what would be the crucial issue of dissent: Catholics might respect the pope and in conscience disagree with his conclusions in *Humanae Vitae*. The next Sunday, Aug. 4, 1968, the 72-year-old Cardinal O'Boyle, still smarting over the reinstatement of Father Curran at Catholic University the year before, distributed a letter to be read at all masses in his archdiocese, demanding total compliance with the encyclical from his priests.

This was the first in a melancholy series of incidents that, bitter for all parties, would symbolize the conflict in the still not fully adjusted post-conciliar era between those, such as O'Boyle, who believed in old-fashioned unquestioning loyalty to every statement of the pope, and those, such as a new generation of scholars, who believed both in exploring the theological reasoning of papal documents and in the ultimate primacy of the individual conscience as well. On that hot Sunday morning O'Boyle had drawn a line in the dust, forbidding his priests to step across it. Bernardin was soon drawn onto the battlefield, like those of the Civil War clustered around Washington, on which the blood of men who had once been brothers and comrades would be spilled.

O'Boyle, a down to earth, highly intelligent, but, like many bishops of his generation, nonintellectual leader, saw the issue as that of maintaining legitimate authority in the church. It was a summer in which other shrewd, successful Irish-Americans, who had always seen loyalty to authority as an element in their nationality's becoming true Americans, would make similar judgments. Chicago's Mayor Richard J. Daley, at 66 a few years younger than O'Boyle, would decide that public authority had been placed at risk by wild and taunting demonstrators and that, at whatever cost, good order had to be restored in his city.

Just as the Chicago mayor clamped down half way across the country, so O'Boyle, particularly concerned that the Catholic University, of which he was chancellor, remain orthodox, decided that strong measures had to be taken to reinforce episcopal control of its faculty, even if this meant he had opened a two-front war. His strong letter of the first Sunday of August may have been influenced by the statement that had been issued by 20 Catholic University theologians on July 30. In it, they had asserted that it was ''common teaching in the church that Catholics may dissent from authoritative noninfallible teachings of the magisterium when sufficient reasons for doing so exist.''

Meanwhile, Bernardin, aware of the explosive nature of the Washington situation, succeeded, within a day, of getting the telephonic approval of the body of American bishops for a restrained statement that underscored the authority of the pope while respecting the consciences of believers. Most American bishops did not want to press their priests or people strongly for public declarations of loyalty to the pope. Aside from Buffalo, Washington was the only major American city in which the conflict was to flare so painfully. As General Secretary of the bishops, Bernardin was deeply concerned about the maintenance of the pope's teaching authority. He would do everything he could to support it but he was keenly aware that forcing public confrontations on an issue as sensitive as birth control might diminish rather than enhance that authority.

The 40-year-old South Carolinian was also well acquainted with the outlook of younger priests and of the new generation of theologians. They needed to be listened to rather than disciplined without a hearing. Some sensible compromise, Bernardin felt, along with most other bishops, could be worked out to respect both papal authority and the integrity of dissenting priests and scholars. For the moment, he could do little about the situation except to counsel patience on both sides. The problem was that each side was in the mood for a good fight.

Bernardin, who had grown up surrounded by Irish-born or Irish-American clergy, was now well acquainted with what at times seemed contradictory qualities of leadership in the American Catholic Church. Although his first mentor had been the gentle, intellectual Hallinan and he was now working with the urbane and cultured Dearden, he also had come to know the scrappy O'Boyle, unyielding as a character out of O'Casey, and James Francis Cardinal McIntyre, the archbishop of Los Angeles who, a few years before, had forced one of his dissenting priests, Father William Dubay, to pledge renewed obedience in public ceremonial fashion.

Now, as Bernardin knew, the 82-year-old McIntyre, as solemn as the Wall Street businessman he had been before entering seminary, had informed O'Boyle that he would withhold his large annual donation to Catholic University until its theological faculty was brought back into orthodox formation. Bernardin felt the toughness of these men, powerful incarnations of the bygone churchmen who had fought for the rights of their immigrant flocks and who brooked no opposition in their administration of the church. He also understood the enormous contributions they had made, according to their lights and in their time, to the development and stabilization of American Catholicism. He would, as part of a summer that would be prophetic for his later career, soon find himself as the mediator between two groups equally dedicated to the church: these larger-than-life traditional archbishops and the new generation of priests whose lungs were filled with the fresh air of Vatican II.

O'Boyle, meanwhile, had summoned his dissenting priests for individual interviews, quickly reducing their number from 60 to 40 and then to a remnant of 19, suspending some of these, and demanding, like the allies in World War II, unconditional surrender as his price for their full reinstatement. When one group of 353 parishioners sent him an appeal to revoke his suspension of one priest, O'Boyle dismissed them as ''good and simple people'' who didn't understand the situation. While totally ignoring a petition from another group of more than two thousand lay persons, he prepared and issued, on September 20, a pastoral letter in which he predicted that the curse of Deuteronomy would descend on all who insisted on following their own consciences instead of God's law. If priests did not recant, they would find themselves outside the priesthood. This document followed O'Boyle's move, agreed to by 20 other bishop trustees of Catholic University, to suspend the 20 theologians who had issued the dissenting statement of July 30.

That the world had changed drastically from the age in which the command of any bishop received prompt and quiet compliance became clear when the episcopal trustees of the Catholic University found themselves facing an unfamiliar thicket of issues including due process and academic freedom. The bishops were soon parties to an inquiry conducted by a committee of Catholic University faculty that, after a year of testimony and deliberation, exonerated the 20 accused professors and criticized the bishops for their arbitrary approach to the problem. They also noted that the accused scholars were "compelled to some kind of honest response" and that "a concerted silence would have been more truly improper."

The body of the bishops accepted these findings, despite the dissatisfaction of the cardinal archbishops of Washington and Los Angeles, at their spring meeting in Houston the next year. O'Boyle who, winking at a layman who had yelled a cheer for him as he entered a Washington church at the height of the turmoil, said that the "professors are good men but they have more depth than they have width," found himself embroiled in an increasingly oppressive and painful controversy. According to a priest who was close to him at the time, O'Boyle did not want to battle with his priests but he felt that a principle of loyalty to the pope was involved that he could not ignore. He remained sensitive about the incident for the rest of his life, peering through the curtains of the cathedral rectory on the day of his 50th anniversary of ordination, needlessly fearful that few priests would show up to celebrate with him.

In the autumn of 1968, however, as Hubert Humphrey strove to disentangle himself from Lyndon Johnson's Vietnam policies as he battled Richard Nixon for the presidency, the young Bishop Bernardin was asked by Pope Paul VI, through Secretary of State Cicognani, to mediate the dispute between Cardinal O'Boyle and the priests who, in the Catholic press, had been named, in the fashion of the day, the "Washington 19." If this was a vote of confidence in Bernardin, it was also a diplomatic assignment whose conditions made success problematic. Bernardin was forbidden to disclose that he had been given this assignment by the Holy See. As he moved into negotiations, he had to accept silently the immediate impression that he had been invited to intervene by Cardinal O'Boyle. This made the priests wary of him, for, fearing that he was O'Boyle's man, they bit hard on the coin of his intentions, testing and making more difficult his role as an impartial mediator.

Bernardin, as he would do in many subsequent situations, accepted the conditions without complaint. He would rely on his own integrity in trying to establish a process of dialogue that would minimize and outlast the impact of the involved personalities, including his own. Both the priests and the cardinal would have to make their own judgments about his even-handedness as the discussions progressed. Although O'Boyle cooperated and a number of scenarios to resolve the impasse were developed, the cardinal, who felt that the measure of a man was how much steel there was in him, could never bring himself to agree completely to any of them.

Bernardin, however, retained the confidence of all parties as the conversations continued, employing the patient approach that would grow to seem second nature to him in the years ahead. Always conscience of wanting to act correctly, Bernardin masked his own feelings, submerging them through the habitual self-control that he had learned early in life. Nor would he ever give any indication to others of the internal cost to him of not allowing his own emotions to interfere with the process of negotiation. He might express frustration privately, for he was not without feelings or personal opinions, but he always did this discreetly and nonjudgmentally, according to those who knew him well, and never in ways that would attract publicity to the matter at hand. His capacity for self-control and for maintaining confidences was admired by his superiors in the church for these were the features, smooth as the time-worn stones of Rome, that the Vatican valued in its emissaries. Those with whom he worked identified his talent for listening to both sides in disputed matters, refusing to be drawn into the often irrelevant if satisfying arguments that arose, ever ready to begin again after tempers cooled. These soon became the hallmark of his style.

"Perhaps," a priest friend observed at the time, "we are finally seeing the gifts of the Italian temperament emerge in the American church." The "Washington 19" skirmishes revealed Irish-Americans, for the most part, deployed for battle. That national group had supplied most of the priests and, therefore, most of the bishops in American Catholicism. O'Boyle found his dissenting priests led by men named O'Donaghue and Corrigan. The Irish-American ethos and the echoes of both its proud loyalty to and feisty challenges of authority were being illustrated at about the same time in Chicago. Father David Tracy, one of the exonerated scholars from the Catholic University faculty, had accepted a position at the University of Chicago. John Cardinal Cody had asked him indignantly what kind of an Irishman he really was. "I'm the kind of Irish," Cody had proclaimed without waiting for the bemused theologian's answer, "who, when people attack the pope, he fights."

Not the least of the new truths about American Catholicism that could be discerned in that turbulent year was the emergence of men without Irish names in positions of leadership. John Krol had, only a few years previously, become the first priest of Polish descent to head an important archdiocese when he succeeded John Cardinal O'Hara, who had succeeded Dennis Cardinal Dougherty, as archbishop of Philadelphia. Only a few months before O'Boyle and his priests stood off against each other, Francis J. Mugavero became the first Italian-American to lead a large diocese when he took over Brooklyn from Bishop Bryan McEntagart who had been preceded by bishops named Loughlin, McDonnell, and Molloy. In that year in that same Brooklyn diocese, a young lawyer named Mario Cuomo, a first generation Italian much like Bernardin, was beginning to make a name for himself as a skilled negotiator and public servant.

Something was beginning to happen in American culture and in American Catholicism. Perhaps it was not unexpected that the Irish, as in Washington, D.C., would, like estranged sons battling their fathers in many a Gaelic tale, display their forthrightness and their readiness for a good fight. Bernardin represented not only a new generation of bishops but, like Cuomo, a way of approaching the politics of church and state with a combination, rich and sun-warmed as Italy's ancient vineyards, of subtlety and realism. If Bernardin did not reflect on such matters, his emergence as General Secretary of the bishops and as a mediator chosen by the pope himself was an indicator of transformations under way in the distribution of power in the American Catholic Church. In 1970, when Portuguese-American Humberto Medeiros succeeded Richard J. Cushing as archbishop of Boston, a cabdriver would offer a footnote to the changes taking place by saying to Bernardin, as if mourning a loss on the day of Medeiro's installation, "If you ain't Irish here in Boston, you ain't anything."

Bernardin discovered that O'Boyle was quintessentially Irish in his stubborn reluctance to compromise, lest he compromise loyalty to the pope. To a question as to whether he would reconcile with the priests if the pope told him to, O'Boyle replied, "Right away." It was a genuine disappointment for Bernardin when his mission of arbitration did not succeed. "He was given an impossible assignment," observed Monsignor George Higgins who, as head of the department of Social Action of the bishops' conference, observed the proceedings at first hand. "They wanted him to make bricks without straw, expecting him to work a miracle without giving him any portfolio. He had no real authority but he worked very hard at the problem. And he took great pains not to hurt anyone."

The National Federation of Priests' Councils energetically took over the pursuit of a solution, investing enormous amounts of time and over $30,000 in what its chairman, Father Patrick O'Malley of Chicago, understood as a historical effort to vindicate the canonical rights of individual priests in relationship to church authority. Some months later, the case would be referred to the Sacred Congregation for the Clergy in Rome, headed by another Irish-American, the former bishop of Pittsburgh, John Cardinal Wright, who was as determined as O'Boyle to resist the democratization of the priesthood by a successful challenge of O'Malley's group to a sitting cardinal archbishop. As Bernardin later recalled, the ultimate, long delayed resolution of the case "followed one of the plans we had worked out in secret in Washington." He also learned that none of the compromises he had transmitted to Rome had ever been referred to the Congregation for the Clergy which was ultimately to settle the matter. His efforts had been doomed all along.

By the time of the disposition of the matter in 1971, many of the "Washington 19" priests had withdrawn from the active ministry and O'Boyle was left to nurse the wounds of the encounters for the rest of his days. The event could, like many an Irish family estrangement, be understood as a battering fight that exhausted the combatants and ended with no clear victory, only sadness, for both sides. If the lives of the Washington priests were irrevocably changed, O'Boyle's was also, for never again was he as self-confident or self-complacent as he had once been. He would almost apologetically ask the priest who was to give the luncheon talk at his golden jubilee "not to mention the troubles."

Pope Paul VI did not, in the succeeding years, criticize the bishops' conferences that issued statements acknowledging the primacy of individual conscience in making moral decisions. Nor did he ever punish theological dissenters. The American bishops repeatedly pledged their loyalty to the pope but dealt with birth control, as they do to this very day, as a pastoral rather than a disciplinary matter. The issue gradually moved away from being a test of public authority in the church to being the proper concern of the theologically informed private conscience.

The major incidents with Father Charles Curran, the Catholic University faculty members, and the "Washington 19" suggested that the American church had, in Yeat's phrase, "changed utterly." As Robert Blair Kaiser wrote, "It was a good lesson for many American Catholics, who had never before realized that any Catholics could dissent from an authoritative papal teaching and still be loyal to the church.... In the post-conciliar church, as the inquiry board put it, it was apparent that 'theological reflection must develop in dialogue with the entire church and with others.' " (*The Politics of Sex and Religion,* pp. 208, 209.)

Bernardin's main administrative task, to implement the Booz Allen blueprints for structuring the National Conference of Catholic Bishops according to Vatican II theology, was, amidst many absorbing and time consuming distractions, his central preoccupation. One of the added jobs he was given by Archbishop Dearden was that of making sure, in that period of tumult, that the multidisciplinary study of the American priesthood went forward. The bishops were, after all, just getting accustomed to the idea of working together and the notion of involving themselves with research scholars, even though they were priests, was only one of many projects on their agenda. The priest-scholars were anxious to begin but their research designs first needed episcopal approval as well as adequate funding.

The preparations dragged on, catching on bureaucratic snags and other uncertainties. Although John Cardinal Krol would soon be asked by Archbishop Dearden to oversee the studies, Bishop Bernardin assumed the task of coordinating the bishops' relationships with the priest chairmen of the involved disciplines. On September 7, as the country and the church within it boiled over with the events of the summer, Bernardin arranged a meeting during a stopover at O'Hare Field with Father Greeley, who headed the sociology team, and the author of this book, who headed the psychology team. The bishop displayed an understanding sympathy to the problems of the researchers and promised his support as he urged them to keep their work on track and to submit detailed proposals to the bishops. Greeley expressed dismay about the possible episcopal censorship of the findings of the investigations. Bernardin, his briefcase bulging with other urgent business, reassured the scholar-priests about their independence and they agreed afterward that Bernardin had been a helpful, well prepared, and trustworthy intermediary.

Working with the holdover staff personnel back at the office required as much or more tact as negotiating with scholars. As Archbishop Thomas Kelly of Louisville, who served at the Apostolic Delegation during that period, recalled, "Many of the veterans were good men but were not really capable of adjusting to a whole new way of doing things. The period of implementing the process was a very painful time. Bernardin displayed his finest characteristics in dealing with and reassigning them. He was always kindly, never wanting to hurt anybody's feelings, and he was never petty. He was very forgiving of human foibles."

Although Bernardin was assisted by, among others, John O'Neill, a layman who had once been a Trappist and later a business executive, in putting the new structure into place operationally, the main responsibility was his. The original National Catholic Welfare Conference provided a shaky basis for a national organization on the scale of the conciliar vision of the bishops' renewed collegial function in the church. The prototype structure that had been put somewhat hastily into place during the First World War had a small budget, paid low salaries, and, as Archbishop Kelly, who became the new organization's third General Secretary in 1977, later recalled, "needed to be turned into a real professional organization, a healthy bureaucracy with all that that implies—reviews, salary scales, rules about who could make statements—and Bernardin, along with those he selected to work with him, solidified the conference."

Just as 1968 had brought Bernardin into close contact with persons who would reappear later in his life, the challenge of building the conference did the same. In 1970, he recruited a 44-year-old priest from Minnesota, Father James Rausch, to function alongside him as Associate General Secretary. Rausch, who was just completing his doctoral dissertation, accepted the position, developing a smooth, practical relationship with Bernardin and, in 1972, succeeding him as General Secretary when the latter became archbishop of Cincinnati.

Rausch, with a profound interest in politics and in international affairs, proved to be a hard driving administrator, a man who could also be fascinated by the details of establishing, for example, a counterpart civil organization to the national conference, the United States Catholic Conference, through which the bishops could address public issues in a systematic way. Its members were to be the bishops but the committee and staff of its departments of communications, education, and social development would be made up of priests, religious, and laypersons. These, with subdivisions of their own, would, among other things, prepare curriculum materials for Catholic schools and adult education programs, write articles for Catholic newspapers and journals, and represent the church before various branches of government.

The National Conference of Catholic Bishops would communicate in its own fashion, through joint pastoral letters, formal statements, special messages, and resolutions and brief statements. While Rausch labored with Bernardin to get these associated organizations firmly established, he also helped recruit people to serve in the various offices. In 1971, he recruited the young priest who had been spokesperson for the striking Boston seminarians not long before, Father Bryan Hehir, who would, in Archbishop Kelly's opinion, become the "intellectual mainstay of the organization."

Indeed, the conference structure was becoming solid enough

now to bear the weight of the pastoral letters on nuclear war and the American economy that would rise from it, along with heavy Vatican criticism, ten years later. It would remain, as a theological and bureaucratic entity, at the center of Bernardin's later work. Individuals like Rausch, Hehir, and Kelly, along with Krol, O'Boyle, Dearden, and a galaxy of other American clerics, including a Navy chaplain then stationed in the Far East named John O'Connor, would also appear and reappear constantly. At times they would assume leading roles and at other times supporting parts, sometimes as allies and sometimes as adversaries, in the unfolding drama of Bernardin's life—a life whose personal and public aspects would be increasingly difficult to separate from one another.

In his first years as General Secretary, Joseph L. Bernardin had, in a real sense, survived an Irish brawl, undergone an extraordinary test of his faith and convictions, and experienced the scrutiny of Roman authorities, his fellow bishops, and American priests without being diminished in the sight of any of them. His mission to the "Washington 19" had failed but he had not. Bernardin, keenly aware that he was being evaluated by all parties, emerged from his baptism by immersion in the international church believing more firmly than ever in the importance of process over personality in resolving disputed issues within it. During that stormy year he completed a rite of passage that increased his trustworthiness, or "credibility," as this intangible but vital quality came to be called in the American church.

Bernardin had, above all, met every expectation of Conference President Archbishop John Dearden. The Detroit prelate and the General Secretary deepened their relationship so that it came to have the characteristics of that between Bernardin and the late Archbishop Paul Hallinan. It was not exactly intimate friendship; it was more that of a father with a dutiful son who was proving to be an ideal inheritor of his vision and beliefs, that of the head of General Motors comfortable in gentlemanly comradeship with a younger executive much like himself, a man who would carry on for him.

If Bernardin, in his mannered, talented ways, his reluctance to hurt others, and his devotion to the institution as well as the people of the Catholic Church, closely resembled Dearden, he also learned that summer the fierce lessons of being an ecclesiastical administrator that his mentor had come to accept years before. For Bernardin felt in the depths of his being the tensions that were inevitable for a bishop who was completely dedicated to the church and its traditions yet keenly aware of its own stirring inner impulses for growth. He could never, he realized, sacrifice one for the other.

V

In 1968, the scientific vessel *Glomar Challenger* was the platform for drilling through the crust of the ocean floor to extract cores layered with information supporting the theory of a plate-like geological formation of the earth. That the continents floated on such vast drifting islands surprised nobody who lived through that earthquake year. The windows had been sent rattling in every institution that supposedly anchored society, from government to education to the churches. The major professions, once secure in their self-understandings and autonomy, began to suffer what many of them described as identity crises. Among these was the priesthood. If the dissent and confrontations of the year had not been enough, many clergyman came openly to express their doubts about their relevance in society as well as about the formerly unquestioned disciplines of their calling, such as celibacy. Ann Landers, reflecting on the problems of the day, wryly observed that "people go to see the priest to arrange their marriage only to find out that he's arranging his own."

Priests and nuns, once the symbols of an orderly, providentially guided world, withdrew in large numbers from their rectories and convents. Many who remained, like Fathers Philip and Daniel Berrigan, became active in the anti-war protest movements, performing liturgical burnings and splatterings of draft records, their sketched portraits at their multiplied trials becoming commonplace on the evening news. Other priests, nuns, and brothers, emerging from once hidden lives, involved themselves in social crusades, marching and demonstrating for civil rights, engaging in draft counseling, and other radical movements of the time.

Bishop Bernardin was not insulated from the shocks and aftershocks that radiated through the church. He understood that, although he often played a background role, at times mediating between protesting priests and their bishops and religious superiors in order to keep them in good standing, these events made more urgent his primary task of reorganizing the bishops' conference and expediting its projects. The restructuring, he later observed, went according to plan, especially with the assistance of Father Rausch, but "the real difficulties came from other sources." Taking on behind-the-scenes negotiations in delicate matters was sometimes "like kneading dough" and tested the deepest reserves of his patience and diplomacy.

Some of the conflicts, such as the standoff between Cardinal O'Boyle and his priests, were not fully resolved but others, bubbling with as many difficulties and bound by confidentiality, were brought to quiet and satisfactory conclusions. Bernardin's discretion—he never violated a confidence, told others only as much as they needed to know, and displayed an almost strenuous impartiality in discussions—gained him a reputation not only in the United States but among the men who labored beneath the frescoed ceilings of Roman congregations. Bernardin's sensitivity and capacity to keep secrets, according to a priest who worked with him at the time, was "an investment that was paid back by the Holy See's attitude of trust toward him."

The transformation of the bishops' conference into a practical, working instrument of collegiality was not only the fulfillment of the decrees of Vatican II but also, on a pragmatic level, a development essential for the survival of the church in a period during which relationships of authority were being reworked, sometimes thoughtfully but often haphazardly, all across society. Bernardin believed, along with Dearden, that the large scale study of the American priesthood that was just getting under way would not only demonstrate the concern of bishops for their clergy but would, if prudently managed, yield findings that would be of great benefit to them and to the entire church. His charge was to floor manage this project, to negotiate whatever difficulties arose between the scholars and the bishops who had commissioned them, and to oversee the details of the professional contracts by which the bishops had, for the first time, committed themselves to contemporary research that was focused on their priests and, in effect, on themselves. Not every bishop was convinced that the vocation they deemed sacred should be subjected to the methodologies of the social sciences, or to modern historical or theological analysis. What, they asked, could sociologists and psychologists or historians, for that matter, possibly discover with their natural approaches about a calling whose character, in their judgment, was undeniably and unassailably supernatural?

One prelate who eyed the researchers skeptically through his silver rimmed glasses was John Cardinal Krol who had accepted Archbishop Dearden's request to be general chairman of the project. There had been intense speculation that Dearden had asked Krol to take over the job not only because of his high regard for the Philadelphia archbishop's administrative abilities but also because the doubting Krol would demand high standards and thoroughness. Politically speaking, it was also thought wiser to have him inside the tent of the studies, responsible for their success, rather than on the outside as a shrewd and vocal critic who might tear it down. Years later, Monsignor John Tracy Ellis would ruefully smile as he recalled the meeting of the bishops in St. Louis at which the appointment of the chairman was announced. "Father Andrew Greeley came into breakfast, threw up his hands dramatically, and said derisively, 'Well, they've given us Krol!' as if the whole project had been betrayed."

Bernardin, aware that a genuine crisis existed in the American priesthood, wanted the studies to succeed. He did not want an additional crisis fomented by overreacting scholars. Although he understood their uncertainty about Krol's commitment to research procedures, he also understood the Philadelphian's viewpoint. Cardinal Krol was a traditionalist; he had been formed in the rigid seminary system that had evolved after Modernism had been suppressed; he believed in a priesthood built on uncomplaining rugged individualism, above all immune to any probing of the inner psychological experiences of its members. Real men did not talk about their emotions, didn't complain about their problems; they exercised ascetically heroic self-control instead. In short, the powerful, subtle Krol was a man of his time who was reluctant to lessen masculine spiritual demands on the priesthood or to open it to an examination by "liberal" scholars who might be too revolutionary, too "modern," or perhaps too influenced by theorists such as Weber or Freud, in their willingness to disregard its privileged, sacred character.

Krol, as Dearden well understood, nonetheless wanted to succeed in this new assignment. Bernardin welcomed Krol's appointment because he respected the decisive nature of the cardinal whose episcopal origins, like his own, could be traced back to Archbishop Edward Hoban of Cleveland. But the young bishop also appreciated the uneasiness of the priest-researchers who, including the then 65-year-old Monsignor Ellis, shared a Vatican II outlook on the church. The scholars were unsure of how to interpret Krol who ordinarily opened conversations with a prickly observation or an unsettling question. Was this a probing hostility or a gambit that enabled Krol to take the measure of others before he exhibited what could be a hearty clerical friendliness? The investigators were not sure whether Krol liked them or merely wanted to contain them within what he considered the acceptable bounds of inquiry. To the generally younger team of priest-professors, Krol also represented the generation of lordly bishops more attuned to the medieval Council of Trent than to the recently concluded Vatican II. The outcome of the conjunction of these very different stars was by no means predictable.

Although one of the original team of researchers, Monsignor William Baum, went on to become a cardinal archbishop and later a Vatican official, most of them, including Greeley, were not interested in or destined for bureaucratic ecclesiastical life. Greeley often spoke to his peer academics of his ambition to live in the same residence with the cardinal archbishop of Chicago as a gray eminence who directed the destiny of the archdiocese by teaching the prince of the church sociology at mealtimes. Like the others, he wrote books, lectured widely, lived, as only they could as priest academics, on the "margins" of the official church.

The scholars were typical, then, of a class of bright, talented men who, unlike their classmates destined to be bishops, were creative, independent, self-supporting, and, to some extent, difficult to classify or to employ in the ordinary day to day operations of the church. They symbolized a unique problem of the Catholic clergy at what was its high point in numbers and prestige. In a real sense, the official church did not know exactly what to do with them, and some of them had no official assignments from their superiors at all. They were superfluous, overqualified for routine priestly assignments and unsuitable, by their temperaments and creative interests, for the administration that was the core of a bishop's work and the locus and source of real power in the church. Influence existed on the margins of the church where they lived but authentic power was rooted deep in the heart of the ecclesiastical organization where the bishops functioned.

Such scholars, or other specialists, might talk of wanting to be like the parish priests they were studying but they could not and would not surrender their freedom or their special interests in order to accept that life on a full-time basis. Of Bernardin's generation for the most part, they had been sifted out of the last great post-war harvest of vocations to the priesthood. Most of them, like Bernardin, had entered seminaries near or immediately after the end of World War II. Because they shared so many similar interests, the difference between administratively-oriented bishops and creatively-oriented priests was not at first obvious. It was not a question of intelligence, for the bishops were, almost to a man, keen and knowing individuals who in school had, like Bernardin, scored at the top of their classes. Intellectual curiosity, a capacity for distractability and the endurance of disorder while searching for order in a mass of data: these were characteristics of the priest professors and writers that were not common to the bishops. Indeed, their possession of the characteristics was one of the reasons that the priest academicians would never fit the criteria for becoming bishops themselves. But neither they nor the bishops understood this fully at the time.

This group of scholars provided a symbol of changes on a larger scale that were just becoming evident within American Catholicism. The bishops had for decades enjoyed status as exemplars of the best and the brightest of Catholic young men who had, by choosing the seminary, pursued almost the only avenue of higher education available to a largely immigrant people. Now the very Catholic higher education system they had supported had begun to produce men and women startlingly different from previous generations of Catholics in their general learning and in their theological competence. Their presence became unmistakable in the excitement over Vatican II, in their wide participation in church matters, and particularly in their conscientious dissent after the issuance of *Humanae Vitae*. Because of them, American Catholicism, once distinguished for its unity in discipline and belief, had become, as Monsignor John Tracy Ellis observed, a "shattered fixity." The almost radically differing internal intellectual dispositions of bishops and priest academics made them as contrasting beneath their clerical shirtfronts as, say, Hollywood studio heads and their writers and directors. This filled their novel partnership with every possibility of misunderstanding right from the start.

If Bernardin did not speculate on the varying philosophies of Krol and these scholar-priests, he understood that their relationship demanded his steady support and intervention if the entire project were not to collapse. He assumed the intermediary role again, reassuring the priests about Krol's good faith and willingness to cooperate while working closely with Krol in vetting the administrative details of the investigation. Bernardin would resolve a number of impasses over the two-year span of the studies, often through a combination of emotionally controlled personal interventions and unruffled public behavior. He was a friend to many of the scholar-priests and sympathetic to their problems but his official responsibilities enjoined him to act consistently and reliably in behalf of the bishop contractors of the scholars' services. Once again, he was gaining experience for the silent skillful reconciler's role that he would assume consistently in the years ahead.

Bernardin at times, therefore, had to absorb quietly the charged complaints of the priests, not allowing them to involve him personally, for the sake of the overall undertaking. He would also become familiar with the style of Father Greeley, characterized by even some of the Chicago priest's friends as strident but by Greeley himself as that of a fighting Irishman. The General Secretary was, in effect, mediating more than the priest study, or one of the other projects of the bishops. As with the "Washington 19" and Cardinal O'Boyle, Bernardin was attempting to manage a major cultural change in ecclesiastical Catholicism. Its ingredients included an old generation of largely Irish bishops, truculent and traditional, and a new generation of progressive and impatient Vatican II priests, many of whom lived in a kind of hitherto nonexistent academic no man's land that stretched between the fortress of the organized church and the heavily populated territories of a newly sophisticated Catholic laity.

Bernardin was trying to steady the bridge that swayed above the generational transformation that, in the general culture, was footnoted by the death, on Mar. 28, 1969, of former President Dwight D. Eisenhower and the occupation, 12 days later, of the administration building at Harvard by the Students for a Democratic Society (SDS). Richard M. Nixon's words, on being sworn in as the country's 37th president the previous January, seemed to ring true everywhere. "We are torn," he had said, "by divisions, wanting unity." The sense of a dangerous rending of the fabric of the national life was heightened by the rise of the counterculture which, with free sex, drugs, and rock music, would celebrate itself the following August on a farm near Woodstock, New York. Bernardin studied other reports, one of which noted that, in the two previous years, more than 700 men had left the American priesthood to marry. Roman officials acknowledged that more than 10,000 requests for dispensation from the priesthood had been received from all over the world. Nobody could examine such statistics without realizing that the future of American Catholicism was already being seriously affected, that it might regain its balance but never the well-ordered, seemingly serene character of its immediate past. A Gallup Poll that year indicated that, of those responding to its survey, 70 percent felt that the influence of religion was declining in the United States.

Bernardin was convinced that the priesthood studies would help the bishops understand and respond more effectively to the racking problems of the clergy. One of his most delicate tasks was to negotiate the acceptance of the psychological and sociological protocols from Cardinal Krol who had expressed reservations about any effort to examine the sexual dimension of the lives of American priests. In part, Krol's concern was that the findings might be used politically by groups agitating for a change in the discipline of celibacy. That, he felt, would compromise the value of the research completely. Krol was also hesitant, as many of his peers were, to allow anybody, under the aegis of the bishops, to ask questions or to make interpretations about the sexual feelings, attitudes, or behavior of priests. Neither did Krol approve the sociological questions about the prayer life of priests. He felt that inquiring about whether they read the prayers of what was called the Divine Office every day was a conscience matter just as sexuality was and that the investigators might unwittingly urge men to confess that they had committed sins.

Krol was correct in claiming that hardly any other profession had subjected itself to an examination as thorough as the one that had been proposed by the scholar-priests. The psychology panel, located at Loyola University in Chicago, received an inquiry from the American Bar Association about a similar study of lawyers and judges. When they discovered the detail into which the psychologists, and the sociologists at the National Opinion Research Center (NORC), hoped to go, the legal officials backed off, saying they did not want to learn that much about themselves.

Bernardin respected the priesthood as deeply as Krol but he also understood the need to look at the areas of spirituality and sexuality about which many priests were expressing conflict. In this instance, as in many others, the future cardinal displayed what some termed the Italian gift for earthy realism that balanced and sweetened his obsessive bureaucratic dedication. While nothing seemed to please Bernardin more, as an associate later observed, than a briefcase jammed with reports to review, he could also take real if infrequent pleasure in music and art and he never expected anybody to be perfect. He listened to the sociologists and the psychologists as they explained their research plight. He also heard clearly Krol's *caveats*, uttered from the depths of his traditional experience, and echoing the sound of great doors slammed shut centuries before in the official church on anything but the most guarded, idealistic, and antiseptic discussion of sexuality in the life of priests.

Mediation between Krol and the academics was not made easier by the style of some of Father Greeley's statements and letters to the Philadelphia cardinal in particular and to the bishops in general. While his peers sometimes winced at Greeley's explosive tone and need to control, they also recognized his intelligence and, beneath his protean brashness, a dedication to the church and a true generosity of spirit. In May 1969, Greeley wrote, in one of his milder letters to Bernardin, "I have been upset by letters from both Cardinal Krol and Cardinal Dearden recently raising issues about the personal garb and attitude of people on my staff. If this sort of fear and harassment continues, I simply will want no further part of this study."

Bernardin would become even better acquainted with this approach in later years. For the moment, however, he ignored the dramatic flourishes and threats, and patiently continued to seek the freedom of inquiry that he, no less than the scholars, thought essential to the success of the investigations. In the end, he was successful in gaining this and the studies went forward with no censorship from the bishops at all, something that, as one of the scholar-priests observed, "could not have taken place in any other profession, institution, or business in the land."

Background events, like the subtle shifting of scenery behind the actors, continued to reshape Bernardin's world, opening up unexpected opportunities, confirming his approaches, and revealing in ever finer detail the actors whose entrances and exits would become increasingly common in his career. Archbishop Dearden was made a cardinal in the spring of 1969, an elevation that had been scheduled two years earlier, when Krol, O'Boyle, and Cody had received their promotions. While nobody is now certain why Dearden was not made a prince of the church along with them, there was speculation that some old guard churchmen had intervened to prevent the honor from being bestowed on the president of the National Conference of Catholic Bishops at that time. Dearden's joining the College of Cardinals in 1969 validated his strong but undramatic leadership style and placed him on the same high ecclesiastical plane with McIntyre of Los Angeles and Cody of Chicago as well as with such prominent figures as O'Boyle and Krol. It was also at least an indirect approval of the manner in which the restructuring of the conference of bishops was proceeding and, therefore, a seal on Bernardin's work, too.

Bernardin was doubly delighted at the honor that his mentor had received. He and Dearden had deepened their association, sometimes taking trips together, as they did after a bishops' meeting in San Francisco by driving down scenic Route One to Los Angeles together. Bernardin also began to join Dearden for a week's vacation every summer along with a few other bishops in a cottage near Harbor Springs, Michigan. These gatherings, good natured but slightly formal, matched the dispositions of the two men very well. A friend came close to the truth when he said jokingly to Bernardin, "Joe, that's like going on vacation with your father." These holidays, as stately in their correctness as in their underlying warmth, would continue until Dearden's death in August 1988.

In October 1969, the robust, 52-year-old bishop of Evansville, Indiana, Paul F. Leibold, was named archbishop of Cincinnati, succeeding the 84-year-old Karl Alter. Alter, an authentic product of what some termed the triumphalist era in American ecclesiastical history, had lived, as bishops of previous generations had, with the hearty approval of their immigrant flocks, in a splendid mansion into whose marble floored foyer his intertwined initials had been artfully worked. Returning from a visit there, the famous television preacher of the fifties, Bishop Fulton J. Sheen sat in the red silk wallpapered study of his New York townhouse, and observed in rolling theatrical tones, "Why, the man lives like a king!" Within a few years, Bernardin's future would become as entwined as the old archbishop's initials with the archdiocese of Cincinnati.

Earlier that summer, auxiliary bishop James V. Shannon of Minneapolis–St. Paul had resigned and married after the full weight of the old guard of the American hierarchy, led self-righteously by Cardinal McIntyre, had fallen upon him because of his pastoral dissent to the teachings of *Humanae Vitae*. At the time, Shannon, unusual among his peers because of his Yale doctorate, his true intellectual interests, and his extraordinary presence, had been considered a future candidate for one of the cardinalatial sees of the country, the perfect successor, for example, to the already embattled Cody in Chicago. Shannon's convictions that he must reveal to Rome his misgivings about the birth control issue were met with a medieval response that doomed his ecclesiastical future while suggesting that he seek literal exile in a university, South America, or Israel.

The sensitive Shannon chose the difficult path of conscience, withdrawing from the institution without uttering a word of criticism or complaint. While his departure was lamented by the progressives in the church, Shannon was judged by most of his brother bishops, even those who admired him, to have broken the code of institutional loyalty. Bishops, by their commitment to the church, were expected to do what it asked of them and to deal with their inner conflicts in personal, nonpublic ways, sacrificing their expression, if necessary, in order to carry out their calling as churchmen. Being men of the church meant being men of the institution, carrying out what it asked of them without hesitation. So deep was this self-understanding of bishops that Shannon, by leaving, even quietly, seemed to his colleagues to have violated a condition as basic as bone and blood to their lives. His previous accomplishments, his personal qualities: These counted for little now that Shannon had stepped out of the episcopal circle. Only a few of his brother bishops would keep in touch with him in subsequent years.

Shannon had also removed himself from the top of the list for preferment in ecclesiastical assignments. Bernardin, saddened by the kind of decision against organizational Catholicism that, whatever the inner conflict, he would never make himself, moved up a notch on the roster of prospective leaders of the church in the United States. Bernardin already understood that as a bishop his duty was to do what the church asked of him. He had thought long and hard about the obligations of being a bishop. His appreciation of the personal renunciation it might require of him was one of the reasons that, along with Dearden, he emphasized collegial process over personality in the governance of the church. He also understood, again along with Dearden, that progress in helping the church to grow organically demanded the maintenance of a sometimes achingly difficult balance between institutional expectations and personal conviction and integrity. This could only be carried out if a bishop kept a long view of history and was willing to labor in the darkened back part of the stage rather than in the spotlight.

Only the previous April, Bernardin had seen another progressive young bishop, James Malone of Youngstown, Ohio, rise at the bishops' meetings to discuss the issue of celibacy that, from the results of the priesthood studies, seemed to demand exploration. Malone was right in his subject and his intentions but, by asking the question when and as he did, he lost some invisible but real esteem in the eyes of his brother bishops. The pope expected their unhesitating support of the discipline of celibacy in their official conference gatherings. They must stand together on that or they failed the organizational church they had sworn to serve.

Malone, who, like Shannon, had been considered a likely candidate for a major American diocese, had, for the moment at least, lost a measure of credibility with the very men he sought to influence. This stamp of credibility, or general trustworthiness, was the greatest validation the bishops could bestow on one of their own. But, as with Dearden at the time and gradually with Bernardin, its conferral depended on a steady constellation of factors, including a sense, as keen as that of Ecclesiastes, of a time for speaking and a time for remaining silent. Bernardin may have perfected his own style by observing Dearden during the April 1971 bishops' meeting when Malone had proposed that the question of optional celibacy be included in the document to be discussed at the forthcoming Roman synod.

Dearden, who understood as well as anyone the need for some ultimate discussion of celibacy, knew that the moment was not right for it. He did not want the bishops to vote on it and he dealt gently but firmly from the chair with Malone's proposals. He downplayed the possibility that the Roman document meant to exclude such discussion, weaving connections for the bishops, referring to the Roman document as "highly compressed....a working paper....not a final document." Reviewing the draft's restatement of the traditional position on celibacy, Dearden, aware that nothing good would come of discussing this on the floor, accepted it, reassuring the bishops who had become mildly tense over Malone's intervention. Such intuitive and undramatic constancy appealed to the bishops; they felt comfortable with a bishop who might nurture progress but never by a sudden, disastrous overturning of the past. Just as Dearden's credibility rested on such skills, so, too, would Bernardin's.

Bernardin, however, was not thinking about that as he stuck, in 1970, to the interconnected items on his agenda: the rebuilding of the national conference and the ongoing priesthood studies. Early in 1970, Pope Paul VI declared that celibacy, questioned world-wide by priests, was a "fundamental principle" of the Roman Catholic Church. The Synod of bishops later the next year, to which Dearden and Krol would be two of the elected American delegates, also reaffirmed the discipline. Significantly, Bishop Malone, who had raised a good question at not quite the right moment, would not be chosen as a delegate even though he had been considered a likely candidate at the opening of the spring 1971 meeting.

In the fall of 1970, Bernardin was negotiating the successful conclusion of the priesthood studies, the reports of which would supply the context for Malone's observations the following spring. If the bishops would be hesitant about anything but a public affirmation of the church's teaching on celibacy, they were quite open to learning the truth about clerical problems and discontents in the nearly completed research. Strangely enough, the problems of the studies, during 1970, came to center, not on the bishops, but on Father Greeley's leadership of the sociological committee.

As recalled by his NORC staff members, Greeley, involved in a number of other projects, inexplicably lost interest in the day to day work of the study during the late spring and summer of 1970. He left it to the talented project director, Richard Schoenherr, and remained at his summer home in Grand Beach, Michigan, did not seem eager to return staff members' phone calls, and left unresolved the conflicts that had arisen about the progress of the research. Greeley would later complain that the bishops did not give him enough time or money to complete the study as he wished while, in fact, during the long season before the reports were due to be presented, he remained aloof and indifferent to associates who became increasingly concerned about his behavior and the fate of their work.

The restlessness of his NORC coworkers came to the attention of other scholar-priests and Bernardin, all of whom attempted to reassure them and to encourage them to keep the study on track. Father Greeley, Bernardin was learning, could be surprisingly unpredictable in his professional attitudes. In December, Greeley, as reported by members of his research team, took the data to his Michigan retreat and dictated the draft report in less than a week. The staff members felt that the remarkable amount of information they had acquired suffered from Greeley's herculean but necessarily hurried treatment of it.

The scholars were to offer their reports at the bishops' meeting in Detroit in April 1971. All the findings were, by mutual agreement, to be kept confidential until the release date. Greeley, however, chose in mid-March to give an advance copy of his report to the *New York Times*. When a colleague remonstrated with him that he was doing exactly what he had repeatedly accused the bishops of, violating a professional agreement, he replied, ''It's more important for me to get my name in the *New York Times* than to keep some agreement with the bishops.''

Cardinal Krol, informed of the situation, was exasperated and, at first, was disposed to react publicly to what the bishops considered a breach of faith. Bernardin was well aware of the public relations explosion that might follow such a move and was concerned about its effects on the results of the sociological survey and the other studies as well. He also understood how damaging Greeley's behavior was to the fragile bond that had been established between the bishops and the research community. An untoward incident might sour the bishops completely on further collaboration with academics. Bernardin wanted the studies to be published successfully and without censorship or misgiving. He and Krol agreed that the best course, for the overall good of the conference as well as the best use of the scholarly findings, was that the bishops remain silent even in the face of Father Greeley's continuing public accusations against them for professional ineptitude.

Greeley would subsequently protest mightily about the fact that his study, along with the others, was, at the bishops' request, going to be subjected to outside professional evaluation. His own disputes with his NORC staff continued as he again charged that the bishops were unfair in their choice of outside evaluators, even though he had submitted two of the three names of those selected for this task. The evaluation meeting, to which all the other chairmen readily agreed, would be held, under the chairmanship of Archbishop Philip Hannan of New Orleans, at an O'Hare Field hotel on Feb. 1, 1972. Greeley, angry at some of the criticisms of his work, decided not to attend. Instead, he sent a 40 page critique of the bishops to the major news services and to the *National Catholic Reporter,* with a release hour that coincided with the 9:00 a.m. convocation of the meeting. His accusations that the bishops were ''morally and spiritually bankrupt'' undercut the meeting and were given major attention in the news media. The bishops winced at what they perceived as a defensive and unfair maneuver that clouded their attempts to weigh the merits of the studies objectively. But once again, in an example of Henry Ford's dictum ''Never complain, never explain,'' they remained silent.

Bernardin felt that salvaging the useful aspects of the studies was more important than dignifying Greeley's actions or comments with a reply. The body of the bishops, however, felt that their first in-depth partnership with the church's so-called professional scholars was anything but a happy experience. They would be in no hurry to avail themselves of their services in the future. Keeping the best face on things and maintaining the integrity of the developing conference became paramount concerns for Bishop Bernardin. This was particularly crucial in view of the forthcoming autumn election of a new president of the National Conference. It would almost certainly be Cardinal Krol and Bernardin was anxious that the restructuring be as complete as possible when Dearden yielded his leadership after his unique five year term was concluded in November.

Such matters as temperamental and unreasonable academics could not be allowed to damage that, no matter what irritation Bernardin, or any other bishop, felt about what appeared to them to be a manipulation of their good faith. Bernardin decided to see that the studies were published in book form so that their results could be available to bishops and priests across the country. The academic community would use its own channels to appraise the studies. In an ironic but little noted development, when the revised and corrected sociological research was printed, the NORC staff insisted that their major contributions to the work be fully acknowledged in the preface to the report. And, contrary to his heated predictions, the bishops allowed the results, even those concerning priests' personal emotional problems and intellectual conflicts with church teaching, to be issued without censorship on their part.

Bernardin was too preoccupied to react publicly but, even in private, his close associates recall that, despite the needless grief the bishops had encountered, the General Secretary never uttered one word of criticism about Greeley or about any of the other participants in the priesthood research. Through this episode, his patience and understanding had been tested and grown deeper and more secure as a result. Bernardin would later observe that one of the qualities he had admired in Cardinal Dearden was that, no matter what the development, he "never panicked." He was perfecting the sublimation of self that enabled him to maintain openness and control in public, the special virtues of the administrator that would help him during the increasingly demanding years that were given ample foreshadowing before 1971 came to an end.

VI

In September 1971, as Bernardin worked, in effect, to polish the fittings on the new structure of the bishops' conference, a few miles across the District of Columbia Leonard Bernstein's Mass was given its premiere performance. It took place in another recently completed structure, the John F. Kennedy Center for the Performing Arts tented in white marble along the Potomac. Bernardin, a music lover, was far too busy to attend as he checked the fine details of the freshly implemented plans of the fraternal twin conferences under his charge. The civil arm, the United States Catholic Conference, would incorporate many laypersons and members of religious orders into its varied departments and committees. The National Conference of Catholic Bishops, concerned strictly with church matters, drew its membership solely from the ranks of the bishops, although it made ample room for the use of consultants. Some observers would, later and not uncritically, compare these related structures to the United States Congress and the members of its large support staffs who wield great influence through their preparation of research, documentation, and position papers.

Bernardin was also overseeing the development of a National Advisory Council, whose members would offer advice to both organizations. The mechanics of fairly selecting its participants so that they truly represented laypersons, priests, and religious, was as bureaucratically demanding and absorbing as the careful definition of its role and function. The young bishop well understood that what might seem the boring and inconsequential tasks of organization were, in fact, as important as the preparation of painstaking blueprints for the ultimate integrity of any contemplated structure. If the basics were taken care of thoughtfully and thoroughly, later stresses would be borne successfully. A mistake at this fair weather level, however, could well lead to a disaster when once-a-century storms blew up.

During this period, Bernardin, whose skills and discretion as a mediator had been increasingly valued by the Holy See, was again entrusted with confidential trouble-shooting missions to various points in the United States. A true churchman not only does what the church asks of him through his superiors but he must do so despite every possibility of misunderstanding and every likelihood that someone else will claim credit for what he achieved. Bernardin, of course, understood that important Roman authorities were pleased with his judiciousness. But he also remembered an old proverb from the Eternal City, "The Roman Catholic Church is never grateful." Still, Rome began to signal its confidence in him. In 1969, he was asked to be an associate secretary of that year's Synod of bishops. At Bishop Ladislas Rubin's recommendation, Bernardin was appointed by Pope Paul VI to assist at the October synod at which Cardinal Dearden was an *ex officio* delegate. This was valuable experience for him. From 1974 on, he would have an important position at every Synod.

In 1971, Bishop Bernardin was also responsible for preparing for the annual bishops' meeting that would be convened in November. One of the most important pieces of business on the agenda was the election of a new president for the organization. Cardinal Krol, who had been serving as vice-president, was expected to succeed Cardinal Dearden. For his part, Dearden felt that the major objectives of his five year term had been achieved. The Booz Allen plans, thanks largely to Bernardin's executive ability, had been implemented, several serious crises had been surmounted, and the bishops had begun, for the first time in their history, to work cooperatively together on the business of American Catholicism. As Dearden watched Bernardin quietly and effectively completing the enormous job he had given him he felt, as he told this biographer later, that he would like to see the General Secretary appointed soon as a bishop to a diocese of his own.

Americans and American Catholics were becoming inured to both scenes of battle and protest. The surreal had become commonplace. Father Philip Berrigan, Sister Elizabeth MacAlister, and a small group of Catholic peace activists, were indicted for a plot to kidnap Secretary of State Henry Kissinger, to blow up utility buildings in Washington, D.C., and to vandalize draft boards along the East Coast. In April, as Attorney General John Mitchell had watched in Dickensian solemnity from a balcony, 200,000 protestors, many of them formerly unquestioning patriotic Catholics, had marched in the nation's capital against the still dangerously sputtering Vietnam War. The once staid Catholic Church seemed, through the consciences of its members, everywhere present in the peace movement. If its spiritual influence seeded the quest for peace, its efforts to seek reimbursement for nonreligious education in its vast network of schools was struck down in June by an 8 to 1 vote of the Supreme Court.

Bernardin lived in a city seething with the discontents of the age. This was part of his education, for if his personal sympathies were often with the earnest seekers of peace, his official commitment was to the institution, which he hoped, through the transformations he was overseeing, would become more capable of reflecting on and expressing its own moral ambitions to the nation at large. But that would fail if it depended only on dramatic public demonstrations to assert its points. As Cardinal Dearden observed, when urged against his own collegial convictions to speak out individually, ''I am president of the bishops' conference, not czar. . . . It's better to have something to say than to have to say something.'' Bernardin shared Dearden's convictions, sometimes unappreciated by those who felt they should be marching under banners in the streets, that, in forgoing public drama for private bureaucratic planning, they were securing the foundation for the collective pulpit from which the bishops would one day speak with authentic moral authority on the pressing issues of the day.

As the bishops' meeting approached, Bernardin also continued his direct involvement with the bishops of Canada and South America. Dearden had initiated these contacts, which led ultimately to the Inter-American Bishops' Meeting. These exchanges, rooted, as the national conference was, in careful preparation rather than just personality, have kept up to this day. One of the serendipitous results of these new associations was Bernardin's becoming well known and trusted by churchmen throughout the hemisphere.

Although President Nixon had withdrawn another 45,000 American troops from Vietnam just a few weeks before, and, for the year 1971, casualties would drop to less than 10 percent of what they had been in 1968, the bishops' meeting was threatened with demonstrations by various activist groups. The bishops, stolidly entering a Washington, D.C., hotel as bands of protestors raised a garden full of placards along their path, were not, in general, marchers any more than they were scholars. They were administrators, doing what they did best, carrying out, as any deliberative body must, the intrinsically dull tasks of assembled legislators everywhere.

With the exception of the then 42-year-old auxiliary bishop of Detroit, Thomas Gumbleton, none of the prelates participated directly in the peace movement. They might support its aims but they did not yet have an effective way to speak in their true voice on the tangled problems of the nuclear age. They did something, following their own limited bureaucratic instincts and procedures, that gave the only kind of signal administrators can offer; they took a vote on Dearden's successor, the implications of which, like tea leaves crusted on the bottom of a royal cup, had to be read carefully for their message.

The raw-boned Krol, his Slavic features slightly pock marked so that he resembled a grand duke in a daguerreotype, accepted the gavel as the incoming president of the conference of bishops. It was not an unexpected development and the bishops drew some reassurance from the presence of the highly intelligent traditionalist in the chair of leadership for a three year term. But they gave another signal as well. The 43-year-old Joseph L. Bernardin, only five years a bishop and three years as General Secretary, a prelate with no diocese of his own, received 94 votes for the office of president. The bishops were unmistakably expressing themselves, in a crab-like shuttling motion that seems to be getting nowhere as it seeks leverage for an impressive sideways move. They were not traversing much ground by electing Krol; they were, however, getting themselves and Bernardin in position for a more significant transit in the future.

Nineteen seventy-two winked like ruffled water with the lights of changing times. Cardinal McIntyre had retired the year before and Cardinal O'Boyle would retire in the next year. Across the Atlantic the 85-year-old Lord Fisher, who had forged pacts of friendship with Pope John XXIII when he served as Archbishop of Canterbury died, and so, too, did the spade bearded, 81-year-old Eugene Cardinal Tisserant who had sealed everything after the death of Pope Pius XII, preserving order at a moment of perilous transition for the church. If in February President Nixon sought a place in history through his visit to China, in June he courted his own downfall by his handling of the arrest of five men inside the Democratic National Headquarters in the Watergate complex. The ironies of the age were not spent, for although the last American ground forces left Vietnam in August, Nixon resumed bombing there in December.

Time and chance dissolved into each other everywhere. J. Edgar Hoover, who had reportedly sent FBI folders on peace activist priests to Cardinal Krol, died before the jury in Harrisburg found that it could not convict the priests and nuns on the major charges Hoover had brought against them. George Wallace was shot in a Maryland shopping center and, in the Vatican, a deranged man shattered Michelangelo's *Pieta* with a hammer. And in Cincinnati the May Festival prepared to perform Bernstein's Mass in the city's sold out Music Hall.

Cincinnati's newly appointed archdiocesan vicar for communications, Dan Kane, a man with long experience with the church and the media, consulted with Archbishop Leibold about his possible response to the impassioned demands that certain traditional Catholics were making for an official condemnation of a composition that they considered sacrilegious. Archbishop Leibold had given strong support to Caesar Chavez and the grape boycott, these outraged right wing Catholics argued, now he had to stand up for one of their causes. Kane prepared several scenarios for the archbishop's consideration and arranged an interview with him for Maggie Carson, Bernstein's representative. The gentle Leibold read the text of the mass, was disturbed by the desecration of the host and chalice described therein, and conferred with Ms. Carson. Carson upon leaving his office, said to Kane, ''You prepared me for every possibility but one about your archbishop. He's a saint.'' She understood his uneasiness and that, in the mild expression of criticism he felt compelled to make, he intended no condemnation of the mass.

Leibold's intentions foundered on the explosive reaction of the media to his carefully worded statement. He was portrayed in the May 30 editions of the newspapers and on television as a censor of art rather than a religious leader who had asked about an artist's right ''to use the elements of our central act of worship as a vehicle to present his theme and, further, may they be vandalized in the expression of his theme?'' A storm of controversy broke over the city that, heavily German in population, ordinarily sat as complacently on the Ohio as any of its ancient counterparts on the Rhine. The archbishop, known for his enthusiasm for the reforms of Vatican II and a champion of ''the common church of man'' was stunned by the reaction. Two days later, he suffered a stroke in his residence at Mount St. Mary Seminary and died that afternoon at Good Samaritan Hospital.

The highly regarded Leibold's sudden death shocked his brother bishops. It was not long after his burial before the institutional corridors of Catholicism buzzed with a sample of perhaps its most richly savored speculation: Who would succeed to Cincinnati and what would it mean on the map of changing Catholicism? It had been unheard of until Vatican II for powerful archbishops to surrender their sees until death. Now they were required to resign when they reached 75 years of age. Even cardinals were granted no exemption. Within a relatively few years, Spellman and Cushing had died, McIntyre had retired, O'Boyle would be next; the power structure of the American church was being rapidly transformed. While Cincinnati was not in a class with New York or Los Angeles, it was a venerable and important archdiocese and the bishop who was placed there would almost certainly play a significant role in the future of American Catholicism.

Most observers expected the affable, charming, highly intelligent bishop of Youngstown, the prematurely silver-haired James Malone, to move to the Queen City on the Ohio. But, in the late summer, Malone, whose brave words at their April meeting had raised subtle doubts about him among his brother bishops, was diagnosed as having stomach cancer and, at the time, the prognosis was grave. His health removed him from consideration for the Cincinnati appointment. He would shortly travel to the Roswell Clinic, a famous cancer center in Buffalo, New York, for special treatment that would ultimately prove successful. At that moment, however, Providence seemed to be arranging the career of Joseph L. Bernardin.

John Cardinal Dearden realized that the 150-year-old archdiocese that embraced 19 southern Ohio counties needed a vigorous young man. Cincinnati would be an ideal place for Joseph L. Bernardin who had proved himself exactly the kind of patient, collegial leader that Dearden felt was needed in post-conciliar American Catholicism. If Bernardin was only 43, Cincinnati would benefit from his relative youth and Bernardin himself would, as an archbishop, gain stature in the American hierarchy whose members, as witnessed by their 94 votes for him for conference president the previous year, already regarded him highly. What his first mentor, Paul Hallinan, had envisioned—that Bernardin would not only serve well as General Secretary but be prepared through the assignment for other things—was about to be fulfilled by the recommendation of his second mentor, John Dearden.

Just before Thanksgiving, on Nov. 21, 1972, Archbishop Luigi Raimondi, the apostolic delegate, announced the appointment of Joseph Louis Bernardin to become archbishop of Cincinnati. On December 19, the day after President Nixon ordered U.S. forces to resume bombing North Vietnam, Bernardin was installed in the Cathedral of St. Peter in Chains as head of the archdiocese of Cincinnati. The forces of history would soon come into play once more in the young archbishop's life. Among other transitions in 1973, Raimondi, the softspoken career diplomat, would be recalled to Rome and named a cardinal. He would be succeeded by Jean Jadot, a Belgian born prelate with a Devil's Island haircut who would play a major role in the American church and exert a profound influence on Bernardin's career.

VII

D an Kane, then archdiocesan vicar for communications, remembers the sudden burst of interest on the part of the national media in Cincinnati's new archbishop. This wrote an early signature, as clear as that for the theme of a symphony, on the decade of Bernardin's service there. He would never be regarded only as the archbishop of a midwestern archdiocese, no matter how respectable that title was in itself, for he was already perceived as a man whose substantial influence in the broader ranges of Catholicism could only increase. If Cincinnati was not a "bully pulpit," it was already a strong and well constructed platform that would give sturdy support to Bernardin's plans for the future.

His immediate predecessor, Paul Leibold, had generously built on the Vatican II reforms that his predecessor, Karl Alter, had implemented, immediately and dutifully, as the church's will expressed through that ecumenical council. Alter's prompt action defined, in a sense, the notion of "churchman" that, born long before Vatican II, still retains its meaning in Catholicism. A true churchman—the bishop fulfilling his calling—does what the church asks him to do as, for example, in the decrees of an ecumenical council or in the expressed wishes of the pope. The bishop's task is not theological speculation but administrative implementation. What the church asks can, however, be carried out in a variety of ways. The pastoral mode may be understood as doing things *humano modo.* That describes the special sacramental sense of the imperfection of men and women that seasons idealistic expectations with profound understanding of the irregular and unpredictable course of the human struggle. This was the "medicine of mercy and not severity" of which Pope John XXIII had spoken at the opening of Vatican II.

If Alter and Leibold stood ready to do what the church wanted, they did so with that kind of pastoral appreciation of the members of their flock. Bernardin came with a feeling for human frailty that, perhaps because of his Italian sense of history, may have been richer than that of the men he succeeded. What he brought to the organizational apparatus he inherited from them was an almost intuitive sense of what it meant to be a collegial leader. Alter and Leibold, like Cardinal Dearden, accepted the church's revival of this approach, learning it, in a sense, in midlife. Bernardin, on the other hand, was perhaps the country's best example of the generation of leaders whose consciousness of the church had been thoroughly informed by the conciliar debates and decrees.

In the waning days of November, Bernardin, accompanied by two of his Washington associates, Fathers James Rausch and Michael Sheehan, quietly visited Cincinnati to meet the diocesan officials and to discuss the preparations for his installation. He also wanted to raise a divining rod above the almost score of counties that saddled the twisting river border of southern Ohio and the 500,000 Catholics who lived in them. Despite Bernardin's manner, finely tempered on the open hearth of his Washington years, the tempo in the archdiocesan offices picked up noticeably as he made the rounds. Something dignified rather than sensational was beginning. Bernardin's arrival was like that of a conductor with a technical mastery of the score to a well prepared orchestra. In leading it, he would employ only the slightest, disciplined gestures with the baton.

Just as Bernardin had been immersed in the Irish culture of the priesthood and bishopric in his previous experiences, he now entered, again as an outsider, a tradition as solidly German as the furniture and drapes of Moeller Hall, the archiepiscopal residence. Connected by a portico to the pale stone buildings of the seminary of St. Mary of the West, its architecture was described by one of the professors as "early Renaissance with a touch of the Inquisition." Stolid as the city, the hall hearkened back, as did the splendid house in the College Hill section of the city in which the 87-year-old retired Archbishop Alter lived among fine furnishings and oil paintings, to the period in which immigrant Catholics were still establishing themselves in the United States. Bernardin would never feel entirely comfortable there, although he enjoyed the close association it afforded him with seminary faculty members and students. He was too far removed from the real center of archdiocesan administration in downtown Cincinnati. Within two years, he would move into an apartment on the fifth floor of the chancery building that also served as the rectory for St. Louis's Church and begin to consolidate the scattered archdiocesan offices into that central location.

Cincinnati, established in 1819, had long been a busy port city on the broad brown waters of the Ohio that, linked to the veins of the canal system, was a main artery for the growing nation's commerce. Spread on bluffs and hills, the city worked and played like the Bavarian homeland of many of its citizens that it so closely resembled. Hard work and dark beer were favorites in the metropolis that had survived monumental floods and a scourge of civic corruption that had led it to adopt the city manager system half a century before Bernardin became its archbishop. About a third of the population was Catholic when Bernardin arrived, a stranger to the traditions and folkways of a clergy with a strong Germanic identity. Had he not succeeded a bishop named Leibold, and had not Archbishop Alter before him reigned as confidently and benignly as a Junker patriarch?

The Italian-American Bernardin was warmly received, however, in a city that had lost its previous archbishop suddenly and on an unsettling note of unfair and undeserved controversy over the performance of the Bernstein Mass. Bernardin seemed a calming influence during a period that remained tortured for all Americans. Richard Nixon, who, along with his running mate Spiro Agnew, had been pictured at the Republican convention smiling fixedly, their hands upraised on either side of John Cardinal Krol, had been reelected in a smothering landslide over Senator George McGovern. That picture of the candidates with the president of the American Catholic bishops had been no more an accident than had Secretary of State Henry Kissinger's claim, shortly before the election, that "Peace is at hand." Although fewer than 25,000 American troops remained in Vietnam at the end of the year, the country's cries of anguish had not diminished; they had only been muffled like those of a biblical woman worn down by mourning.

The exultant Nixon had begun a helicopter shuttle between the White House and Camp David, announcing, on each return landing, personnel adjustments for his second term whose triumphant conclusion he foresaw coinciding with the nation's Bicentennial celebration in 1976. The first change he announced was his dropping of Notre Dame University President Theodore Hesburgh from the Civil Rights Commission. Hesburgh, aware that his liberal progressive credentials had made his discharge as politically attractive as Nixon's televised bonhomie with the conservative Krol, observed that "Thoreau once said that the best place for a man when the government is unjust is in jail." Nixon's action was, in his judgment, a kind of negative endorsement.

In any case, it was clear that the American Catholic Church was valued by the still bristling and bright eyed Nixon as an entity to be manipulated routinely for political purposes. The 1972 campaign had seen the first full scale development of "ethnic" desks, a code word for operations to woo the Catholic vote. Nixon had read the signs with his brooding shrewdness and had made inroads into the once reliably Democratic Catholic camp. It was politically safe for him to stand with Krol and to jettison Hesburgh. On Dec. 18, 1972, at Nixon's orders, bombs once again began falling like clutches of candles from B-52s onto targets in North Vietnam.

The next day, Bernardin thought about this renewal of the air war as he prepared for his installation in Cincinnati's weathered cathedral of St. Peter in Chains. The large turnout of nearly one hundred bishops and cardinals was yet another indication of the high regard in which Bernardin himself was held by his fellow churchman. They liked him and genuinely wanted to wish him well. But their presence in large numbers was also a signal, ringing off ancient coils of instinct in the institutional church, that this was an event to attend and at which to be seen. No canny churchman wanted to be marked absent from a significant transaction of ecclesiastical power. Bernardin was someone to watch in the American church. And so the day could not be completely shadowed by the resumption of the Indo-China bombing, and, in the classical style of high clerical culture, it was well and comfortably celebrated at a banquet at a downtown hotel.

Bernardin's mother Maria, still vigorous, practical, and keen eyed, proved, in her down to earth presence and observations, the hit of the day. The large crowd of black suited clergymen laughed and applauded appreciatively as the new archbishop told them of his mother's advice on the day he had first become a bishop, six years before, to walk straight and not to look too pleased with himself. For a moment, the cares of the troubled nation faded away and history paused to have its picture taken. It was as familiar a snapshot as any from the thick album of pre-conciliar American Catholicism. A relatively young archbishop with a devoted and engaging mother had received the pallium, the band of wool cloth whose tradition dated from the sixth century, signed with six black crosses and worn around the neck. For Bernardin, it signified something at the very core of his commitment to the church, his union and obedience to the pope as well as his own authority as an archbishop. These notions were permanently fused in his heart and mind. Bernardin, surrounded by the most powerful figures in American Catholicism, looked out at the priests and people he would lead before, as everyone silently and contentedly expected, he took an even higher step in the hierarchy. This stop-time event carried the comfort, for the length of the day, of earlier and more peaceful and spacious periods in American Catholic life.

As Bernardin settled behind his desk at the chancery office, he was joined by his secretary Octavie Mosimann. She had worked with him since his years in South Carolina and, a decade later, would go on with him to Chicago. Her Southern accent and rare talent for discretion leavened with unfailing pleasantness were already well known to everyone who did business with him. Perhaps nobody understood and responded so quietly and effectively, almost intuitively, to the archbishop's work habits as she did. Bernardin tapped the obsessive reservoirs of character he shared with almost every other Catholic of his generation to deal systematically and swiftly with the mounds of paper that, like the Indian burial grounds a hundred miles north in Ohio, were prominent features in the landscape of any bishop's life. The Loyola University research on the priesthood had revealed that bishops truly enjoyed administrative work, that they experienced a profound gratification of doing their duty by making decisions and clearing their desks. Bernardin was *primus inter pares* in this regard.

It was the beginning of the age, as a priest associate later recalled, "in which we came to recognize the poetry and power of the interoffice memo." Dan Kane remembered that the use of written memoranda quickly became the best way of communicating with the new archbishop. "He might come in late at night from a confirmation or a trip to find a huge pile of mail on his desk. And I would be astounded to receive a response from him the next morning." Such swift administrative action was possible because Ms. Mosimann, known as Tanchie, understood and adapted so well to Bernardin's style.

During his first week as Cincinnati's archbishop, Bernardin was preoccupied about his forthcoming Christmas sermon. Father Thomas Nolker, who later served as his priest secretary, remembered that it was Bernardin's habit "to focus on some major issue in the world at Christmas, to spend a great deal of time preparing a statement on some aspect of the meaning of the incarnation for the world today. It was part of his general desire that the views of the local church not be too narrow." Bernardin reflected on the troubled and ambiguous hours that were piling up like a snowdrift of woe on the crown of the year. What could he say, what *should* he say from his heart as the city's new pastor, that would illuminate these days whose early darkness and long nights seemed a metaphor for the shadowed soul of America at large?

Bernardin consulted with some of the priest professors at the seminary adjoining his residence, using their skills, as he would with other experts in future years, to assist him in drafting his first midnight mass sermon in his new position. The central thought, however, was to be his own. He read the text over again, decided to rewrite the last two pages on his own typewriter. He climbed into the pulpit, into the white brilliance of the television lights in that first chill hour of Christmas day, 1972, with a carefully thought out message. It was addressed to a broader audience than the throng of worshippers in the squat cathedral that loomed like a frontier fort in the heart of Cincinnati. And it dealt with more than the Christmas pieties that Catholics expected.

Bernardin addressed the issue that had so absorbed his attention, the fresh bombing in Vietnam. He also spoke directly to the Nixon administration whose maneuvers he had observed closely during his four years in Washington, D.C. In a passage that startled his immediate listeners and that drew wide attention in the media, Bernardin evoked the sadness that gripped the world on that Christmas night. "In Vietnam, especially," he said, "we can only feel grief and dismay that the long and tortuous journey which seemed so close to peace has again been interrupted by violent force and massive bombing. It is not my intention at this time to assign blame for this latest turn of events. However, on this birthday of the Prince of Peace, I do issue a plea to the leaders of our nation and to all parties in the Vietnam conflict to halt the hostilities and to resume the negotiations quickly and in good faith so that this devastating conflict might soon be ended."

The young archbishop's challenge to the Nixon administration policies was not the cry of an emotional anti-war activist. Bernardin never put anything down on paper, or made a public utterance, without thinking through its every implication. Because of the enormous concentration, reflection, and caution that went into their preparation, Bernardin's statements resembled archeological digs: every level contained discoverable meaning. So here, in less than melodramatic terms, Bernardin was not only condemning this new flare of warfare but making it clear that the Catholic Church was not a silent, malleable force that Nixon could use as he wished for his own political advantage.

This was further underscored when Cardinal Krol, along with a few other Catholic bishops and a small ecumenical group of religious leaders, protested the reigniting of the conflict in Vietnam. President Nixon could hardly discount these prelates as speaking from some offshore island of liberalism. Their voices rose from the mainland of American Catholicism. So Bernardin understood that, with Krol taking a similiar stand on one side and Bishop Thomas Gumbleton, a well known peace activist, taking it on the other, he was on firm and ecclesiastically safe ground in enunciating his position. Still, it came from his heart and marked him clearly as a man of conscience.

Perhaps Bernardin had read the history of one of his distinguished predecessors, William Henry Elder, Cincinnati's second archbishop, who had served from 1883 to 1904. During the Civil War, he had been bishop of Natchez, Mississippi, and had been arrested for refusing the order of the commander of the occupying Union forces to have prayers offered for the president of the United States in the Catholic churches of the diocese. Elder's conviction by the military court was later reversed in Washington. His forthrightness had not been lost to local memory.

The popular anti-war tactic of the time, civil disobedience, was not Bernardin's style. But then, preaching his first major sermon in Cincinnati against the government's policy was not what people had expected from him either. The public pursuit of peace had been added to his agenda and his words on that cold Christmas midnight did more than challenge the government policy in Vietnam. It offered a prophecy of the positions that the entire conference of bishops would take against nuclear war almost a decade later in the pastoral letter, *The Challenge of Peace*. The chairman of the committee of bishops who drafted it would be Joseph L. Bernardin. By then, the American bishops, operating collegially through their conference, would be characterized by one Washington columnist as the greatest obstacle the Reagan administration faced to the free use of arms in Central America.

An ironic invitation arrived shortly thereafter at the archbishop's residence in Cincinnati. Bernardin was asked to preach, along with evangelist Billy Graham and Hollywood Rabbi Edgar Magnin, in an ecumenical service to be held in the White House on the Sunday immediately following Nixon's second inaugural.

VIII

Bernardin pondered the presidential invitation carefully. Although he could read the manipulative message between its engraved lines, he decided to accept it. Nixon's staff explained that Bernardin had been chosen because he was so well known in Washington. But the president's efforts to co-opt religious leaders for his own purposes—to dazzle them with the grandeur of the East Room, and to envelope them in the atmosphere of being insiders in the Wasp temple of power—were obvious to the archbishop of Cincinnati. He also understood that he would be teamed with religious leaders whose sympathies for the Republican administration were well known. Billy Graham was perhaps the most famous preacher in the world, a familiar figure at White House prayer breakfasts, a minister of unquestioned sincerity who strongly supported what he perceived to be the righteous causes of the Nixon administration. Edgar Magnin was the dynamic reform rabbi to the stars and the studio heads. He held Hollywood enthralled by his speaking ability and his talent for combining religion and patriotism.

"Why didn't they ask Krol?" one of the archbishop's aides asked wryly. Bernardin smiled philosophically. He felt uncomfortable, he acknowledged, but he did not think that he had any choice in the matter. He would represent the church at what, after all, was a national celebration, but he would not be easily incorporated into an all-faith endorsement of Nixon's second term. Bernardin would approach this matter in a characteristic fashion. He would think, pray, consult, and thoroughly prepare his remarks, anticipating the possible vagaries of time, chance, and misinterpretation as if drawing up a plan for D-Day. Although some progressives and peace activists envisioned this setting as a dramatic opportunity to confront the president over the war that Bernardin had just condemned, he resisted calmly, saying "I will not insult the president in his own house." No, he would be correct in every way, but his remarks would not lack a real message, he would acquit the conscience of the church—and his own—with honor and pastoral subtlety at the same time.

As the sunlight stretched farther across that January's bleak white face, the new archbishop was kept busy acquainting himself with the personnel and administrative operations of his new assignment. Dan Kane had already suggested a series of visits to the deaneries, geographical subdivisions of the archdiocese, that would enable Bernardin to get to know the priests and the parishes in an orderly fashion. Eager to do this, he scheduled his first such pilgrimage for Springfield, Ohio, in the week that followed his preaching at the White House.

Bernardin surveyed the post-Vatican II structures already in place in Cincinnati. These included almost a dozen vicars for departments ranging from the traditional canonical concerns of the diocese to those of modern communications. Archbishop Leibold had held monthly luncheon meetings in the Cathedral cafeteria with all the heads of offices and bureaus. This had been designed as an informational exchange, with Leibold making his own observations at the end. Some of the structures, such as the Pastoral Council composed of 25 laymen, 25 laywomen, and the 10 deans and representatives of religious orders, were basically refashionings of organizations that had flourished in the generation before the council.

Bernardin inspected these groupings with the eye of an executive who had just supervised the streamlining of the bishops' conference. In classic fashion, he would live for a few years with this inheritance of assemblies, scattered in various locations in the archdiocese, and then, after his accustomed consultation, he would replace them with a centralized and simplified arrangement that, for example, would reduce the number of departments to six and re-name their heads as directors instead of vicars. While he would continue issuing a financial statement every December, he modified other traditions, such as large, unwieldly meetings, preferring to have the six departments heads relate to him in cabinet-like fashion.

Bernardin's collegial approach to this restructuring would be Cincinnati's first experience of a way of handling things with which it would become very familiar in the ten years of his presence there. A tissue sample of the archdiocese would have revealed the strengths of its Germanic genetic structure: A willingness to accept, be comfortable with, and loyal to, good order. If anything, the new archbishop was certain of his own goals in restructuring the governance of the archdiocese. But Bernardin had to draw on his every gift of subtlety, to promote a challenge to, and transformation of, already proven structures by the gifted Bismarcks and Metternichs of his ecclesiastical territory.

Cincinnati's Catholics, priests and laypeople alike, were soon to be involved in the kind of consultative process that would be Bernardin's hallmark ever afterward. He was not, it must be emphasized, a bishop without ideas clear enough to delight Plato about the direction in which he wished the archdiocese to move. But he would never, in any circumstances, impose his own notions by ecclesiastical fiat. He would, rather, initiate what he deemed the most effective practical means of implementing collegiality: He drew everybody into reflection and deliberation that emphasized the process of participation rather than the personalities of the participants.

In practice, this meant opening broad and deep consultations that were designed to entertain almost every possible course of action. As Father Nolker later recalled, ''he had a tremendous desire for consultation, looking at every possibility. In a controversy, he wanted every viewpoint expressed, making everybody feel that they had input. The archbishop had a real commitment to his belief that everybody was a part of the church. He very quietly made sure that this was *the* working principle of the discussions. It was frustrating and tiring at times but everybody's opinion mattered whether it belonged to the director of a department or a secretary.''

Bernardin, however, did not believe in what Nolker characterized as "pooled ignorance." Indeed, Bernardin, listening carefully, speaking softly, generally knew exactly where he wanted to go and what he wanted to accomplish, even though he might not know every detail in the collegial journal or every detail of what would be worked out. "If there was a clear goal," Nolker remembered, such as reorganizing the archdiocese, "he would reconcile differences by letting people talk through their different opinions. He always emphasized the positive in order to get a consensus on the issues about which everybody could agree. Then he would deal with the disagreements, guiding them often to a path they could walk together. 'Well, what about this?' he would ask, as he led the discussants very gently through the obstacles. Often, the answer would emerge, seem to be discovered, as the outcome of the process."

In short, quintessential Bernardin. If he knew what he wanted, he was also sincere in allowing every option or problem to be examined minutely. This process, as fire eating into roughly mined gold, burned out the dross of congested emotions, unacknowledged prejudices and uncertainties, letting them be dissolved as they were expressed, so that the issues might emerge as purely as possible. This patient listening, with meetings multiplying like chain letters, was one of Bernardin's pastoral ways of handling the often unnamed inner resistances to change that, carrying the special curse of every hidden agenda, destroyed the chances for real agreement. That the final conclusions were not unlike those that he had foreseen was the exact signal of a leadership style that was tested and proven by the very process through which it expressed itself.

All that was, however, in the future as Bernardin reviewed various drafts of his forthcoming White House talk. Events that symbolized the generational change in America continued to counterpoint his own emergence at the head of a new cohort of leaders in Catholicism. Harry S Truman had died at 88 on the day after Christmas and Lyndon B. Johnson, his gray hair tumbling like some eternal Texan's to his shoulders, stood solemnly at the graveside, his own death less than four weeks away. And Richard Milhous Nixon was the improbable figure of transition, ending the war in Vietnam, reopening America's relations with mainland China, proposing to reform welfare, and finally undo the social effects of the Democratic New Deal on American life.

The full shadow of the Watergate scandal had not yet fallen across his smiling but anxious and unsynchronized features. The president had obliterated the news coverage of the end of the first Watergate burglars' trial on January 11 by ending the second phase of the price control program he had put into effect the previous summer. The event was knocked off the front pages and off the top of the newscasts. Nixon seemed, for the moment, to have mastered the dark possibilities of scandal's tainting his new term in office.

Nine days later, at his second inaugural, the self-complacent president enunciated a primitivist Republican theme of rugged individualism, of prosperity, in effect, as God's reward to the Puritan strivings of Wasp America. The country, which had voted for him in every state but Massachusetts and the District of Columbia, was behind him. "In our own lives," Nixon said, "let each ask not what will the government do for me, but what can I do for myself?" The thrust of his intentions was clear. His new administration would take aim at what he perceived as the humanitarian excesses, the soft liberal concerns for the community at large that had characterized the Democratic overtures from Franklin D. Roosevelt to Lyndon B. Johnson.

Bernardin studied the final draft of his talk for the religious service that would be held in the White House's East Room the next day. He packed and flew to Washington, aware of the approaching moment when, in front of the most powerful people in the nation, he would stand as the spokesman for the Catholic Church. He and his fellow speakers, Billy Graham and Rabbi Magnin, were received warmly and brought to the Nixon's private quarters, where coffee was served in the living room into which sun streamed through the fan-shaped window at its end.

The religious leaders chatted cordially with members of the Nixon family and then, surrounded by the smartly disciplined pomp of White House protocol, were escorted to the East Room. The highest ranking members of the administration, along with senators, congressmen, and the justices of the Supreme Court packed the spacious room that had been the setting for moments of tragedy, such as presidential wakes, and moments of triumph, such as this in which the very atoms of the Republican triumph seemed to glisten like decorations in the solemn yet festive atmosphere.

Rabbi Magnin, at ease with the powerful, knew what to say to them, too. His remarks, made without a text, were of unrelieved praise for President Nixon and his accomplishments. Then Billy Graham, the sound of his voice as soft as woodsmoke from his Carolina background, endorsed the president's political morality. Graham, also speaking without a text, made a strong case for teaching the ten commandments in the nation's schools. The president beamed at such endorsements of his carefully contrived agenda. All eyes turned to the dark-haired Catholic archbishop as he unfolded his text and began to speak.

True to his vow, Bernardin delivered a talk that was appropriate for the occasion. It was not, however, full of praise for Nixon or his programs. But, in phrases whose meaning could not be misunderstood, Bernardin counterpointed Nixon's emphasis on rugged individualism. The task, he said, catching the president's dark hooded eyes, "is to eradicate that enervating individualism, based on selfish interests, that often works against the common good. That kind of individualism is illustrated in the demands for *absolute* rights for individuals without due concern for the rights of others, in the apathetic turning-off of politics because it is not immediately self-fulfilling, in a God-and-me theology that ignore the institution and the realities of social concern. . . . The philosophy of this extreme individualism is directly counter to the spirit of biblical religion which emphasizes our relationship to others, our responsibility to neighbors which is the expression of our response to God."

Nobody missed the point of what he said; Bernardin's style had been gentlemanly but clear and, since he had brought copies of his carefully worded text, it was carried on the wire services and was featured in coverage of the event around the world. He mixed pleasantly with the great and near great as, satisfied that he had undramatically but unmistakably delivered a message both about Catholic values and about the manipulation resistant character of the church, smiled as a reporter asked him what he thought of Billy Graham's idea of teaching the ten commandments in school. Bernardin paused, caught Vice-President Spiro Agnew's sloe eyed, half jovial glance. "I certainly support the teaching of the commandments," Bernardin said softly, "but I think the Reverend Graham's proposal might run into some constitutional questions." President Nixon's smile seemed a little more forced than usual as he handed Bernardin an autographed bible and bade him farewell.

IX

The year would quickly turn so phantasmagoric for America and the world that, at its conclusion, a gas station in Chicago would mourn its passing on its sign just off one of the city's busiest expressways: *1973, Farewell You Bastard*. The seeds of this streetwise judgment had sprouted beneath the snows of its first month. Bernardin had just returned from his White House sermon and begun to implement the regional pastoral visitations that Dan Kane had proposed to him. On Tuesday, January 22, he travelled to Springfield, Ohio, to meet the pastors, religious brothers and sisters, and delegations of lay people from the cluster of surrounding parishes. That very day, the United States Supreme Court issued its first ruling on *Roe v. Wade*. Although this was widely interpreted as conferring not only legality but an aureole of moral acceptability on abortion, the decision actually confined itself to a constitutional question, saying that individual states could not prohibit abortions during the first six months of pregnancy.

This court action inscribed another lasting signature note on Bernardin's career as a leader of a new generation of American bishops. He would not only join his colleagues in a lengthy counterculture effort against abortion but, three years later, when he was president of the bishops, the issue would involve Bernardin, in an uncharacteristically uncomfortable way, in the 1976 presidential campaign. And 10 years later, after he had become a cardinal, he would assume the chairmanship of the Pro-Life committee of the National Conference of Catholic Bishops. Throughout the decade, the question of abortion, as complex and mysterious as the issues of birth and death that were its parameters, was to blaze like a town square fire from which extremists on either side lighted their torches. Bernardin, ever the orthodox centrist, would feel the heat not only from the vigorous proponents of abortion who framed it as a rights issue but also from the most impassioned legions of its opponents who viewed it as the finest test of every loyal Christian's soul, including Bernardin's. On this hearth Bernardin would ultimately hammer out the mesh shield of his consistent ethic of life whose links included not only opposition to abortion but the defense and promotion of life in a range of other questions, including those of modern warfare, genetic engineering, and capital punishment.

On that raw January day, however, he was taking the first steps on a pilgrimage of leadership initiatives that would, along with the strengthening and preservation of the bishops' conference and the development of its letter on nuclear war, constitute the distinctive triad of his pastoral accomplishment. Arriving in the small Ohio town, he was pressed by the newspaper and television reporters for a reaction to the Supreme Court decision that had just come over the wires. Bernardin, in consultation with Kane, quickly drafted a statement defending the church's traditional teachings on the matter. Then in a minor but brilliantly symbolic incident, they encountered the complications of life in a nation that obsessively prized the separation of church and state.

The Ohio legislature had passed laws that allowed the subsidization of equipment for religious schools as long as it was not used for religious purposes. The mimeograph machine had come to the local Catholic school as a portion of state aid with such restricted uses. Bernardin encountered a Catholic conscience as finely attuned to moral probity as his own when the nun in charge of the machine refused to use it to reproduce copies of his statement. While his expansive Italian appreciation of life's ironies allowed him to smile, his aides scrambled for another acceptable way of getting copies of his words to the representatives of the media.

That evening, on the CBS news, Walter Cronkite interrupted

himself to take a phone call in the middle of the program. He then solemnly shared the information that was yet another sign of the transition point America had reached in generational leadership in both church and state. Former President Lyndon Baines Johnson had suffered a heart attack at his Texas ranch and died on his way to a Houston Medical Center named after himself.

Bernardin's carefully planned visits to various sections of the archdiocese not only acquainted him with his people but gave them an opportunity of observing him—affable, approachable, ever correct—at first hand. As he would in the far more sensitive situation of succeeding the embattled Cardinal Cody a decade later, Bernardin paid tribute to his predecessor while gently and gradually taking his own place in the imagination of his people. In this, he followed the human instincts that undergirded and gave warmth and light to his administrator's preoccupations and planning. Taking a lead from Pope John XXIII, Bernardin had, for example, offered masses on Christmas day and throughout the week at homes and centers for the aged and poor in Cincinnati and, later, in the other large city of his ecclesiastical territory, Dayton. He also initiated a Christmas mass at the Cincinnati Workhouse for prisoners, something no previous archbishop had done.

It was at such moments that the pastor who lived just beneath the surface of the obsessive archiepiscopal official emerged freely and naturally. Indeed, people began to understand that these aspects of Bernardin's personality were always present together, that what they saw, in the phrase of the day, was exactly what they got, Bernardin just as he was both in public and in private. He was, as some coworkers noted, consistently pastoral even in his role as the decision-making bureaucrat, for he never imposed decisions and was always understanding of the shortcomings and failures of others. A photographer with an eye for just such telling moments, caught a spontaneously smiling Bernardin as he received a Black Power handshake from a black prisoner on one of his workhouse visits. On another occasion after mass, a prisoner asked him for his bishop's cross. Bernardin nodded and grinned, yes, he would be glad to do that. As he handed it over, prison officials quickly informed him that they would "place the cross with the other items to be returned to the individual when he was released." Priest aides shuddered at such characteristically unaffected responses. "Thank God," one of them murmured, referring to an historic cross only taken out of the archdiocesan archives for special occasions, "he wasn't wearing the Purcell pectoral cross."

Through such incidents, like a succession of candid camera shots from different angles, the dimensions of Bernardin's unique character gradually became clear. If there was closeness, it could not be completely separated from the distance, as in a view of mountains that seem within reach even when they are still a day's march away. Trustworthy impressions began to coalesce about this man who prized managerial efficiency but appreciated human frailty and the disorder it could cause at the same time. Bernardin, it became evident, was consistently more demanding on himself than he was on others. He was also keenly intelligent, a quick study who grasped the proximate and long range implications of proposals immediately. But he was also a man who, no matter the opinions or advice of others, trusted, as St. Thomas Aquinas had once put it, "the authority of his own instincts." Indeed, there seemed to be a steady ongoing dialogue between these two aspects of his being, between the keen and confident executive who loved nothing more than a few unobstructed hours in which to attack his correspondence and the benign and undefensive man who interpreted people and events as much through his reliable internal reactions to them as through their stated claims and resumes. If he was a man who strove to avoid the smallest mistake in his own work, he was quick to understand and avoid embarrassing others for the errors they committed in their own. Priests and people began to think that they had never met anyone quite like him.

As Bernardin continued his get acquainted journeys throughout the archdiocese, he sensed that, although he was warmly greeted everywhere, he was being measured against the memory of his much beloved predecessor, Paul Leibold. Some priests and people wondered how the new archbishop would evaluate the progressive post-Vatican II structures whose justifying documents had been voted in just the year before Leibold died. These had grown out of diocesan-wide participation at every level of church membership and, in the judgment of Father Carl Modell, who worked closely in various posts with Bernardin during his Cincinnati years, "were very forward looking. The guidelines for parish councils, for example, called for decision by consensus and provided for a detailed appeal process."

Indeed, so progressive were some of these developments that they seemed to exceed, or at least anticipate the reform of, the church's official canon law. But the priests and the people were immensely proud of them. They had been wrought with the same German thoroughness that had given the world machines and automobiles so finely engineered that they hardly needed lubricating oil and barely showed the stress of use. As Father Modell, who had been deeply involved in their planning, remembered, "We were still mourning Archbishop Leibold, a native son of Cincinnati, and some of us felt that we had to defend his accomplishments against any change by the new archbishop."

Bernardin also ran the danger, according to Father Modell, of seeming, because of his Washington background, to be "the bishops' man," an outsider with plans of his own rather than a man like Leibold whose Ohio River roots guaranteed his sympathy for the achievements of the local church. "Bernardin stepped into that," Modell recalled, "and it was difficult for him to do. I don't think that he was totally comfortable with the work of the synod, especially with the structures that didn't fit into canon law. And I don't think he was enthusiastic about implementing a plan that he had no hand in producing. He dealt with this through his administrative talents and his enormous sensitivity to the feelings of others. He did everything he could to overcome being perceived as a stranger or a representative of the bishops. He struck the theme of being the 'pastoral bishop' and insisted on that notion in everything he did."

So the new archbishop, confronting an array of newly minted procedures, approached the situation by "listening sincerely," according to Modell, "to what everybody had to say. He projected a genuine interest—nobody could fake this—in individuals and their work. That's where you could observe one of his distinctive abilities.

Through the power of his open-minded and fair personality and his approach, he could get the best out of people, draw out their best ideas and their best performance so that they even got greater satisfaction out of their work.'' Gradually, Bernardin modified his inheritance of structures, achieving what he wanted through this patient evocation of the cooperation of others. This cooperation, Modell recalled, was the fruit ''of his consultation. He listened to everybody's ideas so they felt that they really added something to the matter under discussion. Finally, I, and others, realized that we didn't have to defend the archdiocese against him.''

In all this Bernardin was following his deepest blood knowledge rather than some how-to-do-it manual from the Vatican. But he achieved the kind of good order in procedures that was, in his judgment, essential for any archbishop who aspired to be a ''churchman'' in the classical sense, that is, a man who does what the church asks of him. He could never be comfortable with arrangements that did not match ecclesiastical legislation but neither would he ever administer his territory in concrete literalistic fashion. His goal was to reorganize the already reorganized archdiocese, trimming and simplifying its plans, consolidating its offices, and bringing its practices into harmony with the official regulations of the church. He also wanted to make himself present as a pastoral figure, that is, as one who mediated between well honored Vatican expectations and laws and the people who were enthusiastic for a more open, participative experience of the church.

Bernardin's pastoral sense was also characterized by compassion for the struggles of imperfect human beings. This feeling for the way people really were, and his lack of being scandalized or disappointed when they fell short of this, informed his collegial attitudes and his manner of exercising his authority. There was, however, no question about who possessed the authority in the archdiocese and no question in Bernardin's mind about the ultimate authority of the Holy See. Harmonizing diverse interests, giving people room to talk out their differences, reaching accords that preserved values even in striking compromises: these were elements of what priests and people soon came to recognize as the classical Bernardin approach, a commitment to the process of dialogue to resolve past disputes and to make plans for the future.

Father Modell compared Bernardin with his predecessors in their way of meeting their ideal of being churchmen, bishops obedient to the church's wishes. "Archbishop Alter would, if convinced that the Holy See did not understand a local situation completely, on occasion say *no* to Rome. Archbishop Leibold would do what Rome asked him to do, no matter what it was. Archbishop Bernardin would do what Rome wanted and would never say *no* directly. But he would raise questions about interpretations and timing, about the circumstances and prudence of implementing certain things, getting Rome to see things in a better light. That's exactly what he was so good at in Cincinnati, finding middle ground, reaching a solution that respected everyone's rights and was acceptable to all sides."

The priests and people of the archdiocese soon recognized Bernardin's nonauthoritarian leadership, coming to accept the nature of collegial collaboration on matters even as they marvelled at his capacity to listen until the last voice had been heard at meetings that stretched far into the night. The clergy, in their ironic fashion, soon dealt humorously with Bernardin's untiring readiness for consultation as well as his thorough preparation for meetings. He always thought things through before-hand and was, therefore, able to guide the discussion rather than let it drift aimlessly. In short, he often entered what he knew would be a long meeting with a very good sense of the direction the conversation would take and the decisions that would be made.

"Spontaneous and unrehearsed," Father Joseph Goetz recalled, "were never the words that came to mind about the Archbishop." Still another said that, "So carefully prepared was the archbishop for every occasion that, if he were asked to say grace at a banquet, he would probably read it from a file card so that nobody could misinterpret him." Father Modell, commenting on charges made several years later that Bernardin had conspired with Father Andrew Greeley to oust John Cardinal Cody from Chicago, said, "The idea of Bernardin's conspiring was ridiculous. He couldn't be part of a conspiracy because he would first have consulted with 10 other people."

If Bernardin's personality and approach to issues were becoming clearer to the Catholics of his archdiocese, so, too, was his presence to Cincinnati at large. "He raised the level of visibility of the church in the city," Father Thomas Nolker recalled, "although he did not intrude directly into many civic matters. He endorsed the school tax levies publicly but otherwise worked through the diocesan and other church structures." One of these was the Metropolitan Religious Coalition of Cincinnati whose members focussed on the issues, such as poverty and homelessness, that reflected the moral tenor of the city. Bernardin also used his column in the Catholic newspaper to comment on local issues and on matters of general concern, such as gun control. It was, however, within the environment of the church itself that the new archbishop functioned most comfortably. "He loved it," Father Modell recalled, "he loved his involvement in the national and international church. It was the main, perhaps the only, interest in his life."

This flowed, in part, from Bernardin's conviction that the influence of Catholicism could be best expressed through the people who constituted its essential mysterious nature. Their capacity to bring Catholic values to bear on society would be best served through parish and other administrative structures that encouraged collegial deliberations and expressions of their convictions in their work and in their lives. The Catholic Church as a People rather than just an organization was a reality envisioned by Vatican II but, in Bernardin's judgment, this would be a diffuse community that, without effective structures, would never discover its true identity or speak in its true voice.

Bernardin's methodical way of proceeding built on his past experience as an administrator. In Cincinnati, however, he was able to tincture this heavy bureaucratic emphasis with many pastoral activities. He worked sincerely at fulfilling his ideal of being a "pastoral bishop." He not only presided at the many official liturgical ceremonies that were an essential part of any bishop's life but also made room for the unprecedented visits and masses at the jails, hospitals, and nursing homes as well. When he was apprised of criticism that the people saw more of this pastoral side of him than the priests did, he arranged to conduct a series of days of recollection with the clergy. He was therefore able to mix with them on these occasions reserved only for them, reinforcing the hearty male bonding and sense of fraternity that were then such prominent features of clerical life. This was, in fact, another classic Bernardin solution to a difficulty, for he initiated and institutionalized a process aimed at deepening his contact with his priests and providing them a forum for collegial discussions with him. He has continued this process, in the form of overnight gatherings, with the priests of Chicago.

Occasionally, something of the parish priest in him could also be observed as when, with a refreshing simplicity and self-effacement, he ignored protocol to respond to some spontaneous religious need, often that of a stranger. One evening, for example, a woman called, saying that she was having difficulty contacting a priest to come and hear the confession of a friend of hers. Bernardin responded, ''When would you like me to be there?'' The next day, he made the pastoral call without fanfare or publicity. Cincinnati quickly lowered the defenses it had initially raised during its period of evaluating its new Catholic shepherd. His capacity for wielding authority in the subtle but purposive manner of a post-Vatican II prelate was tested in and through his letting himself be known and in negotiating the pattern of administrative services that he desired. If Bernardin's authority survived such close and occasionally skeptical examination, it was not so for authority in America at large at the time.

Immediately after Secretary of State Henry Kissinger announced, on January 27, the signing of a four party pact in Paris providing for a Vietnam cease-fire, the withdrawal of U.S. troops and the release of prisoners, President Nixon's approval ratings rose to 68 percent. Despite that fact, he was entering the shadows of the Watergate scandal that would destroy his authority and severely compromise that of his office as well. On Feb. 7, 1973, the United States Senate established a Select Committee on Presidential Campaign Activities to be chaired by the 77-year-old Sam Ervin of North Carolina. Its public hearings into what was termed the Watergate Conspiracy would begin on May 17. Near the end of March, James McCord, one of the defendants in the first Watergate trial, wrote to Federal Judge

John Sirica of the pressures exerted against them to be silent and accused Attorney General John Mitchell of being the "overall boss" of the coverup. Less than a month later, Patrick F. Gray, head of the FBI, would admit destroying evidence at the request of Nixon aides and resign. On the last day of April 1973, President Nixon would attempt to salvage his authority by accepting the resignation of aides John Erlichman and H.R. Haldeman, and dismissing White House counsel John Dean.

The trustworthiness of government was suspect everywhere as the sad, solemn parade of revelations continued throughout the long summer of nationally televised hearings of the Ervin Committee. The existence of White House tape recordings became known as did information about secret raids in Cambodia in 1969 and 1970. The air was charged with melancholy as the president isolated himself progressively as the pages of the calendar fell away. October 1973 would see a renewed war in the Mideast, the resignation of Vice-President Spiro Agnew, and the "Saturday Night Massacre" following Nixon's decision to oust Special Prosecutor Archibald Cox. The oil embargo resulted in the discontent of long lines at gas stations. American life had indeed grown shadowed for the office of the presidency, that central symbol of the republic's authority, was ensnarled in such deceits that on Oct. 23, 1973, Congressional leaders agreed that the House Judiciary Committee should begin investigating impeachment charges against Richard M. Nixon who had been overwhelmingly re-elected only fifty weeks before.

In Chicago, the largest archdiocese of the country, the dissatisfaction with John Cardinal Cody had also grown to a new intensity. His arbitrary dealings with laity and priests, his seemingly punitive decisions, his technique of dividing his critics by a combination of flattery and threat, his secretiveness and imperiousness: These were only some of the particulars in the long bill of complaints that was being compiled against him. Still, it was felt that, no matter the way in which he exercised his authority, a sitting archbishop with a wide network of friends in the city of Rome that he visited several times a year was secure in his power. The church had lived through such incidents many times in its history. It would never remove an archbishop merely on the strength of rumor or complaint. That would lessen the authority of the entire structure of the church. No, the church could wait out the situation, and eventually absorb Cody and his critics into its seemingly eternal tissues.

That summer, however, Father Andrew Greeley watched the Watergate hearings with fascination. He would call his friends to discuss the investigation and to raise the possibility that, if a president could be drawn close to impeachment by such public inquiry and publicity, then pressure might also be brought successfully to bear against a cardinal archbishop. Church authority in the most populous and richest of archdioceses would soon be the subject of an unprecedented campaign of letter writing and protest. While some observers felt that Chicago's priests were too absorbed with the father figure of their archbishop, flooding their imaginations and conversations with his controverted presence, thus making an already bad situation worse, Father Greeley decided that he would use his polished writing skills and his contacts with the media to make life for Cody as uncomfortable as possible.

X

Archbishop Jean Jadot, fresh from Vatican diplomatic posts in the Far East, arrived in Washington, D.C., in the summer of 1973. With a crew cut above his lean, preoccupied features, he could have been a resistance general dropping behind the lines of a city under siege in the Watergate war. He was, in fact, a middle-aged Belgian with vivid memories of the Second World War and a good working knowledge of the universal church from his years of service in the equivalent of its foreign service. Jadot had been entrusted by the aging Pope Paul VI with perhaps the most sensitive and important of all Vatican diplomatic assignments, that of apostolic delegate to the United States.

Jadot moved quietly into the handsome granite residence and office complex on the stretch of Massachusetts Avenue dubbed Embassy Row that stretched northwest away from the center of the city. The delegation headquarters looked across a stretch of Rock Creek Park toward the Naval observatory dwelling that would soon be the official vice-presidential residence. He settled into the comfortable quarters that, in their location and style, reflected the Catholic striving for respectability in Protestant America every bit as much as the grand bishops' houses in which the immigrant Catholics had once taken such pride. American Catholics, although by now educated and prosperous, still aspired to national influence in proportion to their presence as roughly a quarter of the population.

That the Vatican's official representative lived and functioned in the same neighborhood and circles as the world's most powerful ambassadors bolstered the church's position even though the United States hesitated to establish full diplomatic relations with the Vatican. President Harry Truman's effort to do that barely a quarter of a century before Jadot's arrival had been frustrated by vigorous protests that had not lacked the acid overtones of anti-Catholic fears and prejudice. Although it was thought that the election of John F. Kennedy as president in 1960 had dispelled much of the heavy opposition to Catholic advancement, the fact that few members of the Roman Catholic church had yet received national appointments suggested that the mighty fortress of American power was still overwhelmingly Protestant. At the time of Jadot's arrival, America was almost two hundred years old, yet only seven Catholics had served on the Supreme Court and one of those, Sherman Minton, had become Catholic only after relinquishing his chair. In the first 150 years of the nation's history, only seven Catholics had served in the cabinet. Only 17 had served since 1939.

The United States, Jadot realized as he looked toward Capitol Hill where the Ervin Committee was involved with the momentous constitutional possibility of finding evidence that might unseat a president, was deeply committed to the constitutional separation of church and state as well. Jadot, aware that in Europe constitutional crises were settled swiftly and that governments rose and fell with regularity, observed that Americans, for all their emphasis on individuality and freedom, were restrained in their behavior and respectful of their governing institutions. The Catholic church had grown in this Protestant republic as it had in no other country. The American brand of Democracy, Jadot reflected, had much to recommend it. He also understood the persistent Roman suspicions of the United States; these resembled western Europe's resentment of the superpower status of the United States and certain curial fears that the newly developed National Conference of Catholic Bishops might become a superpower among the churches.

Still, Jadot's function in Washington was far more weighted toward institutional Catholicism than to relations with the government. The apostolic delegate was the pope's emissary, transmitting the wishes of the Holy See on a wide variety of matters, some of them merely regulatory in nature but others, such as the selection and placement of bishops, crucial to the stability and theological awareness and emphasis of American Catholicism. Although he understood the loyalty of American Catholics to Rome, he had a finely tuned sense of the moment of change that had arrived for their church. The generation of powerful, highly individualistic American prelates, had all but passed from the scene. The National Conference of Catholic Bishops had been set on firm foundations and was functioning reasonably well. True, many bishops were unhappy with the manner in which Philadelphia's John Cardinal Krol had carried over his disregard of the very advice he had solicited from them in his function as its current president. Krol was, however, considered an ultimately fair and honest man, and, as one bishop observed at the time, ''I would rather have a dispute with Krol, who is open and forthcoming about the terms of disagreement, than with someone who keeps a secret agenda. You can have a fair fight with Krol.''

But Krol's term was up in the fall of 1974 and much would depend on the bishop who succeeded him. The time had come, almost a decade after the close of Vatican II, to look beyond the transitional problems to the future shape of the world's richest and most powerful church. Nonetheless, a certain portion of Jadot's time would have to be devoted to stabilizing the Catholicism that was still dealing with the internal problems and external yearnings that the council had generated. Priests and religious nuns and brothers had left their work in large numbers, there had been a drop in church attendance, and severe polarization had developed between so-called conservative and progressive Catholics.

The latter, to some extent, followed the conservative-liberal split within the nation itself. Many earnest Catholics felt bewildered, and to some degree, betrayed by the rapid changes that had taken place in the church. The new liturgy seemed shallow and flat to many, and the seeming embrace of protoplasmic and undemanding moral positions, especially in sexual matters, convinced others that Catholicism had lost its vigor and its clear sense of identity. Progressives, on the other hand, felt that the rigid institutionalism that had characterized preconciliar Catholicism had kept the church insulated and infantile. Poorly as much change had been managed, they felt, it was as essential as an individual's passage through adolescence for the church's growth into adulthood in the modern world.

Despite these difficulties, nobody could doubt the energy or generosity of American Catholics or their leaders. The National Conference of Catholic Bishops, whose solid, still developing sense of themselves as cooperating members of this organization was the fruit of the collaboration of John Dearden and Joseph Bernardin, was entering a crucial phase of its maturation process. It could become a truly collegial body, implementing the theology of Vatican II successfully and providing a model for bishops' conferences throughout the world, or it might, under hesitant or passive leadership, stall and never achieve its full development.

At that moment, the conference was, to some extent, preoccupied with the kinds of questions that were natural but vexing, if not inflaming, during the difficult adjustment years that followed the conclusion of Vatican II. So, for example, there were lengthy discussions about the new liturgical provision that allowed Catholics, as a symbol of their adult status, to receive the Eucharistic wafer in their hands rather than having it placed on their tongues by the priest. Such an intramural issue proved to be a glinting lens that focused the varied rays of dissatisfaction on a question that came to be symbolic of the rifts that had rippled the tiles on the once smooth marble surface of Catholic life. To some conservative Catholics, communion in the hand was a desacralizing sign of the generalized failure of discipline that had crept into church life. To Catholics encouraged by conciliar reform to practice their faith by attempting to influence the major issues of the time—war, racial relations, poverty and hunger—such an obsession with a minor issue was emblematic of an older, closed, and self-complacent Catholicism. Church leaders learned that in this period, no matter what stance they took, it was not difficult to get into an argument.

As Jadot came to know the American church leaders, he developed an admiration for the young archbishop of Cincinnati. Cardinal Dearden thought well of him, as did Archbishop Benelli in Rome.

From all that Jadot could learn, Archbishop Bernardin seemed to have settled well into his new assignment on the Ohio River. It was interesting to observe Bernardin's implementation of collegiality in administering his diocese. Cincinnati, after all, suffered the same aggravations as every other diocese during this period of transition. These troubles had been multiplied by the high expectations that had been built up through the synod called by Bernardin's predecessor. If Bernardin had decided to bank those fires of enthusiasm in order to design procedures more congenial to him and more responsive to his control, he had done these things with a remarkable degree of finesse. His willingness to listen and to reconcile opposing viewpoints in a pastoral manner had gained him considerable respect.

Those accomplishments, which had the side effect, surely pleasing to Rome, of reining in extra-canonical innovations, recommended Bernardin as a man who kept obedience to the church's wishes at the center of his concerns. These fit in, Jadot appreciated, with Bernardin's previous record. Not only had he succeeded, as general secretary, in reorganizing the bishops' conference, but he had been used by the Holy See to carry out a number of highly secret and sensitive missions in the United States. Archbishop Bernardin, who had received 94 votes for the presidency of the bishops in 1971, was widely spoken of as the likely successor to Cardinal Krol at the next election in November 1974.

Bernardin's reputation had also been rising in Rome where, during Dearden's tenure as conference president, he regularly visited to carry out the business of the American bishops. Cardinal Krol preferred to deal with Roman congregations himself but Bernardin would, in November 1973, be elected along with Krol as a delegate to the 1974 International Synod of the Bishops to be held at the Vatican the following autumn. He would be asked by the secretary of the synod, Bishop Ladislas Rubin, to prepare a report in Latin, based on the reports previously submitted by the bishops of the English speaking world, on the synodal topic of evangelization, the general efforts of teaching and preaching for the purpose of converting others to Catholicism. Bernardin did present that during the early fall of 1974. He was subsequently elected by the other synodal delegates from around the world to the Council of the Secretariat of the Synod of bishops. The Cincinnati archbishop was the only prelate so chosen on the first ballot. His star, as attested to by general and Catholic newspaper coverage of the time as well as by ecclesiastical lore, was clearly rising.

North by northwest from Cincinnati, however, storms were rising violently around the planetary orbit of Chicago's archbishop. His priests complained of his failure to implement true collegiality in his relations with them and found him so distant and ambitious that a saying became current among them: "Cody is the only man who looks on the papacy as a stepping stone to higher things." John Cardinal Cody stubbornly resisted any modification in his style of leadership. Those who knew Cody appreciated his tenacity in a difficult situation and predicted that, if he felt under siege, he would only dig in further. Cody would touch his pectoral cross and raise his eyes to heaven during an interview at that time and say, "As long as I'm alright with God, I don't care what my critics say."

Among Cody's most outspoken adversaries by the time 1974 dawned was Father Andrew Greeley, who frequently attacked him in his syndicated column in Catholic newspapers. Greeley actively attempted to enroll others in the public assault on Cody, urging priests and laypeople to write letters of protest to the apostolic delegate, Archbishop Jean Jadot. For his part, Cody isolated himself further, giving rise to rumors that he no longer lived in his large North Side brick residence but had taken an apartment nearby. He visited Rome regularly, keeping up his long established contacts there, and bringing substantial donations to the Holy See. He was dealing with a kind of contemporary upheaval that he did not understand. He relied on methods out of those previous imperial generations when a measure of arrogance was not unexpected in powerful American churchmen.

The publicity that the situation was attracting was, in the judgment of many Catholics, helping Cody. They felt that Rome, following the wisdom of every ancient institution, would never remove a cardinal archbishop while he was under fire. Dan Herr, for example, a well known Catholic publisher who lived in Chicago, remonstrated with Greeley, urging him to give up what Herr judged to be excessive and, at times, even distorted criticism. "Andrew," Herr observed to an associate during this period, "is going to do more harm than good by these attacks on Cody." Greeley was not, of course, alone in his critique of Chicago's then archbishop. Cody was the source of an enormous morale problem for his priests. He chose to ignore, or fend off, their complaints, just as he chose to pay little attention to Greeley's use of his column to give voice, even in exaggerated style, to the discontents many Chicagoans felt. The unrelieved nature of Greeley's accusations, however, was soon to come to the attention of Archbishop Jadot who agreed with publisher Herr that the delicate business of informing Rome accurately about Cody was being impeded rather than moved forward by this barrage of charges.

Cody's embattled state was a counterpoint in the year that separated the summers of 1973 and 1974, within Catholicism, to the larger numbing crisis of authority centering on the Nixon presidency and the gradually crumbling lines of defense that gave way one by one. Texan Leon Jaworski had replaced Archibald Cox as special prosecutor and the Supreme Court ruled that Nixon had to surrender additional secretly recorded White House tapes to him. The House Judiciary Committee, acting, ironically, under the resolution first proposed by priest congressman Robert Drinan of Massachusetts, solemnly recommended three articles of impeachment for consideration by the full House of Representatives. An additional tape that revealed the president's early involvement in the cover-up efforts of the Watergate burglary dissolved the last membrane of resistance and Richard M. Nixon resigned, wigwagging the peace signal as he climbed into the helicopter that lifted him away from the White House lawn at noon on Aug. 9, 1974. The nation, racked by the inflation that had been loosed by the artificial elevation of oil prices during the embargo of the previous year as well as by the extended drama of its chief executive under siege, breathed a sigh of relief as Gerald Ford, newly sworn in as president, announced that "the long national nightmare with Watergate is over."

Yet the year 1974 was not free of other ecclesiastical problems that also concerned the exercise of proper authority. To immensely ambivalent reaction Pope Paul VI, facing Cold War realities, removed the exiled anti-Communist Jozsef Cardinal Mindszenty from his position as primate of Hungary. Eric Sevareid wondered, on his analysis that evening on the CBS news, what price had been paid for the elimination of a man who had been such a consistent believer all his days. The Church of England called the Archbishop of York, Donald Frederick Coggan, to assume its highest authority as the Archbishop of Canterbury. Its Episcopal counterpart church in the United States witnessed a wrenching episode of revolt against authority when four of its bishops defied ecclesiastical law and ordained 11 women as priests.

Joseph L. Bernardin, just completing his revision of the administrative procedures in Cincinnati, was being mentioned not only as the likely successor to John Cardinal Krol as president of the American bishops but, given the turmoil reported from there, as a possible successor some day to John Cardinal Cody in Chicago. One of those who often spoke favorably of a Bernardin accession in Chicago was Father Greeley, who saw him as the only kind of bishop who could restore integrity to the church there. And, Greeley frequently added in conversations with friends, he would be able to help him do it. Such gossip and rumors quickly became common in Catholic newspapers and in the secular press in Cincinnati. Their archbishop, who had so carefully and subtly refashioned the church bureaucracy into one that responded to his control, was increasingly perceived as a man of destiny. He was also accused of being a man of ambition.

Asked about that after his election to the Council of the Secretariat of the Synod of bishops, Bernardin told an interviewer, "In the local papers there were a lot of stories about me.... They made it sound as though I were a politician who knew how to run a good campaign. These stories really hurt me. What I try to do is what I think a good pastor would do. So these stories annoyed me. They hurt and upset me. Of course, these reporters wanted me to look good and many people didn't interpret it badly." He paused for a moment in his answer, as if realizing that he had not fully come to grips with the issue. "Now, to answer more directly, I would like to think that what I do, the drive I have, stems from the deep conviction that I am doing the Lord's will. Being human, I have to admit that there may be an ambitious streak in me but I don't let it dominate me or determine my actions or positions on things. But you can't rule out ambition. There's some of that in everybody.''

Such soul-searching, obsessively carried out, was characteristic of Bernardin's approach to himself and struck his interviewer as sincere. But his statement did not stop the speculation about him. Such ambition as he had would face its own purifying tests in the years ahead when he was accused of conspiring with Greeley to overthrow Cody. In the fall of 1974, Providence seemed again to be arranging his career without his having to do much about it.

While Bernardin was in Rome with Cardinal Krol at the synodal meeting, Archbishop Leo Byrne of Minneapolis–St. Paul, the vice-president of the National Conference of Catholic Bishops, died suddenly. As the second to Krol, many thought that he would be the Philadelphian's logical successor and the only real contestant, aside from Bernardin, for the presidency. Bernardin returned from Rome to head almost immediately to Washington for the bishops' meeting at which the election of the new president was to be the most significant item on the agenda. The hallways of the Capital Hilton, however, rang with speculation about the uncertainty of the outcome. Bernardin was still considered young and the balloting would, in effect, symbolize the passage of leadership out of the hands of an older generation of church leaders. Gossip had it that John Cardinal Carberry, the precise and conservative archbishop of St. Louis, who had evinced great concern about the potential abuse of the reception of communion by hand, would be put forward as the candidate of the senior and more cautious bishops.

As the bishops convened, the trial of Nixon's closest associates, H.R. Haldeman, John Erlichman, and John Mitchell, was being held a few miles away in the courtroom of Federal Judge John Sirica. As the bishops began to ballot for their new leader, the spectators in court heard through their earphones the anguished voice of President Nixon contemplating the wreckage of his own authority as he spoke to Haldeman and Erlichman, ''Despite all the polls and the rest, I think there's still a hell of a lot of people out there, and from what I've seen, they're, you know, they want to believe. That's the point, isn't it?'' To which Haldeman quickly responded, ''Why sure. Want to and do.'' Back in the hushed ballroom of the Hilton, the assembled bishops, earnest as schoolboys at their desks, inscribed their votes for their own new president.

The first ballot, although overwhelmingly for Bernardin, did not give him the majority that he needed for election. The outcome was sure, yet there was measurable tension in the hall as the process was repeated. A frowning Cardinal O'Boyle rose and made his way to the exit. Another elderly comrade joined him as they pushed through the panelled doors. ''I only came,'' the other bishop whispered hoarsely as he pulled on his overcoat, ''in order to vote against him.'' O'Boyle glared uncertainly at his companion and stepped into the hallway.

But, back on the floor, the choice of Bernardin for a three year term as president of the conference was quickly assured and greeted with strong applause from his confreres. The first bishop to reach him and shake his hand was his beaming fellow Italian-American, Francis J. Mugavero of Brooklyn. There was, as the bishops took a break before choosing Carberry as vice-president, an air that something fresh and momentous had begun for both Bernardin and the bishops themselves.

That night, Archbishop Jadot entertained all the bishops at a buffet dinner in his spacious Massachusetts Avenue residence. When asked about the election results, he replied with a trace of satisfaction in his voice that ''Bernardin is a very modern churchman, representative of a new and alert kind of bishop. The American church is not really authoritarian, with a few exceptions, but now we have turned the corner.''

Across the bishop filled room, Cardinal Dearden, watching Bernardin's head nodding near Jadot's, smiled broadly as he said to a friend, ''Now, Joe can move!''

XI

As Bernardin went to bed that night he thought of the way the newspapers had dealt with the election three years previously in which John Cardinal Krol had become president, for he himself, the young man from South Carolina, the General Secretary with no diocese of his own, had received a remarkable 94 votes on the first ballot. The *Washington Post* had headlined its story *Krol Wins Decisively.* The paper back in Columbia, South Carolina, had bannered its story with the phrase, *Local Priest Nearly Wins.* He smiled in recollection of the way in which the angle of vision affected the media's interpretation and display of events. The news, he understood, lived an urgent life of its own. A leader had to appreciate its moods and movement and measure his actions and words carefully if he wanted his message to get across clearly. The president-elect of the bishops would have further reason to reflect on the intense and demanding environment of the media before his three year term expired.

Bernardin had heard the gurgling backwash of talk about Cardinal Carberry's having been chosen as vice-president in order to balance what some bishops identified as his own relative youth and his progressive, if not liberal, tendencies. "They wanted St. Louis," one priest journalist had said omnisciently, referring to Carberry, as was the frequent clerical custom, by the name of his archdiocese, "in order to keep Cincinnati in line." Neither Bernardin nor most of the bishops accepted that translation of events but it opened a good news angle and, in the generally dull bureaucratic universe of the bishops, gave off the aroma of gossip as rich as that of the Thanksgiving dinners about to be prepared across the country.

The main argument against the gentle, soft-spoken Carberry's having been elected for such a guardianship role lay in the historical meaning of the vice-presidency of the conference. During their terms the previous holders had been only tangentially connected with the conference's main activities. They had accepted such responsibilities as the conference president chose to give them as, for example, when Dearden had asked Krol to oversee the priesthood research. Archbishop Leo Byrne, however, had practically nothing to do during Krol's term and had never even been invited to the briefings on conference business that were regularly given at the headquarters offices in Washington, D.C. Carberry, who had been a diocesan official in Brooklyn before becoming a bishop, came from a generation different from that of Bernardin but did not conceive of his task as that of balancing the latter's ecclesiastical views with his own. He was as realistic about his role as most vice-presidents of the United States were about theirs.

Bernardin acted immediately both to end the rumors of potential conflict and to demonstrate his good relationship with and intentions toward Cardinal Carberry. Immediately after Carberry's being voted in, Bernardin had said to him, ''I want you to collaborate with me in the work of the conference.'' As soon afterward as possible, Bernardin arranged for Carberry's being present at all headquarters briefings and initiated a policy of informing him in advance of what policies he planned to undertake. Carberry, described once as a man as reserved as the one in everybody's family album who was photographed at the beach wearing a cap and a long sleeved white shirt buttoned at the neck, was delighted by Bernardin's openness and talked to his clerical friends, among whom he numbered Cardinal Cody of Chicago, about the younger man's positive dealings with him. He was grateful to Bernardin for making him a part rather than an adjunct to the conference's projects.

The incident illustrated two sides of Bernardin's approach to problems. Ever sensitive to areas of potential difficulty, especially those that might arise from a clash of personalities or outlooks, he attacked his partnership with Carberry directly if not entirely guilelessly. Aware that a good intention could never be completely spoiled by at least a slight tincture of pragmatism, Bernardin squelched the rumors by opening up the responsibilities of the office of the vice-presidency and expanding his own relationship with the vice-president himself. Such gentlemanliness, instinctive to him and much prized by the almost Victorian Carberry, revealed, as it had in very similar fashion with Cardinal Dearden, a largeness of spirit that would immediately be recognized and admired by the body of the bishops. It was also, at the practical political level, a very effective dose of preventive medicine. With Carberry's working closely with Bernardin at the latter's invitation, the heady gossip of their being pitted against each other, in howsoever dignified a fashion, quickly evaporated.

Secondly, Bernardin looked beyond his own and Carberry's personalities to the office and the function of the conference vice-president. It was, in his judgment, a position that deserved more respect and one that should receive more responsibility for the overall good of the conference itself. Its holder's function should not be redrawn every three years in terms of the personal relationship between him and the president. In short, Bernardin, in accord with his career-long commitment to process over personality and his recent experience in reshaping the conference organization, began to institutionalize the role of its vice-president. Within a few years, the bishop holding that position would be fully involved in the overall business of the American church. In his dealing with Cardinal Carberry at the very outset of his own leadership of the conference, Bernardin was actually continuing the work of effectively bureaucratizing it that he had begun as General Secretary. He was also manifesting a style that was both refreshingly public and thoughtfully shrewd. Bernardin, his colleagues realized, never did things on impulse or whim.

Bernardin also remembered the unresolved question of the conference president's relationship with Rome and the various curial departments. Although Cardinal Dearden had asked Bernardin himself to handle Roman business when Bernardin was General Secretary,

Cardinal Krol had visited the Vatican directly on official business during his tenure in office. Bernardin felt that whoever held the presidency should have regular relationships with what were called the dicasteries, or departments, of the Roman Church. He wanted not only to solidify the character of the conference which he had worked to develop but to institutionalize as many aspects of its functioning as possible. He therefore coupled his up-grading of the vice-presidency with a formalization of much of the work of the presidency. What began as somewhat ad-hoc decisions were formalized into policies. A few years later, Rome accepted the notion of regular visits by the president and vice-president, and other relevant officers, of the National Conference of Catholic Bishops from the United States.

This structural stabilization insured, in Bernardin's judgment, that sound policies and procedures would outlast the personalities who established them, thus building an arch under the conference's bridge of continuity. Making sure that the conference was on a solid footing was, however, only one aspect of Bernardin's presidential agenda of implementing the conciliar decrees in the American Church. The documents of Vatican II, although almost all of them necessarily compromises, aimed at the reform and revitalization of the church throughout the world. As the outcome of an ecumenical council, they had the authoritative character of the church itself telling its bishops what was expected of them.

Perhaps understandably, not all bishops were enthusiastic about them, and many of these hesitated to put the council's recommendations into effect. John Cardinal Krol, for example, for years resisted the council's liturgical provisions for Saturday evening masses that fulfilled the traditional obligation of Catholics to go to mass on Sunday. He may have decided that abandoning the requirement that Catholics must not eat meat on Fridays had caused enough adjustment problems for his flock and did not want to introduce yet another radical transformation in their experience of church life. Whatever the reason, such hesitations and inconsistencies led to a broken pattern of response in the American church, something Bernardin wanted, as gently and fully as possible, to correct during his years of leadership. The best way to guarantee that the American church would reflect the mind of the council would be through the appointment of new bishops whose whole sense of the Catholicism was permeated with the spirit of Pope John's quest for what he called *aggiornamento,* or updating, of its institutional presence in the world. It was here, for Bernardin was already a member of the Roman congregation that appointed bishops, that his collaboration with Archbishop Jadot would be crucial.

In an interview with this biographer six weeks after his election as president of the bishops, Bernardin had sat in his three room apartment in downtown Cincinnati in carpet slippers and sweater reflecting on his new role in general and on his ideas about new bishops. "The president of the conference," he had said as carefully as a man laying tiles, "is consulted on most appointments of bishops in the United States and I am a member of the congregation in Rome. I intend to seek out the best men possible through as much consultation as possible to be bishops in this country. I will look for high-caliber men with a broad outlook but, most important of all, with a pastoral sensitivity. There is only one way to select bishops and that is through a great deal of consultation. What people want is somebody who can be a real pastor to them. They don't want just an administrator or someone who is a glib talker. They want someone who understands where they are, what their concerns are, and what the church can do in order to help them live their lives."

As he continued his exploration of the pastoral needs of American Catholics, the biographer noted then that "control can be sensed in the quiet, subdued tones of the room, even in the dun-colored tones of a Wyeth-like painting of an abandoned farm on one wall. Control is part of the explanation for why he is where he is. He seems attuned to his own psyche the way an expert mechanic is to a motor's hum. He can hear the first dissonance, the initial squeak of imbalance, and knows what to do about it. The Mediterranean is in his warm smile but it is a careful hand that opens a can of root beer as the proper sipping drink in a long interview." The description holds up a decade and a half later, just as his conversation of that cold January evening still reflects the themes he continues to pursue. In that quiet, thorough way, marked by carefully shepherded consultation,

Bernardin began the collaboration with the apostolic delegate that brought dozens of moderate, pastoral, Vatican II bishops into the American church. These men would come to constitute the great central cohort of bishops who would not only put the conciliar decrees into effect but would also work together on major pastoral statements on peace and the economy that attracted world-wide attention.

Bernardin was very much himself that evening, the clear thinking administrator who, much like his mentor Cardinal Dearden, had a long and undramatic agenda aimed at strengthening the body of the bishops and American Catholicism in general. He also revealed his own characteristic way of dealing with others when, half way through the conversation, he was interrupted by the ringing of his private phone in the adjoining study. One could hear silence of the intense listener and then the soft accents of the understanding pastor as they drifted back across the hallway. "No, no, don't think it was in any way your fault. . . . No, I'm sure you did your best and that you couldn't expect things to be any different. . . . Anyway, I think it was all right."

It was not surprising that the national conference was near the top of his list of concerns as he reflected on the objectives he hoped to achieve within the opportunities of his new office. "The conference gives the bishops a forum for discussing internal church problems and expressing the Catholic opinion on questions of general interest to society. It's more important, as a result of Vatican II which stressed the principle of collegiality which means the bishops have to work together. The president is not a man who can give orders; he must develop a consensus on major issues."

Acknowledging that the conference attempts to influence national policy on important questions, Bernardin returned quickly to the business of building the base of collegial process the bishops needed to employ in their common pastoral tasks. "Certain tensions exist in the conference. When the bishops come together they really come as representatives of local churches. They should, then, reflect the hopes, aspirations, and difficulties of their people. That is why they need to do a lot of consultation before they come to a general meeting. It isn't just a private club of bishops who issue edicts. That is not the purpose of it at all.

"We have a body of religious teaching that should affect policy. It is best to do this through the education of people who constitute the church so that they, in turn, through the way they vote and influence their own communities, can do something about it. That is the whole idea of the Vatican Council's statement on the church and the modern world. We have to try to educate our people so that they are a leaven in society for the values we believe in."

Bernardin, again like Dearden, wanted the bishops to collaborate rather than strive for dramatic effects for the sake of their then just broadened openness to coverage by the press. "I think we have a lot of trouble with our meetings. I am completely committed to an open church. I think we should have open processes for discussing and reaching conclusions on all our issues. I will never back away from that. But having said that, we bishops have been programmed by the media to do something sensational or newsworthy every time we meet. The media, in a sense, won't let us be ourselves. Their pressure results in a lot of artificiality around our gatherings. This destroys the best instincts of the bishops."

The further development of the pastoral process of collaboration was, as he saw it then, the only way to deal with what he perceived as the growing disparity between what the church actually taught and the way many Catholics made their moral choices and led their lives. The fundamentally orthodox churchman part of his make-up asserted itself as he said that "the Catholic Church loses its identity if it doesn't seem to believe in anything or if it seems to believe in everything. I don't think you can travel very far on a cultural kind of Catholicism that is very vague in its meaning." A few moments later, he shifted to another aspect of his concerns. "There is a lack of confidence in the church as an institution. We are perceived like the other institutions. We are grouped with them and people don't listen to us. We have an enormous problem in reestablishing our trustworthiness as an institution and the church has to cooperate in helping to restore this confidence."

Bernardin had shifted in his chair as he summed up his reflections on the challenge to close what he perceived as something like a belief gap among Catholics. "I think our basic question comes to this: How is the church going to speak seriously to human experience? I think we have to meet people where they are, show them that we are interested in them and very much one with them in their struggles and their problems. The basic position I believe in and the one that I think represents the Catholic Church's commitment is this: We won't abandon people, no matter what. We are going to stand with people in their struggles. We are not going to judge them harshly or turn our backs on them. We want to help them to find themselves and to find happiness and we want to do this even with people who disagree with some of our teachings. We are committed to people and to their well-being."

It was obvious that the newly chosen president of the bishops had thought long and hard about the pastoral and practical possibilities of that organization's intervention in the personal and public lives of Americans. The conference, he telegraphed, was not yet at ease enough structurally, or in the glare of publicity, to meditate in an effectively collegial way on the moral dilemmas of the day. The Catholic people needed to be drawn into simultaneous reflection with their leaders on their own beliefs and practices and on the manner in which they wanted to influence the beliefs and practices of the nation at large. More patient building would have to take place to make this possible. But Bernardin did not lack a finely shaded understanding of what had to be done.

He also searched, that chill midnight, for a unifying approach to dealing with the bishops' approach to moral teaching. "We are going to press the pro-life issue," he said as he poured a goodnight brandy. "We are going to seek some kind of legislation, preferably a constitutional amendment, that will change our public stance on abortion. We are going to give that top priority. But there are many other pro-life issues which we must address. We want to emphasize the need to respect all life and to focus attention on all issues that are connected with such respect. We intend, in other words, to build up the context of our pro-life commitment."

Bernardin was, in fact, sketching the preliminary outline for the "consistent ethic of life" theme that he would give formal public voice to in a lecture at Fordham College almost nine years later. By that time he would have accomplished many of the other goals he had discussed on that long evening early in 1975. A phalanx of new bishops would be in place, including Thomas Kelly, a Dominican priest who had worked at the Apostolic Delegation and who would become General Secretary of the bishops and a close collaborator of Bernardin's; the national conference itself would be mature enough as a collegial body to issue historic pastoral letters on nuclear war and the economy. And Bernardin would be the Cardinal archbishop of Chicago by the time his "seamless garment" of interconnected pro-life issues begin to infiltrate the consciousness of serious Catholics and other believers across the land. He would, however, have passed through a grueling season of frustration with the media in connection with the bishops' pro-life objectives during the 1976 presidential campaign and an even more severe test by headline five years after that when he was suspected of having conspired in an ecclesiastical *coup d'etat* against Chicago's Cardinal Cody.

In that city 300 miles northeast of Cincinnati, Father Andrew Greeley was as enthusiastically applauding Bernardin's rise in the American church as he was systematically damning John Cardinal Cody's stewardship in Chicago. Greeley spoke openly of his admiration of and friendship with Bernardin, the kind of man, he told priest friends, who should succeed Cody in Chicago. But first, he would counsel, Cody must be ousted just as Nixon had been. Greeley would become increasingly displeased that the Chicago priests did not take more revolutionary action, such as the strike, or the "black flu," a job action he had endorsed, through which priests would refuse to say masses on some chosen Sunday to express their displeasure with their ordinary. The priest-author was also frustrated at not being chosen by his fellow priests as one of their elected representatives in any of the national or local clerical organizations. Many clergymen, he confided to friends, were jealous of him and took it out on him in various ways. He felt on the outside both with his archbishop and his confreres in the archdiocese in which he longed to have some positive influence.

Many other reform minded priests and religious men and women supported a more democratic church and viewed the new bishops, especially Bernardin, as more progressive than they actually were. Their lofty ideals which, for example, included a revamping of Catholic sexual teachings, were understood but not actively supported by the bishops, again including Bernardin, who perceived the bishops' main responsibility as that of supporting papal authority and traditional church teachings while introducing the modest reforms of Vatican II. It was time, Greeley concluded, to dramatize what he judged to be Cody's tyranny to the new apostolic delegate and the new president of the American bishops. His friendship with Bernardin—with "Joe" as Greeley and other long term associates called him—he felt, would be a great help in this crusade.

XII

Nineteen seventy-five witnessed Bernardin's deepening collaboration with Archbishop Jadot in placing younger, conciliar minded bishops into dioceses throughout the country. These appointments were not, however, of a generation of revolutionaries out to make the church into a constitutional monarchy as many more avid reformers hoped. They were progressive, intelligent men who would institutionalize the changes that had been legislated by Vatican II. It cannot be stressed too often, however, that, although they might have been personally sympathetic to even more radical transformations, their agendas were not at all the same as those of the great numbers of energetic Catholics whose imaginations had been profoundly and irrevocably stirred by the conciliar event of the previous decade. These Catholics, many priests and religious men and women among them, were anxious, among many other issues, to explore the possibilities of modifying the priestly obligation of celibacy and of ordaining women. They had responded to the council's definition of the church as a "people of God," a mystery of human relationships that could never be fully codified or properly governed through legal and administrative approaches alone.

Bernardin and the new generation of bishops might have understood the historical inevitability of such developments but they felt that they enjoyed no freedom to pursue or promote changes that challenged positions which the aging pope, Paul VI, had defended many times. This new cadre of progressive, pastorally oriented bishops, very much different in style then their predecessors, would never challenge the authority to which they had committed themselves by accepting episcopal ordination. In fact, these men had been selected according to an ancient process that quickly winnowed out almost any candidates who evinced the slightest equivocation about orthodoxy. If the fresh generation of well educated Catholics delighted in understanding their church as a people, Bernardin and his brother bishops, no matter their theological sympathies, intended to support it as an institution.

Still, freedom and revolution remained in the air of recession struck America. The quadrupling of oil prices had visited economic hardship on America and devastation on the Third World. America was already preparing for its 1976 Bicentennial celebration with hundreds of events that recalled the revolution against authoritarianism that had given birth to the United States. The American bishops planned a series of public hearings across the country to listen to Americans, Catholic and non-Catholic, on the great issues of the times. These would be climaxed in the later autumn of 1976 by the *Call to Action* conference at Detroit's Cobo Hall, the delegates to which would come largely from the ranks of Catholics, clerical and lay, who wanted the church to continue to change. Its messages were to be heard and responded to, however, by bishops, including Bernardin, who felt that there was little give in the official church to the generally liberal aspirations of the participants.

The title of the conference, *Call to Action,* ironically summed up the quandary in which the American Catholic Church found itself. Many of its most devoted people pulsated with a desire for ongoing transformation of church structures but it was governed by bishops whose vision of change was restricted to the already approved documents of Vatican II. Delegates, like interested Catholics across the land, might call for action but there was no way they could, of themselves, initiate it. The church as an institution stood like an almost inpenetrable and imperturbable presence. It shrugged off the enthusiasm of reformers as calmly as a monk deep in meditation ignored distractions. Even in their own meetings, the bishops were often frustrated that, after much debate and discussion, they offered only resolutions that motivated action uncertainly if at all.

Bernardin, the master of process, was becoming keenly aware of this problem and, in a 1976 interview with the *National Catholic Reporter,* implied reflectively that the torrent of the bishops' statements and resolutions seldom reached, much less nourished, the great plain of ordinary American Catholic life. "I think," he said, "that in many instances we've taken a much more progressive position than our Catholics, than the mainstream of the Catholic community. In fact, the teaching in these documents has not filtered down to the grassroots level...We've got the substance, but not the style, perhaps, to attract a larger audience...The fact of the matter is that there's a real problem in communicating. We're not communicating as effectively as we should be." The president of the bishops had come to understand that the conference, barely 10 years old and still finding its way as a collegial body, was not affecting the general culture very much and was not bringing about sufficient response or follow through from its own communicants.

The problem was complex. Bernardin appreciated that, if the bishops took too strong a leadership role, issuing directives, as it were, from on high, they would only be recreating the kind of paternalism that so strongly characterized Catholic life in a previous era. The chick of collegiality still bore fragments of eggshell on its wings and Bernardin realized that a heavy hand would kill it before it learned to fly. At the same time, the bishops had to encourage those Catholics with a real interest in the church, such as the reform-minded delegates to the *Call to Action* conference, but they could not and would not publicly support the pressures brought by these dedicated people for optional celibacy, women priests, and other remedies for the church's problems that the latter considered urgent.

On the one hand, the bishops, just learning to work together, could not sufficiently motivate action on matters of policy in which they were interested, such as federal aid for Catholic schools, and, on the other, they would not authorize it on the range of populist religious issues about which many Catholics clamored for change. Being president of the bishops, to which, according to his own logs, he devoted about a third of his time, was no easy task, for he fervently believed in strengthening the pope and the institutional church while he was also dedicated to the people who wanted that very church to reform its bureaucratic heart once and for all.

To defend traditional church positions while keeping in touch with their increasingly well-educated and less automatically docile or obedient flock was an enormous challenge for the bishops. Its degree of difficulty was multiplied because, little understood by administratively-oriented bishops, this was a demand made on the religious imagination rather than on the will. As a group they were much more comfortable being strong willed. Catholics, whether grouped on the left or the right of the ideological spectrum, were excited about their church. Their interests and enthusiasms could not be blunted nor would they be satisfied forever by reassurance and promises while the procedural gears of the ecclesiastical world ground relentlessly on. Even the renewal initiated in such an attractively spontaneous and human fashion by Pope John XXIII was, in the name of implementing it, being systematically bureaucratized. The spirit always suffered when translated into the fine print of regulations.

The predominant and highly vocal wings of American Catholicism that flared out from the central body of generally silent if thoughtful believers were composed largely of people who, in one way or other, were involved in the church as an institution. That is to say, they were priests, nuns, religious brothers, or laypersons long associated with Catholic education or other movements and activities whose existence was intimately related to, if not totally dependent on, the official, structured American church. Over 70 percent of the delegates to 1976's *Call to Action* conference came from the ranks of such institutionally involved individuals. In a sense, the church was talking to itself about itself in such gatherings. On the other hand, many of the more conservative Catholics, who favored preservation of traditional doctrine and practice, were also connected variously with the public institution of the church. Some of these, including Catholics United for the Faith, would make their presence felt later in Bernardin's career. In the mid-seventies, however, neither Bernardin nor the body of the bishops could please either of these groupings completely and the archbishop of Cincinnati found himself under mounting pressure and criticism from both of these constituencies. He failed their expectations, as they saw them, by being too cautious and aware of the bright Roman moon over his shoulder to encourage radical change, or he was too liberal, too caught up in democratic tolerance for a faith made bland by ill-considered change.

To respond to this problem Archbishop Bernardin emphasized the pastoral approach, both in Cincinnati and in his wide-ranging official and personal relationships with priests and other church personnel throughout the country. The bishops had expressed their trust in him by giving him their overwhelming vote of confidence. He could retain his credibility with other groups best by practicing with them what he preached consistently as head of the bishops. Catholicism could not go forward, as he saw it, through dramatic gestures or highly publicized activities that lacked follow-up. The slow, steady pace of developing the collegial process might not pay off for several years but it would, he was convinced, insure the vigor of Catholicism in the decades ahead.

Meanwhile, he would display his pastoral sensitivity in his dealings with all groups, listening carefully to their demands or complaints, encouraging them to explore solutions that were agreeable to all parties as, with his inimitable subtlety and endurance, he guided the conversations toward compromises that he had anticipated in advance. His personal concern, his capacity to understand and not indict human failings, his own commitment to a reinvigorated Catholicism: These, along with his gentleness and self-effacing manner, came across in the innumerable conferences and meetings in which he took part while serving as conference president. Those Catholics who were dissatisfied with what appeared to be either the excessively rapid, or haltingly slow, pace of renewal continued to respect him as a leader of great integrity and trustworthiness.

The meeting, convened late in October in the Detroit archdiocese of John Cardinal Dearden, the chairman of the project and of course, Bernardin's mentor, was not held without confusion or conflict. Still, it expressed the enthusiasm and commitment of Catholics throughout the country to the vision of the Catholic Church as "a people of God" rather than just an hierarchical structure. Some bishops who had agreed to attend, such as John Cardinal Cody of Chicago, reneged at the last moment and sent substitutes; others, such as Terence Cardinal Cooke of New York, found it convenient to leave before the group voted on its resolutions, some of which called for women's ordination, the use of former priests in church services, the affirmation of gay rights, a public and broadly participatory method of selecting bishops, granting parish councils true policymaking authority, and the establishment of a National Review Board of ecclesiastical initiatives "to promote the practice of mutual accountability on all levels."

Such resolutions disturbed Roman officials and made life uncomfortable for the American bishops who attended the conference. Archbishop John Roach of Minneapolis-St. Paul, generally considered a progressive, illustrated the bishops' dilemma when he told a group pressuring him to support women's ordination, "You're putting me in a box here." As theologian Richard McBrien accurately observed at the time, it was "unrealistic to expect the Catholic bishops to approve any resolution which has an ecclesiastical pricetag, i.e., one that would require a redistribution of power or a rearrangement of internal structural relationships."

Archbishop Bernardin was faced with a difficult, almost a no-win, situation. Although this seemed to pit him against John Cardinal Dearden who said the "process in which we have been engaged has been a marked success as a speaking and listening process," Bernardin chose, as he later said, "to craft a statement" that would allay the concern of many bishops as well as Roman fears, protecting the conference of American bishops from being damaged in the eyes of the Holy See, while tempering the enthusiastic reform-oriented resolutions by analyzing and putting them into perspective. "I had," he remembered many years afterward, "to try to bring the whole thing together by avoiding selling out the *Call to Action* while making its work satisfactory to the Holy See." Of his seeming conflict with Cardinal Dearden, he said, "at the level of what we had to say, we seemed set against each other, but at a deeper level this was not so."

In short, Bernardin felt that he was preserving as many values as possible by the observations he issued as president of the bishops on Oct. 26, 1976. "First, in retrospect," he wrote, "it seems that too much was attempted. Any one of the eight large topics considered would have provided more than work for the limited time available. All of them together overwhelmed the conference," leading to "haste...to formulate recommendations on complex matters without reflection, discussion, and consideration of different points of view." He also criticized "special interest groups" which "dominated the conference," resulting in "a process and a number of recommendations which were not representative of church in this country and which paid too little attention to other legitimate interests and concerns." He issued a response to questions a few days later by saying that he did not "repudiate the conference."

Feeling intense pressure himself and judging that the bold resolutions of the meeting, which passed with hardly any dissent, would do more damage than good at the time, Bernardin succeeded, not without incurring criticism for himself and generating enormous and, in some cases, lasting disappointment in the hearts of some delegates, in defusing the gathering so that both the bishops and Rome could live with it. This was a classic example of Bernardin's acting in what he considered "the best interests of the church." Even if he might have agreed with many of the resolutions, he felt, in the Latin phrase of canon law, that they were *haud opportune,* "by no means opportune." The two thousand year old church could not swallow these notions and there was no use trying to force feed it. Nonetheless, his intervention, while keyed to saving face all around, was unquestionably a letdown for many fervent and active Catholics throughout the country. Ironically, Bernardin was outdone in his critique of the conference by Father Andrew Greeley who heaped scorn on the delegates in his newspaper columns, viewing them as unrealistic visionaries whose ideas were naive and poorly thought out. The bishops, Greeley concluded, should never have gotten into the untenable situation in the first place.

Indeed, Bernardin was, at the request of Archbishop Jadot, keeping in touch with Father Greeley during that long difficult season. Jadot, alarmed by complaints over Greeley's agitation of others to send letters and other forms of complaint about Cody to his Washington legation as well as by the priest's use of his newspaper column to criticize Cardinal Cody while the Holy See was reviewing Cody's performance as an archbishop, solicited Bernardin's cooperation in an effort to restrain the character and frequency of Greeley's attacks. Bernardin was, however, advised against accepting such an assignment by at least one friend who warned that the effect was not only dangerous because of Greeley's prickly sensitivity but could never be successful. Bernardin, however, committed to his understanding of his function as a bishop, agreed to do what the church asked of him.

Bernardin had the limited objective of keeping up a relationship with Greeley, whom he considered a friend, among other reasons to encourage him in an amicable way to pursue the kind of positive research that the priest-sociologist wanted to do on American Catholicism. He even helped Greeley obtain funding from the Knights of Columbus for one of his projects. Greeley would later interpret their relationship at the time as highly offensive and manipulative, maintaining that Bernardin seemed to be taking him into his confidence on substantive matters of church politics and policy. It was, in fact, to be an ill-starred chapter in the melancholy history of the downfall of Cardinal Cody. In the middle of the seventies, however, it seemed a relatively manageable matter to Bernardin in comparison with other situations into which his role as president of the bishops plunged him.

Nineteen seventy-six was an election year and the Catholic vote, the notorious "ethnic" vote that Nixon had so prized, was seen as vital to the eventual success of either Jimmy Carter or Gerald Ford. At their meeting the previous November, the American bishops had committed themselves to a massive, grassroots campaign to overturn the *Roe v. Wade* decision of the Supreme Court. They intended to lobby for a constitutional amendment to bring that about and, in a whole array of proposals, intended to energize their anti-abortion crusade through the Pro-Life committee chaired by Cardinal Cooke of New York. Bernardin supported this thrust of the bishops' conference and continued to reflect seriously on the need to broaden the

Catholic pro-life position by including other life-related causes on its list of concerns.

The then General Secretary of the bishops, Father James Rausch, was deeply concerned that Catholics were being perceived as a single-issue group and felt that, during the election year, some effort should be made, in line with Bernardin's thinking, to widen the base of Catholic concerns. Rausch, according to the later recollections of Archbishop Thomas Kelly who was then in Washington, liked Carter and wanted to help him cope with the strong anti-abortion climate that the American bishops were rapidly generating. Rausch proposed that the executive committee of the bishops, which included Bernardin and Cardinal Carberry as well as Terence Cardinal Cooke of New York, would meet with the presidential candidates in the late summer.

Bernardin had no desire to meet with either candidate. The same message that would later shimmer like heat waves above the *Call to Action* meeting—*haud opportune,* by no means opportune—rose from the coils of his instincts when the proposal was made. He felt, as he remembered the incident more than a decade afterward, that the bishops would "run the risk of being co-opted by one or the other candidate." Father Rausch, whom Bernardin admired and trusted, kept up the pressure, however, suggesting that if some compromise could be worked out with Carter, that is, if the Georgia governor could move closer to the bishops' position about a constitutional amendment, the opposition he would receive from the most voluble of the anti-abortion people would be minimized. The meeting was arranged at the Mayflower Hotel in downtown Washington for August 31.

As president of the American bishops Bernardin issued a statement on August 16 in an effort to put their position into perspective. "The church," he said, using a phrase that he would invoke as if it were the antiphon to the bishops' psalm of protest many times in the weeks that followed, "does not involve itself in partisan politics; it does not endorse or oppose particular parties or candidates." The church had, however, a teaching role to fulfill in regard to political questions and would, moreover, "closely watch all the issues and address them as the occasion demands." The church was concerned about abortion because that issue could cause insensitivity "to the entire spectrum of human rights." Referring to an insinuation in the Democratic platform, he concluded that it was a "disservice" to accuse those who oppose abortion of "being concerned only about one issue."

For his part, Carter gave an interview to Jim Castelli of the National Catholic News Service in which he claimed that the Democratic party's campaign plank on abortion was "inappropriate and was not in accordance with my own desires." He explained his own views by noting that "I do not favor a constitutional amendment which would prohibit all abortions or which would give states local option. But I think abortion is wrong and that the government ought not ever do anything to encourage abortion." He had, he concluded, supported Georgia's earlier "very strict abortion law." Bernardin then commented on Carter's interview, criticizing the latter's position on abortion as containing an "inconsistency that is deeply disturbing." He went on to observe that the bishops regretted "that he continues to be unsupportive of a constitutional amendment." A few days later, after the conclusion of the Republican convention, Bernardin offered a statement praising the party platform's "recognition of the value of life and its protest of the recent Supreme Court decision." It was perhaps understandable that the press pursued the story of the bishops' relationship to the candidates as it did.

In any case, each side had spoken. There seemed no need, in Bernardin's estimation, for a face to face meeting but the pressure from Rausch and others was unrelenting. Something had to be done, such sources felt, to make it clear that the bishops would not seem to fulfill the description of them given by the late Richard Cardinal Cushing to Joseph P. Kennedy during the 1960 campaign. The elder Kennedy had expressed concern that so many bishops seemed to be in favor of Richard M. Nixon. "Don't worry," the Boston archbishop had said in his flat, rasping voice, "the bishops are wrong on most political matters. It's a good sign." So Bernardin and his fellow bishops agreed to go ahead with the meeting with Jimmy Carter. Their mutual sentiments resembled those attributed to an ancient king on dismissing his mistress, "He, unwillingly, sent her, unwilling, away." No spirit of joy engulfed the bishops as they drove to the Mayflower on that final morning of August.

The born again, Sunday school teaching Carter and his aides, perhaps with trace memories of Southern suspicions of Catholic prelates burning like klansmens' crosses on some distant hillock of their common imagination, were as affably wary of the bishops as the bishops were of them. Carter was pragmatic about the Catholic vote, however, and had spent time earlier in the day courting Catholic labor leader George Meany, meeting with Catholic Senator Edward Kennedy, and visiting with a group of Catholic Italian-American leaders. As Rick Casey observed in an analysis in the *National Catholic Reporter,* "Carter hit the three Catholic touchstones of abortion, organized labor, and ethnic concerns." The atmosphere of the Mayflower Hotel meeting was slightly awkward and anxious, like that of the engaged couple's family's meeting for the first time, as handshakes were exchanged and seats were taken. Carter gave his flashbulb smile, his eyebrows flared as if powered by a tick. Bernardin felt uneasy as he took his place opposite him and looked at the Georgia Governor through his outsize glasses. Everybody wanted to be nice. But Carter, contrary to what they had been led to believe by Rausch, declared unequivocally that, although he was personally opposed to abortion, he had not yet read a draft of a pro-life constitutional amendment whose wording would allow him to support it.

Bernardin had characteristically prepared an agenda that included other Catholic concerns on which the bishops were sure that they shared the same sentiments with the Democratic candidate. This included questions about Catholic schools, which Carter lauded, and other issues of social policy about hunger, poverty, illegal aliens, and human rights in foreign policy. Such joint concerns, which were echoed in the Democratic platform that had also rejected an anti-abortion constitutional amendment, had once made Catholic and Democrat almost synonymous terms, especially in the Northern big cities, for many decades.

"You ask hard questions," Carter responded genially as the bishops explored his attitude toward the plank of the Democratic platform that opposed the very constitutional amendment they themselves sought. It did not go as well as either side would have liked for, despite their many overlapping interests, the split on abortion, like that between prospective in-laws about which religion the children would profess, kept opening like a unhealed cut. Perhaps the uncomfortable standoff that resulted from the encounter that had been aimed at reconciliation was a function of the obsessive, detail and control conscious personalities of the two Southern gentleman, Carter and Bernardin, each trying to bow to the other while caught in some kind of paralyzing wrestlers' embrace. Each wanted the meeting to succeed, each was well prepared, each was cautious lest something go wrong or get out of hand. As a result, however, the meeting, as the national and the Catholic press were quick to judge, bordered on the disastrous. For it was the press rather than the participants that would not play within the chalklines where both the presidential candiate and the president of the bishops wanted the discussion to remain.

"I will not ask for your prayers that I win," Carter said as the meeting ended, "But I will ask your prayers that I do the right thing." The participants nodded, the slight awkwardness that had disappeared during the hour long session bobbed to the surface as ominously as a drowned body that had slipped its chains. The bishops had not gotten what they had wanted but neither had Carter. It had, in fact, been a dangerous game for both groups since the media, waiting outside like a mob for a jury verdict, were not interested in the expanded agenda of concerns. They wanted to know where the candidate and the churchmen stood on the question of abortion. The bishops would not, they decided, give Carter what he could have used most, a picture of him standing, howsoever uncertainly, in their midst for the front pages of the next day's newspapers. Bernardin and his confreres stepped out of the funeral parlor quiet of the meeting room into the accident scene excitement of journalists at work. How, they shouted in a dozen different ways, did the bishops feel about what the Democratic candidate had to say on abortion?

The prelates, Bernardin said softly, striving to pry open the closing jaws of the media dragon, mentioned the matters on which they shared Carter's views. But, yes, concerning his stance on abortion, they were "disappointed." This word fell like a slab of bloody meat onto the press monster's tongue and, howling, it hungered for more. Bernardin, who had relied as always on careful preparation to master the challenge of any day, found that he could not impose control on the questioners who surrounded him and his brother bishops. He struggled several times to shift the subject. The "bishops' position as church leaders," he said, "is to address ourselves to the issues. We do not become involved in partisan politics." Still, the reporters sensed that their story was official Catholic disapproval of Carter and that this might be a boost for incumbent Gerald Ford.

The journalistic judgment held, despite Bernardin's strenuous and uncomfortable efforts to regain control of the press conference, and that evening on the television news, and the next morning in newspaper headlines, the storyline centered on the fact that the bishops were "disappointed" with Carter's position. The *New York Times* printed a picture of Carter and Senator Kennedy with a story about the meeting that misfired between the bishops and the Democratic candidate. The Chicago paper headlined the "failure" of the effort at reconciliation between the Catholic bishops and the Baptist governor. The smell of conflict, old and new, curled out of the newsprint and by that nightfall, a storm of angry reaction to the bishops came from Catholic groups and individuals across the land. The prelates seemed to be favoring Ford while neglecting their many disagreements with Republican policy and ignoring the many values they shared with the Democrats.

The hue and cry were echoed in Catholic papers and periodicals. The church was portraying itself, surely against every fiber of Bernardin's theological convictions, as a single-issue entity, massing its influence about abortion while, in effect, letting go of their concern for what many considered equally compelling social problems. For once in his career, the careful preparation to guide the discussion of the issues, failed Bernardin. The press, he learned would always focus on what constituted news, not on a person's subtle explanations, no matter with what good will they were offered. Some time later, when Carter and Bernardin met again, the Georgian spoke ruefully of that meeting, saying, "The press was really out to get me that day." Bernardin nodded noncommittally. He had begun, at the end of that punishing bicentennial summer, to speak to aides of the significance of "the press's perception of you" in dealing with its members. He would never forget what he learned at that time.

The bishops were flooded with critical mail before they travelled to the White House for a meeting with President Ford on September 10. Even the highly esteemed Jesuit Father Timothy Healy, president of Georgetown University, said at a mass at the opening of the school year that "for the church the appearance of identification with any one party, any one candidate, or, above all with any one political strategy is likely to be as destructive as it is useless. Millions of Catholics will simply not accept such identification. . . ." Many other editorial writers and commentators had not been as calm or kind in their own observations. Nonetheless, having reviewed staff reports about the Ford administration's poor record on abortion, Bernardin and five other bishops joined Ford for an hour long meeting. What they did not fully appreciate was that Ford's campaign manager, James Baker, who would later mastermind campaigns for Ronald Reagan and George Bush and become secretary of state, was shrewdly overseeing the then president's handling of what was considered an important visit.

Bernardin brought up the bishops' concern about the federal financing of abortions in the Ford administration. The genial president, well prepared to handle such questions, promised to "make a study of the matter." Bernardin again attempted to broaden the range of the bishops' concerns, mentioning jobs, hunger, and human rights abuses in foreign countries. However, as with Carter ten days before, the focus kept shifting to the abortion issue. Ford had, only a few months before, reversed a Nixon administration decision restricting abortion on military bases. The president had done this even after consulting with several Catholic bishops. Yes, Ford said, following his political instincts, they would study that. The meeting concluded cordially and the bishops gathered briefly in the cabinet room to agree on a statement.

The White House press conference was even more of a hurly-burly than that after the Carter meeting. If Bernardin had used the word "disappointed" to express the episcopal reaction to Carter's stand on abortion, he now chose the word "encouraged" to describe their sentiments about Ford's position. Once again, a single word captured the imagination of the media and of the coverage that was given to the meeting in the newspapers and television. Although Bernardin reiterated that the bishops were not "in total agreement" with Ford and repeated their intention to avoid political endorsements, he carefully avoided any negative words in characterizing the bishops' appraisal of the president. The news conference proved to be more unnerving than the one that had followed the meeting with Carter. Bernardin would, in subsequent days, issue statements trying to free the bishops from the appearance of favoring Ford but the media, having seen to the news core of the story, was not easily persuaded to alter its interpretations.

A greater flood of mail descended on Bernardin and his brother bishops protesting what appeared to be, if not evidence of partisanship, at least a lack of clarity in presenting their views. Two weeks later, Bernardin returned to Washington to preside over a meeting of the fifty member executive board of the National Conference of Catholic Bishops. On the morning that the meeting was to start, the *Washington Post* published an editorial harshly critical of Bernardin's handling of the bishops' relationships with the presidential candidates. Insiders later suggested that the editorial had been promoted by some members of the bishops' staff, that, at a tense moment, some had allowed their frustration to overcome their commitment to support the conference president with silence if not full blown loyalty. It was well known that the staff house had been the scene of many serious disagreements about the bishops' dealings with the candidates. Even the internationally respected expert on social questions and labor, Monsignor George Higgins, had expressed his sharp disagreements directly to Bishop Rausch who had been the architect of the ill-fated episcopal interventions. But Higgins was absolutely loyal and would never be a party to anything that would embarrass the conference or its president.

Whatever the source, the attack stung Bernardin badly. He felt that, in a situation in which he could not control the interpretations given to his leadership by the press, he had acted with complete integrity. He was particularly offended by the possibility that some staff members had failed in their loyalty to him and the conference. If these staff members forgot the central notion of keeping their own opinions to themselves when the good of the church was concerned, the executive board of the bishops did not. They issued a unanimous declaration of support for Bernardin and his committee.

Nonetheless, as the autumn took hold and other issues began to predominate in the coverage of the campaign, the bishops were never able to clarify their intentions to their own or anybody else's satisfaction. Afterward, Bernardin, who described the period as "one of the most difficult of my life," would think long and hard about future episcopal interventions in matters of public policy. What he had previously identified as a major difficulty with communication had resulted in a serious compromise of the bishop's ability to speak out. There had to be a better way for the bishops to address the moral concerns of the nation and to express Catholic convictions on matters of social policy. And, he was now convinced, there had to be a more effective way of linking the question of abortion with the web of other issues that were associated with the sanctity of life. It might take time, he reflected, but he would eventually do something about these interconnected matters.

XIII

T he tumultuous fall of 1976, which gave way to one of the coldest winters on record, was lighted by the flare-like showers of other events hinting at history's change and confusion. Both Martin Heidegger and Rudolf Bultman, scholars who had so affected religious thinking during the century, died. So, too, did the Chinese revolutionary leader Mao Tse-tung, following his opponent, free China leader Chiang Kai-shek, by a year. The first supersonic Concordes thundered off runways in London and Paris on their inaugural flights to Washington, D.C., and the Air Force Academy admitted 155 women into the class of 1980. The Episcopal Church, in its 65th General Convention, voted to ordain women to the priesthood. On November 2, owing nothing to the Catholic bishops, Jimmy Carter defeated Gerald Ford in a close election, taking 297 electoral votes to his opponent's 241. On the last day of autumn, in as clear a symbol as one could get of the passing of Irish Catholic political power and the end of the church's immigrant period, Mayor Richard J. Daley of Chicago died of a heart attack at the age of 74.

Bernardin had concerns enough as he began his final year as president of the bishops. The Holy See had criticized what became known as the "American Norms" for the dissolution of marriages by annulment, or declaration by the church that no true marital union ever existed. American canon lawyers had indeed been pioneers in applying the insights of social science and medicine into the church court procedures that reviewed petitions from those couples who wished to end their marriages. Psychological conditions were taken into account in a more subtle and nuanced way than they had been previously and the number of couples who availed themselves of this new opportunity increased dramatically. As one experienced psychologist noted of the couples who made application in Chicago, few were recklessly or impulsively seeking this ecclesiastical equivalent of divorce. Many had lived in dead marriages for years with no hope that they could ever get out of them. These included, for example, men and women who had met on weekends during the second World War with every possibility of doom hanging over them. They had wed as strangers and lived that way, unhappily but dutifully, for decades. Offering them some relief was hardly an attack on the indissolubility of authentic marriage. Bernardin had played an important role, while he was General Secretary, in working with Bishop Earnest Primeau of the canonical affairs committee in getting these procedures approved by Rome for a renewable term of years.

Some diocesan tribunals, as the courts were called, seemed to move far more swiftly on a greater volume of cases than other tribunals. Europeans who learned about the broader and more rapid granting of annulments in America, sought to have their applications processed there. As with any progressive development, some abuses occurred. These horror stories, as Bernardin later described them, were transmitted to Roman authorities as examples of what was happening on a daily basis in American diocesan offices. Vatican officials, quick to respond to the critical mail being sent in an organized way by the farthest edge of the Catholic Right, became alarmed and the stories, even though they were isolated and excessively dramatic exceptions to the still substantially bureaucratic rule, tended, as Bernardin said afterward, ''to undermine the credibility of the whole process.''

Bernardin, as president of the bishops, had to explain and support these new experimental norms in Rome. He was convinced that, on a pastoral level, they provided much needed relief for many couples who had, in effect, made poor or hurried marriages. It was his obligation to explain the highly sensitive and combustible situation in a lengthy personal interview with Pope Paul VI, the ill and anxiety ridden Holy Father who had already been battered severely by groups on every side for his attempts to carry out the reforms of Vatican II. It was hardly an easy meeting. The pope was deeply concerned about maintaining the sacramental integrity of matrimony and his pale gray eyes were filled first with sadness and then with the irritation as deep as the risks he felt he had taken in allowing this experiment to proceed in the first place.

Bernardin, well prepared as usual, was surprised at the intensity of the pope's feelings, the dismay of a man who felt that, howsoever unintentionally, he might have in some way undermined the indissolubility of matrimony. The Cincinnati archbishop, however, did his best to describe the situation accurately and eventually to allay the pope's fears. Most of the "American Norms" were eventually integrated into the new code that appeared some 10 years later.

In this situation, as in other problems such as those centering on the well publicized use in some dioceses of general absolution instead of individual confession in certain circumstances, Bernardin was called upon to work out a solution that would preserve the integrity of the church teaching while doing as little damage as possible to authentic pastoral intentions. Such matters were always difficult, especially in cases where the pastoral value of such practices seemed to exceed any harm that might come by some minor violation of canons of the church. Bernardin, the consummate churchman, stood on firm ground in managing such ecclesiastical problems. He would never, as he had vowed long before, go against what the church asked of him nor would he, insofar as it was possible, sacrifice a pastorally beneficial project. This stance, pledging loyalty to Rome and steadfastness to well motivated people, seldom pleased everybody but his consistency spoke for itself and marked him as reliable in the eyes of both the Vatican and his fellow American bishops.

Ironically, another side of Chicago's John Cardinal Cody could be observed in relationship to the "American Norms." If his arbitrary pettiness in many other matters seemed that of a poorhouse warden out of Dickens, Cody's wholehearted and generous support of the archdiocesan program to make annulments, once the prizes mostly of the world's wealthy, more reasonable and less painful goals for ordinary Catholics, revealed the pastor who had closed the confessional slide on a thousand melancholy stories. So, too, did his support for inner city schools, even though he was still able, while showing a visiting European cardinal around Chicago, to instruct his priest driver, "Show his eminence a ghetto." Comments like that, including his acknowledging the participation of the Chicago Symphony Orchestra once by saying "I want to thank the band," marked Cody as singulary encapsulated in the universe of his first childhood wonder, the pageant filled, gossip fueled, clerically dominated institutional church.

Some felt that his interest in the marriage court work, as well as his strong support for separated and divorced Catholics, stemmed from his concern for the divorced woman, Helen Wilson, a "shirt tail relative" in the terminology of the Irish Catholic culture, a woman raised with him as his sister in the same house, a woman he referred to as his cousin. There was little that was secret about their relationship or the cardinal's closeness to her family from the days when his clerical star was just lifting above the horizon back in St. Louis. Her children called him "Gi," short for "Giddyap" from their days of riding on his shoulders. When, in August 1965, Father Andrew Greeley first heard of Cody's appointment to Chicago, he telephoned priest friends around the country, observing that his new archbishop's relationship with a woman was "the best thing I've heard about him."

By the mid-seventies, Greeley had revised this judgment and had raised the heat of his newspaper column attacks on Cody to a fine white glow. Cody, riding home from the Chicago Saint Patrick's day parade in 1975, mused in a bored voice to a priest companion, "I wonder, Father, what Father Greeley wants with all this criticism." When the priest riding with him remained silent, Cody looked out the window of the car, removed and replaced his bishop's ring, said dryly, "I intend to ignore him," and changed the subject to the cost of the condominium towers that were rising near his North Side residence.

Cody had indeed become a subject of almost wild speculation inside organizational Catholicism by the time of the 1976 presidential campaign. He had become famous for his isolation in his rambling, ill-tended brick mansion, his peculiar work habits, through which he reinforced a double image of himself—one as the sole first and final authority on all matters, the other as the obsessive executive with no talent for discriminating between what was and was not important in the daily sacks of mail. Their fresh yields, like the catch of the day squirming out of a trawler's hold, fed his need for undifferentiated paper work. Cody had, in fact, changed the mailing address of the archdiocese shortly after his installation in Chicago, elatedly telling an aide that the use of a post office box enabled him "to get mail every day."

Father Greeley, who at the time was not only conducting a major research study on American Catholicism but was also writing books of advice on sexual matters that included the memorable suggestion for wives to welcome their husbands home in the evening naked, holding a pitcher of martinis, contrasted Cody regularly with his predecessor, Albert Cardinal Meyer. Greeley celebrated Meyer as a theologically informed progressive whose career had been cut tragically short by a brain tumor. He was the "good father" as distinguished from the "bad father," the cunning but nonintellectual John Patrick Cody. The incisive Greeley proved something of a puzzle to those who knew him well. At one moment, his eyes twinkling, he could be charming, a little boy of a man almost touching in his earnest quest for friendship through practicing generous hospitality. But his brow might suddenly crack into lines, his eyes turn stony hard and he could seem a remote and unhappy person, uncertain of what he wanted or needed to achieve contentment. Part of this stemmed from the dilemma he shared with other highly gifted clerics. The official church, unsure of what to do with creative persons who did not fit well into bureaucracies, seemed ultimately indifferent to the very talents they wished to express in its service. Greeley, permitted to function without a regular assignment for almost a decade, was left, like many other skilled colleagues, to make his own career in the margins, as he phrased it, of institutional Catholicism.

It was perhaps understandable, therefore, that the restless Father Greeley, feeling unappreciated in the church, wanted to be noticed in the world beyond it. He confided to friends that, although his books on sexual intimacy had not made the best seller list, as he had hoped, his planned book on the papal election that would follow the death of the ailing Paul VI would have a good chance of attracting national attention. Having worked out a publishing agreement with James Andrews of the Kansas City publisher, Andrews and McMeel, Greeley had already begun his research by the time that the 1976 presidential campaign got under way. Following his usual work habits, he dictated his impressions of visits with various European prelates into a cassette recorder, shipping them back to the United States for later transcription. One of those whose judgments he sought out in his interviews was Archbishop Bernardin.

The priest writer perceived these regular contacts, by phone and in person, with Bernardin as invaluable sources of inside information about the politics of international Catholicism in what was considered the twilight of the papacy of Paul VI. What Bernardin and Jadot, who also met and corresponded with Greeley on a few occasions, hoped would be an amicable liaison that would lessen Greeley's feelings of being an outcast from official Catholicism and thereby soften the stridency of his criticism, was interpreted quite differently by the priest himself. Apparently obsessed with pulling Cody down, as he had been with Nixon a few years previously, Greeley read Bernardin's association with him not as that of an interested mentor with a bright but somewhat unpredictable child but as a sympathetic, even encouraging, friend supplying him with material to be used in his public campaign against Cardinal Cody. While both Bernardin and Jadot knew that Cody had created a problem in Chicago that had to be addressed, over the months, Greeley seemed to be reading meanings into communications from them that neither intended.

By the last year of his term as president of the bishops, the ever churning clerical rumor mill had flooded the corridors of the American Catholic church with stories of Bernardin's imminent transferral to Chicago to replace the increasingly remote and embattled Cody. The *Chicago Sun-Times,* in fact, ran a long story by religion editor Roy Larson that reported and gave a certain specious dignity to the spate of stories about the imminent reduction of Cody's authority or his outright removal and possible replacement, one way or the other, by Bernardin. Many commentators speculated on the possibility that Bernardin would soon be appointed as coadjutor archbishop of Chicago, effectively taking away Cody's power and leaving the latter as a crimson clad ceremonial figure. This was, of course, Greeley's fondest dream come true, for he still spoke of the day when, after Cody's departure, he might dwell in his successor's household and advise him on archdiocesan policy.

Greeley presumed, perhaps not without some justification, that he was on the inside of such arrangements, especially in view of the hospitality he seemed to enjoy from Bernardin and the apostolic delegate. Jadot, perhaps not realizing that he and the archbishop of Cincinnati were contributing to rather than restraining the priest's public agitation for changes in Chicago, judged, in view of Greeley's continuing public campaign against Cody, that they should proceed with their relationship with him, ever hopeful of tempering him so that the charges against Cody could be examined in an unhurried and confidential manner. Indeed, Bernardin felt that a real friendship had developed between him and the Chicago priest. Although numerous complaints had been sent to both Jadot and Bernardin by Chicagoans, many of them inspired by Greeley, no official investigation was under way, that is, no special commission or individual had been appointed to evaluate the situation.

During this period, Jadot wrote a letter in French to Greeley in a direct effort to reduce the drumbeat of harsh accusations that Greeley was making, among other places, in a column he then wrote for the *Chicago Tribune*. Jadot's use of the word "report" in this letter, however, understandably made Greeley surmise that a case was truly being made against the archbishop of Chicago, that Rome was finally moving, that the "bad father" would soon topple off his pedestal like the spurned dictator's statue in a Third World capitol square. The missive increased his feelings of being privy to inside information, of having, therefore, a license to hunt Cody in his own way.

Perhaps the priest could be excused for thinking that he was riding point on the investigative forces of Rome itself, that he could not lose by pursuing his single-minded crusade. And, in what he espied, as mistakenly as the early Christians in their expectation of the second coming in their own lifetimes, as an approaching moment of glorious triumph, Greeley saw himself as prepared to accept the rewards that he would surely get from Jadot and Bernardin for his contributions to the success of the ecclesiastical insurrection. As publisher Dan Herr, however, ironically observed at the time, "The only way the bishops can shut Andrew up is by making him a bishop, by making him part of their club. Then he couldn't criticize them."

But Greeley, misreading the signals, not only continued his own denunciations of the cardinal, who remained sphinx silent in his chill and echoing residence, but attempted to get critical news items into newspapers such as the *New York Times,* or into popular columns such as that written by Irv Kupcinet for the *Chicago Sun-Times.* When those outlets were reluctant to use his tips about potential scandals in, or the cracking foundations of, the Cody administration, Greeley contacted other writers, suggesting that they should author exposes of Cody for national or local magazines. To one friend, whom he urged to put together such a piece for *Chicago Magazine,* he promised "everything I've got" for the task.

Bernardin, still carrying out troubleshooting assignments for the Holy See in addition to his continuing efforts to stabilize the National Conference of Catholic Bishops before he concluded his term, was well aware of the rumors that linked his future to Cody's past. As he did regularly with other priest friends, Bernardin maintained his contacts with Greeley through the barren heart of the seventies, not realizing that Greeley's almost daily escalating need to play a role in Cody's downfall was causing him to distort the archbishop's intentions and regard for him. From Greeley's own dictated memoranda of his European research on the book he planned to write about the next papal election, Bernardin began to loom increasingly large in Greeley's imagination as the fruitful and project saving source of the inside information he would need to write a bestseller.

The priest also came to perceive his junkets to Europe as opportunities not only to write about the internal workings of Catholicism, to which his own romantic attachment was as deep as Cody's, but also to influence the potential outcome of the next conclave. He initiated a series of meetings with theologians, including Swiss scholar Hans Kung, to discuss their sources and the possibility of their influencing those cardinals who would be voting for the next pontiff. He may have brought more to these conversations than some of the others, who later rejected the idea that they were joining some kind of freemasonry of scholar-priests out to pick a progressive pope. But they, too, may have misread Greeley's intentions about the project or underestimated his claims to have inside sources of considerable knowledge.

Back in Kansas City, James Andrews, the skillful publishing executive who had always been a vigorous and committed Catholic, studied Greeley's reports and thought that, yes, perhaps some effort should be made to influence the choice of the next pope. The seeds of what was later regarded as a quixotic and slightly comic crusade to affect the work of the next conclave, may have been inadvertently planted by Jadot's efforts to seduce the priest writer into moderation. Within a few years, these developments, like a screwball comedy's turning inexorably into tragedy, would almost destroy Bernardin's own career in the church.

XIV ═══════════════════

B ernardin had, in fact, come to examine his own crowded life against what seemed to be the constantly shifting stage flats of the seventies. For the road companies of the past and the future continued to compete for attention on the battered stage of the decade. Wernher von Braun, the German expert captured at the end of World War II who had played such an enormous role in the American rocket program, died at the age of 65 in the same season that two spacecraft were launched to explore the outer solar system. President Jimmy Carter signed the legislation that would eventually return the Panama Canal to the country through which it had been dug triumphantly under the guidance of the ebullient Teddy Roosevelt. The Nobel Peace Prize was awarded to Amnesty International, a London based human rights organization, and, in a delayed announcement, bestowed for the previous year on two Irish women from Belfast for their efforts to moderate the bitter strife, its roots beyond the memory of the living, between Protestants and Catholics.

And change flickered like flames in the bell tower of the American Episcopal Church when Jacqueline Means became the first woman ordained by that denomination. Was this a sign, one wondered, of that church's being ahead of the times? Or was it, as some supposed, in a moody, prophetic warning to Catholic hierarchs, the evidence of the collapsing discipline of Episcopalian institutional structures? The Roman Church, still involved in the spirited agony of adjusting to conciliar changes, seemed as weary as Pope Paul VI did when he emerged weeping from a visit to the Roman catacombs. And Joseph Louis Bernardin, immersed in national and international activity, stopped suddenly to examine the state of his own soul.

The occasion was a dinner meeting with three young priests in Cincinnati, two of whom he had ordained himself. The priests challenged their archbishop about his own spiritual priorities in a life that was crammed with administrative tasks. "I realized," he said years afterward, "I was counseling people to do things that I myself wasn't doing." As Bernardin listened to the seemingly pure-hearted and enthusiastic young priests, he recognized that "they were more advanced spiritually than I was. They told me I should do something about it." As he subsequently described the occasion, "it was a turning point in my life."

One cannot presume that Bernardin, the master obsessive, the dutiful churchman in every way, experienced a conversion of heart from some ill-spent existence, as, for example, Augustine had. No, here we witness the prelate, just into middle age, who already demanded much of himself, nudging the bar of expectation a little higher. "I decided," he explained almost a decade afterward, "to give God the first hour of my day, no matter what." He resolved to spend first light in prayer and meditation, even though he might feel, in classic obsessive style, the day's work signalling for his attention like a radio beacon from his chancery office desk.

It was, therefore, a victory of the man who preached prayer over the man who loved work, of the priest over the bureaucrat, a commitment to his own spiritual development. This wrestling with the angel of his own inner life was not a small engagement, not another abstract resolution made, but a personal journey into the uncharted desert of reflection from which he returned with both his own humility and his appreciation of the problems of others deepened. Having grappled with his own shortcomings he felt that he could "share my journey with others. It gives them a great boost to know I've gone through the same things." If this was not the *metanoia,* or change of heart, of a great sinner, it was the development of a keener vigilance over self by an archbishop who was already an unsentimental judge of

photo by John H. White

Joseph Bernardin, the Cardinal's father, known as Bepi, was a stonecutter who served in the Austro-Hungarian army as a sergeant before his marriage to Maria Simion, shown below in a picture taken shortly before her marriage.

Joseph and Maria Bernardin, together on their wedding day. They were married in the hamlet of Tonadico in 1927.

Growing up in Columbia, South Carolina, in the depression years of the 1930s, young Joseph had time for play while attending public schools his first four grades.

With his mother working to support the family, Joseph was often given the responsibility of caring for his younger sister, Elaine, here with him and his mother.

Twenty-five year old Joseph with his mother in 1953, the year after he was ordained as a priest. His first assignment: curate at St. Joseph's Church in Charleston and as a teacher at Bishop England High School.

A smiling Maria Bernardin stands with her son at her left in 1966, shortly after he was appointed auxiliary bishop in Atlanta to serve with Archbishop Paul Hallinan (left).

Now a cardinal, but always a son, Bernardin shares a tender moment with his mother at a Christmas Eve Mass at the Little Sisters in Chicago in 1988.

Participating in the worship services during the inaugural activities for President Richard Nixon in January 1973, was Most Rev. Joseph L. Bernardin, then archbishop of Cincinnati, and Rev. Billy Graham (center) along with Rabbi Edgar Magnin.

The Cardinal, at left, chats with young adults at a lawn party, "Theology on Tap," in Chicago, 1983.

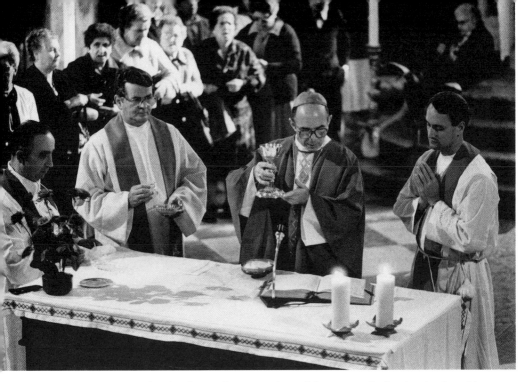

In September 1983, Cardinal Bernardin returned to celebrate mass in the church where his parents were baptized and married in Tonadico, Italy.

Cardinal Bernardin participates in a traditional Holy Week ceremony at the Cathedral of the Holy Name, Chicago. *(photo by John H. White)*

On Feb. 2, 1983, in Rome, Bernardin received the red hat of a cardinal from the hands of Pope John Paul II.

Cardinal Bernardin responds to an ovation at Chicago's St. Hyacinth's Polish Parish on New Year's Day, 1983.

Cardinal Bernardin meets the most important part of the church—the people—during one of his frequent parish visitations in Chicago.

During his 1983 visit to Tonadico, Bernardin visited with townspeople and relatives (above), and led a procession through the streets (below).

Cardinal Bernardin receives an honorary doctorate from Notre Dame University in 1983, with Father Hesburgh at his side.

A solemn moment at the tomb of Archbishop Oscar Romero in 1984, with (from left) Cardinal James Hickey, and, partly obscured, Bishop René Gracida. At Bernardin's left is Cardinal John O'Connor from New York.

During his 1985 visit to Poland, Cardinal Bernardin is greeted by a young churchgoer.

In August 1985, Cardinal Bernardin prayed at the site of the concentration camp in Auschwitz, Poland.

On a visit to Mexico in July 1988, Cardinal Bernardin (center) blesses a parishioner after celebrating mass in Chilapa, displays a tapestry (below) given him by the people of Chilapa, and, covered with confetti, walks with the people during a celebration (above). *(photos by Julio Alejandro Escalona)*

Cardinal Bernardin conducts a mass for the Adoptive Parents Guild in January 1989 and (below) greets one of the participants.

In the kitchen at home, a stately old residence located near Lake Michigan on Chicago's near north side, Bernardin samples food prepared by Sister Lucia and (below) finds time to reflect while answering letters in his study.

The energy of Cardinal Bernardin on a solitary stroll through the mountains near Primiero, Italy, is captured by Photographer John H. White, in 1984.

his own motives and attitudes. This experience inclined him even more to the purification of the vibrations and resonances within himself. It led to a more careful examination of his own goals and intentions, and brought to him a greater sense of self-possession as well. He would need to draw deeply from this freshened well of character in the years ahead.

Bernardin was to visit Poland during 1976. There to witness the rededication of the United States to the Virgin Mary at Our Lady of Czestochowa shrine, he also studied the feasibility of bringing Polish priests to the United States to alleviate what was already an incipient shortage of clerics, yet another sign of the transforming world of Catholicism. He also visited with Karol Cardinal Wojtyla, the archbishop of Cracow. Bernardin came to appreciate that, although Catholicism was vigorous in Poland, it was not immune to the transitional challenges which confronted the church throughout the world. As it was, he was struck that Wojtyla, the strong, Slavic faced leader, was everything his mentor, the aging, strongly anti-communist archbishop of Warsaw, Stefan Cardinal Wyzsinski, hoped he would be—stolid, determined, unyielding to the demands of the secular government whose leaders had striven so hard to shatter the unity of the hierarchy.

Traditional Catholicism was indeed effective in Poland but, had Bernardin consulted them, Polish diocesan officials could have told him, for example, that the rate of abortion in Catholic Poland was in that year running proportionately higher than in the United States. In fact, there was a better distribution of priests to Catholics in the United States than in Poland itself. If Bernardin did not learn these things, he at least became better acquainted, as he did in a visit to Hungary the next year, with the international character of the church and of the underlying human problems that seemed to surface everywhere in its universal experience. Better acquainted, too, with Wojtyla who would be chosen as Pope John Paul II in the second conclave that would be held in 1978.

Father Greeley, in the year before the conclaves, was encountering far more difficulty in learning anything about the internal policies of Roman Catholicism than he had originally envisioned. Nor was he encountering any real interest in his attempts to influence the choice of the next pope by manipulating the electors in advance. Nobody seemed interested in what appeared to be a typically American escapade, a Hollywood scenario at best, a dangerous gossip-driven plot at worst. From his own account, Greeley's effort to translate his understanding of Chicago politics into a pre-conclave grand strategy was getting nowhere. His need to succeed, to be a fashioner of events as well as their chronicler, apparently deepened as his frustration grew. Plainly, another approach had to be devised. Into his cassette recorder, its tape to be mailed back to Andrews and his colleagues in Kansas City, he uttered these words on Oct. 30, 1977:

"I wish we could all be as confident as we all were before we departed about rigging the thing. We can still do a conspiracy in this respect. We can get a lot more publicity beforehand, we can do articles about the failure to think about the election, we can get our job description out and set up our committee. But at this stage of the game, while we can bill it as a conspiracy, and while I'm perfectly willing to have it thought of as a conspiracy, it really won't measure in as one in the same sense as if we could pick the candidate and promote him. Also, let me suggest that one of the points that is important for a conspiracy is getting Joe Bernardin into the College of Cardinals. There is no one I know of... who is more astute in the whole cottonpicking church than Joe. We got to get Joe into the College of Cardinals!

"Then, you see, if we get Joe in, the story can be told. I mean, we won't have to worry about stealing stuff. Joe is going to provide it all for us. In fact, he can become part of the conspiracy. Getting Joe Bernardin into the College of Cardinals is to get our conspiracy into the college...

"Now, gentlepersons, you say 'How the hell can we get Joe Bernardin into the College of Cardinals?' I will tell you how we get him in. We get him to become archbishop of Chicago. Now it happens that this converges with other goals of mine. But multiple birds can be shot down with the same stone.

"How do we get Joe into the College? We get rid of John Patrick Cody soon. And how do we do that? We do an expose soon. We turn an investigative reporter loose on the archdiocese of Chicago, a really good one, maybe an s.o.b. from out of town, and tell him to blow the Chicago thing wide open. They would have to get rid of Cody and they would have to bring in Bernardin. How's that for a clever idea, fellow conspirators?...Investigating Chicago, fellows, will make a superb part of the movie rights.''

Seated at his desk in Cincinnati, Bernardin, who had been named the ''most influential religious leader'' in America in a *U.S. News & World Report* poll the year before, did not have the faintest idea that others were factoring him so cavalierly into their dreams of glory.

Pope Paul VI, speaking to the crowds at his summer residence, Castelgandolfo, on the August 15 feast of the Assumption in 1977, had said, ''I see the end of my life drawing near. I see myself approaching the hereafter...'' Almost a year later, as he prepared at the end of July to leave once more for this villa, the 80-year-old pontiff, racked by arthritis, confided to an aide, ''We will go, but I don't know whether we will return to Rome...or how we will return.'' He died quietly at 9:40 p.m. on August 5, his 50-year-old alarm clock, set for 6 a.m., inexplicably ringing as he drew his last breath. The long expected death—the Roman curial offices had been cautiously expecting it for more than a year, not wishing to make any moves that might put them in an uncomfortable position when a new pope ascended the throne of Peter—had finally come.

Rome moved methodically, if fumblingly, to bury Paul, who had seemed to wear out valiantly in his task, and to elect his successor, whose identity was already a matter of wild speculation. For an event that was no surprise, however, in the heart of the very citadel of ceremony, the fisherman's ring that had to be smashed could not at first be found, and the care of the deceased pope's body, which had caused a scandal after Pius XII's remains exploded in their coffin as it was being carried across Rome, was bungled again. Against the majestic background of the interlude of mourning and ritual, these incidents proved appropriate footnotes to some of the bizarre events that were already taking place.

Not the least of these developments was the arrival of the representatives of an American group headed by publisher James Andrews, the Committee for the Responsible Election of the Pope. Their acronym, CREP, carried memory traces of CREEP, the 1972 Republican Committee for the Reelection of the President, made infamous during the Watergate era. While the Andrews group had named itself with some sense of humor, Watergate and its intimations of thrones overturned and the palace court sent scurrying, were not inappropriate to its goals. As part of their ideological offensive, Father Greeley would offer a sociological description of the job requirements for the new pope at a press conference sponsored at a Hotel Columbus on the day after Paul VI's funeral.

Earlier that year, CREP had produced a book, *The Inner Elite,* published by Sheed, Andrews and McMeel, that contained brief dossiers on the world's cardinals. It was not intended as a handicapper's guide as much as an instrument of the democratic political sentiments of the American authors. The news conference matched the spirit of other groups that had come to Rome with similar motivation, including those who plastered the ancient walls with posters that read *Elect A Catholic Pope.* The gathering turned into a somewhat ungracious affair as the unappreciative journalists hectored Greeley about American positions on other matters.

As the conclave itself drew closer, Greeley again apparently felt frustrated both at what he perceived as the lack of organization for the event that was so crucial for the church and also at his own difficulty in getting more than embroidered and reembroidered rumors out of anybody in Rome. He found it difficult to accept that the cardinals were not organizing themselves along regional or other lines of interest and that they seemed almost naive in their readiness to gather and be guided by God's voice. Greeley reportedly invented and floated a rumor of his own one day and seemed pleased when an American television reporter repeated it.

In his autobiography, Greeley recalled that "during the preconclave restlessness, I phoned Bernardin from Rome and told him how sadly disorganized the preparations were. I pleaded with him to pressure his friend Cardinal Dearden to assume some kind of leadership." (*Confessions of a Parish Priest,* 1987, Pocket Books, p. 322.)

The priest reports that Bernardin said that this was not Dearden's style but that he would try.

From Bernardin's point of view, this was one of dozens of calls he received during that time in which he was asked to speculate about the outcome of the conclave. He was, however, thousands of miles from the Eternal City and without information. He certainly had none from Dearden who avoided gossip on all occasions and took the solemn requirements of his position as an elector quite seriously. Bernardin understood that Dearden would never speak even to him of the secrets of the conclave itself. And, by his every instinct and inclination, Bernardin was avoiding, as he had throughout his carrer, anything that smacked of such impropriety. He had had enough trouble being misunderstood about his position in the 1976 presidential election; he was not about to get involved in talking about the papal election. Still, his gentle handling of Greeley's phone call would earn him, in an opinion the priest writer has never denied, the title *Deep Purple,* the source, resonating again with Watergate memories, to whom Greeley would dedicate his 1979 book on the papal election.

At Father Greeley's 25th ordination anniversary party on May 5, 1979, James Andrews chuckled about the hundreds of papers of manuscript that the priest had dictated and that he had edited down to manageable size for *The Making of the Popes,* which was about to appear. "Andy originally wrote too much about Cody," Andrews said genially, "and I had to take it out or the book would have been twice as long."

Still, the priest writer was hardly alone in his dislike of his archbishop and by that bright springtime Cody had entered fully on his own melancholy way of the cross. Ahead lay the cruel obverse passion and death reserved for powerful figures fallen from grace.

Although Greeley uncharacteristically allowed a chapter of his book to be published in *Playboy* and it was boosted by full page advertisements in the *New York Times Book Review,* the sales disappointed him, according to publisher Dan Herr, to whom he confided his acceptance of the fact that this would not be his long dreamed of bestseller. Nor did the book bring Cody down even though the Chicago archbishop's reputation had already become so compromised for other reasons that he put a public relations firm on a retainer to advise him on how to improve his image. Cody seemed more and more like an archbishop caught in a time warp, a man born into cardinalatial glory out of due time who could not, with his old fashioned authoritarian instincts, harmonize himself with the post-Vatican II church. He was increasingly the victim of the very instincts and gifts that he had used to gain what was still considered the crown jewel of American archdioceses.

The sadness of the situation was multiplied because, in many ways, Cody, howsoever reluctantly, had implemented the conciliar reforms that priests and people had longed for. Almost as soon as he arrived, for example, he started visiting the 420 parishes of the archdiocese, personally calling for the retirement of the older pastors who, in the opinion of younger priests, had constituted such an obstacle to their own development and the work of the church. Yet he did this in a way that made him, as the instrument of the will of the church and his own priests, seem harsh and capricious while it earned sympathy for the unyielding old pastors who, stripped of their authority, seemed ill-treated in their wrinkled and shivering nakedness. Cody did not seem to know how to do the right things in the right way. His reputation as a first rate administrator had preceded him but he had not been in Chicago long when one of his auxiliary bishops said wistfully of him, "He could fuck up a two car funeral."

Cody had, as *Chicago Sun Times* religion editor Roy Larson wrote in the fall of 1978, "established solid insurance programs for lay employees and retirement programs for priests; made appointments by acting favorably on the recommendations of the Clergy Personnel Board in more than 90 percent of the cases, including those involving priests who had sharply criticized him in public;...supported the quality and respected the freedom of the seminary system...; instituted in 1970 a policy of making an annual report of archdiocesan finances;...provided $36 million in 12 years for inner-city schools and parishes;...channeled $1.7 million to hard-up parishes in the 1977–78 fiscal year; quietly supported some controversial people and programs—weekly masses for Catholic homosexuals, and the Ford City Catholic Center experimental parish."

His style, through which, for example, he routinely chose to ig-nore or subvert the advice given to him by many groups of sincere priests, religious, and lay Catholics, ran counter to what had been the progressive spirit of the archdiocese before his ascendency. Cody seemed, in the experience of many, including this biographer, to be casual if not malicious about not keeping his word and in misleading and deceiving people with a sense of impunity, as if, by virtue of his office, he was exempt from the moral requirements forged for those of a lesser class. He lived reclusively, and he had no position or im-pact on the national church except for his disastrous term as trea-surer of the National Conference of Bishops during which he invested in the Pennsylvania Railroad just before it went bankrupt. Cody de-lighted in being archbishop, in being a cardinal, in having an archdio-cese, in a sense, that was his private set of electric trains. He could pull the switches, move the towns, rearrange the inhabitants as if they were plaster and tin instead of living, breathing human beings. It was this autistic manner of ruling that finally wore down even the most patient of Chicago priests and people.

This dissatisfaction was symbolized at the end of May 1979, when a former priest, Walter Imbiorski, died on the Memorial Day holiday. Imbiorski, who had been a beloved and well known priest, had not received official permission from the church to marry and Cody forbade his burial in the Catholic Church. This decision, which seemed heartless and unnecessary, especially in view of the number of gang members and crooked politicians whose coffins had been sprinkled with holy water at funeral masses in his archdiocese over the years, was highly publicized on television and in the newspapers. In response to Cody's mandate that Imbiorski could not be buried in a Catholic cemetery, although Al Capone's remains rested even then at Mt. Carmel, hundreds of Catholics, priests, nuns, brothers, and laypeople flooded the Barr funeral home on the city's North Side for the wake. Having been touched by Imbiorski's spacious Christian soul during life, they were not going to abandon him in death no mat-ter what their archbishop said.

In a remarkable incident, these Catholics, without bitterness but with a sense that they were doing the church's work even if Cody would not, held their own services for Imbiorski and saw him to his grave. The night of his burial, hundreds of them gathered at a huge basilica church on the Northern border of the city and, at the invitation of the pastor, Father C. Robert Clark, whom Cody, in a highly criticized action, had removed as head of Catholic schools, attended a funeral mass for Imbiorski. Among them were some of the city's most distinguished Catholics, including Mrs. Patty Crowley, cofounder with her late husband of the Cana Movement. Afterward, they met, these veterans of many of the formerly vigorous church movements in Chicago, for refreshments in the church basement to celebrate Imbiorski's memory and, without rancor, to mourn the seemingly dead quality of the ecclesiastical bureaucracy in Chicago.

Some expressed surprise that the outspoken Father Greeley, who had known Imbiorski well, did not attend. But others felt that his style of criticizing Cody was as out of tune with their sensibilities as Cody's style of administration was. The mood was bittersweet, a blend of remembrance and conviction, and Cody was not pleased to hear about it, although he made no public comments about the matter. He had his own problems, for his embattled situation had led him to follow the counsel of his non-Catholic public relations adviser and the results had compounded his image problems. It was as if Richard M. Nixon had clumsily attempted to make an unfamiliar religious gesture, the sign of the cross perhaps, before giving an inaugural address. Cody's failure was the greater because of the apparent meagerness of his spiritual ambition.

In the late afternoon on May 25, 1979, an American Airlines DC-10 had taken off from O'Hare Field for Los Angeles. Within a few seconds of its gaining altitude, one of its massive engines tore away from its cowling and the huge plane plunged into a field just beyond the airfield's rim, killing 273 people. At the urging of his public relations firm, Cody, who had never spontaneously acted pastorally at any previous Chicago tragedy, although he, son of a fireman, occasionally stopped to watch a conflagration in progress, travelled to the site of the disaster. His purpose was to be photographed blessing a body bag which, it turned out, was empty.

The effect proved as incongruous as the photo opportunity arranged about the same time by his media guides in which, dressed in a hospital gown, he had raised his hand in benediction over the babies in a Catholic hospital nursery. The old man—for Cody was now well past 70—was going down, it seemed to the saddened spectators, ingloriously, tastelessly, his better side hidden completely by these awkward and unnatural attempts to recapture favor. He suddenly seemed less powerful although still all powerful in the archdiocese, a prelate now without nobility, a grizzled lion too enfeebled to hunt or to be hunted anymore. It was, most people felt, just a question of time before death or the mandatory retirement age of 75 removed him from the scene.

Before the 1978 conclaves were concluded, a story circulated that the papers modifying Cody's authority by appointing a coadjutor bishop had been on Paul VI's desk awaiting his action when he died. It was said that, in fact, Bernardin had been designated for the delicate task of intervening in the troubled archdiocese. While Bernardin denies any knowledge of this, some of his former aides in Cincinnati claim that Rome had been trying to structure this transfer for some months and that Cody, largely through personal visits to old friends in the Roman curia, had bought time for himself. The conclaves, separated by the month long papacy of John Paul I, had been providential as far as the archbishop of Chicago was concerned for no new pope would act swiftly against him. Cody, although battered, was known, in any case, as a tough and unyielding fighter who, in any conflict, would protect his self-interest tenaciously, unconcerned with any rules except those of his own making.

Pope John Paul II's decision to visit the United States in the fall of 1979 gave Cody another interval in which he knew that no action could be taken against him. He had to scramble in order to make his residence ready for the papal trip. By the time the pope's helicopter had fluttered down on the edge of Lincoln Park across from Cody's home, it had been hastily cleaned, fitted with adequate furniture and made to seem relatively normal. The trip, in bright, blue skied October weather, was a huge success and Cody, who reportedly made the pope a gift of $100,000 in cash in a rosewood box during his stay, felt that, despite the difficulties he had encountered, he was not scheduled for early exile, nor would he go gently into its good night no matter who urged him to do so.

Cody was also ailing, the victim of progressive congestive heart disease. His once swaggering corpulence had diminished considerably by the time the seventies had come to a close. With macabre interest, Chicago priests inspected his sallow coloring, his once apple-cheeked face's collapse into the same dark and craggy hollows that had marked Franklin D. Roosevelt's in the last year of his life. An informal death watch was being kept as Cody, more reclusive than ever, began a series of hospitalizations that would increase in frequency and duration in the two years that were left to him.

In 1980 Bernardin, like every other American bishop, had heard about the restless and depressed condition of Chicago, an archdiocese that seemed now adrift, just waiting for the end to come. Cody was proving far different in his stubborn determination to maintain his authority until his retirement at 75 than John Cardinal Dearden of Detroit. After suffering a heart attack, Dearden decided to resign ahead of time "for the good of the church," to surrender his authority, although he was still capable of exercising it, so that an orderly transition could occur in his archdiocese. Bernardin, still preoccupied about the solidity of the bishops' conference and concerned about its ability to speak effectively on contemporary problems, was aware of the continuing speculation that he would ultimately be asked to take over the archdiocese of Chicago. The spotlight of ecclesiastical attention during that uneasy period wandered regularly across the stage of the midwest toward Cincinnati anticipating Bernardin's imminent entrance.

Bernardin, experienced enough to know that he would at least be considered as potential successor after Cody's departure, needed all his self-control to avoid anything that would further stimulate speculation about his future or that might possibly aggravate the already difficult problems of Chicago. Keeping the entire situation under control was an aim that he still shared with the apostolic delegate and other church leaders who felt that nothing was to be gained by publicizing the uncomfortable situation. Still, every day that the enfeebled but hard-eyed Cody remained in office meant further stagnation for the morale of Chicago's Catholics.

According to archdiocese newspaper editor A.E.P. Wall in an interview with writer John Conroy, "Cody hated Bernardin. I don't know why. But there were a lot of people on his list, and Bernardin was one of them. . . . The cardinal threatened to create a lot of trouble if he was removed from office." With his finely honed instincts, Cody, of course, understood perfectly well that Rome was after him and that Bernardin was by far the prelate most likely to take his place. The Lear-like Cody, however, with a combination of papal deaths and papal visits, had managed to keep his throne as the new decade began.

If Bernardin was preoccupied with his own pastoral obligations and concerns about the continuing development of the bishops' conference, Father Greeley was still waging his campaign against Cody, who sat as defiant of those who would pull him down as an ancient pagan idol in a D.W. Griffith movie. Greeley, after a highly publicized battle with the University of Chicago whose faculty he had accused of anti-Catholic prejudice when he had been denied academic tenure at that institution, had accepted a professorship at the University of Arizona in Tucson and purchased a house there on Big Rock Road. His first novel, *Blue in Chicago,* had appeared but had not attracted the readership he had hoped for. He was finishing a second novel as 1980 dawned, one in which he would combine his knowledge of Rome and Chicago as well as his previous research into sexual intimacy. Warner Books thought that with intrigue in high church places flavored with sex he had at last found the ingredients of a bestseller. They planned to publish it in the spring of 1981 under the title *The Cardinal Sins.*

Father Greeley claimed later to have selected personally the photograph of a naked woman viewed from the rear that would decorate its bright red cover. For good measure, he decided that the sex scenes should appear in italics. Greeley was fairly confident that his dream of a bestseller would soon be realized. But Cody had not yet fallen. It was then, in the opinion of many observers of the extended incident, that he reactivated his suggestion of three years before that an investigative reporter should be turned loose on Chicago, "maybe an s.o.b. from out of town."

In any case, and by a course disputed in the memory of the living, the Gannett News Service investigative reporter Carlton Sherwood was assigned to look into the Cody administration of the church in Chicago. Sherwood, a rugged looking Vietnam veteran who sometimes bloodied his fists working out his frustrations on a punching bag, was an aggressive reporter who projected an air of knowingness about the underside of men and events, street learned canniness, and a relish of gossip and danger. He seemed the kind of man who, carrying a drink in one hand, might walk the topmost ledge of a tall building for the gratification of terrifying those watching him. He had collaborated with two other Catholic reporters on a series of stories that had just won the Pulitzer Prize for exposing the massive swindles carried out by a group of monks in Pennsylvania.

"How Greeley joined forces with Gannett is not entirely clear," according to writer John Conroy, but "Carlton Sherwood and his former editor Bill Schmick recall that the prodding of the news service was done directly by Greeley." The priest claims in his autobiography that the meeting occurred more casually. That Greeley had stimulated the recruitment of a tough reporter is, however, suggested by Conroy's reconstruction of executive editor Bob Dubill's giving Sherwood the assignment. "Dubill handed him a piece of paper on which a Tucson, Arizona, phone number was written in red ink. 'Why don't you start with this guy?' he said. The phone number belonged to Father Andrew Greeley." Although he would be delayed in getting down to work by the tour occasioned by winning the Pulitzer Prize, Sherwood did visit Greeley in Tucson in March 1980.

During that same period, the thoughtful and highly regarded religion editor of the *Chicago Sun-Times*, Roy Larson, who had chronicled Cody's star crossed pilgrimage for years, had begun research on the cardinal's background, relationships, and administration. The *Sun-Time's* then managing editor, Stuart Loory, would later say that the newspaper's commitment to a major investigation of Chicago's cardinal had, at some stage, been motivated by the newspaper's anxiety that it not be scooped by the Gannett News Service. According to Sherwood, Larson called him shortly after he arrived, secretly as he had thought, at a hotel near O'Hare Field late in the spring of 1980. "The person who spilled the beans was Andy Greeley," Sherwood recalled to Conroy, "Andy went to Roy Larson, and said, 'You got a hotshot investigative reporter coming into town, he's gonna eat your lunch, he's gonna make you guys look stupid...' "

Sherwood would later claim that not only did Greeley want a public scandal, as he had spoken of three years before, but he wanted it to take place when his novel *The Cardinal Sins* was in the bookstores. That way, according to Sherwood's recreation of Greeley's motivation, the priest would realize his long term goals in one season: Cody would be so embarrassed that he might be forced out of office, Greeley's sex and church scandal book would receive enormous additional publicity, and he would get the credit for slaying the dragon-like Cody as well as for making the way clear for the appointment of Joseph L. Bernardin as archbishop of Chicago. The talented priest, frustrated so far in achieving the recognition he longed for both from the church and the world at large, would therefore gain both at the same time. Perhaps his often expressed desire to rule from behind the scenes as a resident of the cardinalatial household was at last at hand.

Conroy's judgment is that the "the arrival of Carlton Sherwood, however, gave Larson some internal leverage that resulted in the paper's decision to assign Bill Clements and Gene Mustain to work with the religion editor on the story. Mustain, then 32, had just finished...an expose of insurance fraud, that would be runner-up for a Pulitzer in 1981. Clements, 49, was one of the senior investigators on the paper, and had already been advising Larson.... And so a race began between the *Sun-Times* and Gannett. In this case, journalism and the public were not well served by the competition."

A slyly mocking god of irony had not yet finished with the matter. While Sherwood was in Tucson, Greeley welcomed James Winters, then 24, the managing editor of *Notre Dame Magazine,* a distinguished periodical sponsored by the famous University. Winters was to do a profile of Greeley who had happily agreed to the project. As with Bernardin's agreement to attempt to modulate Greeley's attitudes and make him feel more welcome in the institutional church, several friends of Greeley discouraged Winters, when he contacted them, from proceeding with the assignment. Publisher Dan Herr refused to be interviewed, telling friends that no good could come of such a project because Greeley would want to control it from start to finish and that the priest would be furious with anybody who did not give him unqualified praise for everything he did. Undiscouraged and pleased with the rapport that seemed spontaneously to grow between him and his subject, Winters went ahead with his work on the profile.

If, in the course of their research, the *Sun-Times'* team uncovered the fact that Cody had, in fact, placed some of the archdiocesan insurance business with a St. Louis broker named David Wilson, the son of the Helen Wilson with whom Cody had been raised and with whose family he had maintained a close relationship, their inquiries stirred up many people who objected to their looking into Cody at all. He was fondly remembered by many priests who had known him in his native St. Louis and they quickly informed him of the investigation that was under way. The official church in Chicago began a counterattack through its newspaper and through its public relations director, Peter Foote, who, by this time, had a device in his home bedroom through which Cody could signal for him at any time during what were becoming long dark nights of siege. As Cody would claim after the paper finally broke its story, the attacks on him were anti-Catholic in nature. "When you can't attack the church directly," he would say in his sonorous nasal tones, "you attack the shepherd."

As Winters had progressed in his interviews, Greeley urged him to inspect his papers in the library at Rosary College, as, indeed, he had urged a protege of his, John Kotre, to do when writing an admiring biography several years before. As Conroy reports, a dispute that led to litigation, still not resolved at the time of this writing, arose between the priest and Winters about the extent to which Greeley permitted him to look at his materials, but, at the time, according to Conroy, "Winters was surprised at the informality of the Greeley archives...in 18 cardboard boxes that were stacked in a conference room.... The material was not indexed; the only way to determine what was in each box was to open it.... Winters found transcripts of daily memos that Greeley had dictated into a tape recorder on his trips to Rome in 1975, 1976, and 1977, and 10 microcassette tapes from a trip in 1978.''

The young editor had found the motherlode of materials in which Greeley's perception of his seemingly cordial befriending by Bernardin and Jadot in the mid-seventies was described and annotated. Greeley clearly interpreted their interest in him not as a benign attempt to moderate his zeal in denouncing Cody but a validation of his own efforts to uncover material about his archbishop and to influence the forthcoming papal election. As Conroy describes the priest's efforts to expose Cody, "Greeley concluded that Cody had too many highly placed friends to be removed by anything but 'the worst kind of public scandal.' Greeley also said that Bernardin, whom he referred to as 'the great man,' was the only one in the American hierarchy who could get rid of Cody. 'He has to be the one to do it,' Greeley said, 'and he assumes that there are enough people around in Rome who have confidence in him that he will not be thought of as seeking personal promotion for himself. It's a very sticky business, though. . .' ''

The tapes, as quoted previously, went on to give the outline of what Greeley himself described as a conspiracy to oust Cody and ''wire'' the next conclave, replacing Cody with Bernardin, allowing Bernardin to enter the College of Cardinals as the source who would eliminate their need for, as Greeley had put it, ''stealing'' things in order to get the inside story of the election of the next pope. What Greeley did not know, although he was in touch with Sherwood in that thunder and rain filled July of 1980, was that Winters had read these materials, had been struck by the evident outlines of a conspiracy against Cody, and was seeking interviews with others, including Greeley's editor, James Andrews, called a ''co-conspirator,'' and Bernardin himself, to investigate the wild plot to ''rig'' a papal election.

On July 29, according to Conroy, ''Greeley was stunned'' to receive a call from James Andrews in Kansas City, informing him that his private scenarios were suddenly and rudely threatening to become public. Greeley had good reason, as he later said, to be "horrified," for he was now in danger of delivering into the declining Cody's hands the information that would preserve him yet again while it destroyed Bernardin and made Greeley seem, not a sage to guide the policies of the Chicago church, but a calculating and self-interested agitator. Greeley quickly placed a call to Archbishop Bernardin in Cincinnati, near panic at the thought of the worlds, his own and others, that he might be on the verge of destroying.

Greeley also called the Reverend Theodore Hesburgh, president of Notre Dame University, imploring him to intercede in some way with the editor of the university magazine to kill the story and regain control of the explosive materials from his Rosary College archive. Those who were in contact with developments at the time describe the priest's deep embarrassment and depression, his self-dramatizing talk of resigning from the priesthood, his determination to pull every string he could in order to prevent the story of his "conspiracy" from coming to light. Bernardin received his phone calls, expressed astonishment at hearing of the existence of such materials, accepted Greeley's protestations of innocence at face value, but felt, deep within himself, that a major, unnecessary problem had, like a mysterious biblical angel, suddenly and unpredictably appeared in his life.

He remembered Cardinal Dearden's ability to avoid panic in unexpected circumstances. He had been able to deal with surprises, good and bad, with the same restraint and, lover of anticipating the full dimensions of such time fused incidents, he began to prepare for that moment when some member of the media might suddenly ask him, "Is it true, your excellency, that you were part of a conspiracy with Father Andrew Greeley to overthrow Cardinal Cody and take his job for yourself?" He remembered, as he sat at the desk in his private study, the difficult universe the media created and inhabited when a big story was brewing and how difficult it was, as during the 1976 election campaign, to get the full truth heard and accurately reported.

This case of incredible plans to "wire" a papal conclave, a sordid mess with which his own name had been liberally and unwarrantedly associated: This was a grim visitation of God's Providence that was difficult to comprehend and, because of its irrational and sensational character, also difficult to dispel. Father Greeley seemed sincere in his apologies but it was Bernardin, not Greeley, who could be most seriously affected by any public revelation of this freakish scenario. The most ridiculous insinuation, widely published in Greeley's book on the papal election, was that Bernardin, who had been in Cincinnati during the 1978 conclaves, was "Deep Purple," the Watergate-like insider who supplied Greeley with the supposed details of the papal elections. Bernardin realized that he was in the role of the innocent bystander but he also understood that innocent bystanders were regularly the victims of bad shots and poor drivers.

Meanwhile, the *Sun-Times* reporters, unaware of these developments, had tracked down a number of facts about Helen Wilson's family that did not seem to jibe with Cody's stories about her. Helen Wilson, supposedly living on her modest pay as a church worker, turned out to be living in an expensive Chicago high rise, to own a house in Boca Raton, Florida, that had been purchased by Cody, to maintain an apartment in St. Louis, and to dress well and to travel widely. These reporters were beginning to suspect that the real story about Chicago's cardinal was the way he used church funds to support the Wilsons, his "relatives," who, it turned out, were not technically relatives at all. Carlton Sherwood told John Conroy that "Father Greeley would periodically call and tell him what the *Sun-Times* was doing. 'You're gonna have to get movin,' he'd say, 'because they've got the Boca Raton stuff.' Or 'they got Mrs. Wilson down pat.'" Sherwood was convinced that Greeley was playing Gannett and the *Sun-Times* off against each other. Early in August 1980, Greeley informed Sherwood of Winters' discovery of his archival material and that, if others used the material before the journalist, it could ruin his investigation. He suggested that Sherwood contact Winters and carry out what, in Sherwood's retrospective analysis, seemed like a double-agent operation with the young editor.

First, Sherwood was to find out for Greeley what Winters was going to do with the papers he had come across and, through suggesting a possible collaboration, gain control of the material. Winters had already mailed back, at the request of Father Hesburgh, the originals of the Greeley tapes but had kept copies of them as well as Xeroxes of other archival materials. As the flamboyant Sherwood came to know Winters on repeated visits, he realized that he himself was the hired gun, the "s.o.b." of an investigative reporter Greeley had wanted to recruit to expose Cody years before. The reporter sensed, as he studied the outlines of Greeley's fantasied "conspiracy" and his references to "Deep Purple" as Joseph Bernardin, that he had discovered a new story, one richer by far in intrigue than the uncertain information that Greeley had been floating for months about Cody. This was the complex tale, winding and dark as old castle tunnels, suggesting that the archbishop of Cincinnati was a party to Greeley's conspiracy to overthrow Cody in order to succeed to the see of Chicago himself.

By this time Sherwood was acting as a double agent in regard to both Winters and Greeley. He was sniffing a story of Pulitzer-like dimensions and he hugely enjoyed the by-play involved in being confidant to and informer on the principals in the situation. It was all part of the game. Greeley was trying to use him so it seemed only appropriate to use him to some extent in return. In the caverns of his soul, Sherwood sensed that what lay behind these ecclesiastical stratagems was a cover-up underway, another example of a complex master plan that had been worked out in advance by the American hierarchy to squelch church scandals through manipulating the press. "The alarm bells go off," he told this biographer later that year, "and the plan goes into effect nationwide." A fragile balloon of accusation, with Bernardin's name painted on its side, had rapidly been pumped full of air heated by paranoia and sent floating down the Ohio River toward Cincinnati.

When Bernardin was told, a few days later, that a reporter had called, asking to speak to "Deep Purple," it was natural for him to wonder if that strange moment of engulfment by the fevered Roman plotting had not arrived sooner than he had thought. He would not panic, he reminded himself, but neither would he postpone the confrontation with the inquiring media for which he had already prepared himself. He accepted the call and, recognizing Sherwood as the reporter who had investigated the mercenary Pennsylvania monks, agreed to meet with him at his local motel. Bernardin drove himself to the meeting place, determined to put an end to any notion that he had participated in the chimera of conclave manipulation.

Sherwood, relishing the moment in which he expected to uncover the truth about Bernardin's role in the plot to get Cody, dealt aggressively with the somewhat uneasy but resolute archbishop. "I want to know everything," Sherwood said, lighting a cigarette, flipping open his notebook and settling into his chair as slyly confident as the television detective Columbo. The reporter briefly laid out his scenario of Bernardin's involvement and demanded that the archbishop provide him with the dossiers that had been prepared on Cody. This presentation, based on Sherwood's having read fragments of the archival material and listened to Father Greeley's version of events, reflected Greeley's interpretation of Jadot's letter to him in French of some years before. The apostolic delegate's informal use of the word dossier had led Greeley to conclude that formal investigations of the Chicago prelate had taken place, that Rome was preparing to move against the man the priest writer seemed, as one of his friends said, to love to hate. What Jadot had intended as a note to pacify Greeley was misinterpreted as an encouragement to battle. Sherwood had accepted Greeley's interpretation and insisted that Bernardin knew of the existence of these files and that he expected him to produce them for him. Veiled behind his silky insistence that Bernardin deliver the nonexistent dossier was Sherwood's threat to expose what he presumed was the archbishop's knowing complicity in the "conspiracy" that had seemed, according to Greeley's transcribed descriptions, to have been solidly in place in the mid-seventies.

Bernardin blinked at the assured investigative reporter through his large lensed glasses. The world was indeed coming loose, he thought, if such dangerous and untrue fabrications were being treated as fact. There were no dossiers on Cody for, although complaints about Cody, as well as about other bishops, had been routinely referred to the apostolic delegate and to Rome, there had never been a formal investigation of the Chicago archbishop. Bernardin explained all this to the disbelieving journalist. The interview turned swiftly into an intense and uncomfortable 90 minute standoff. Sherwood, fresh from an investigation that had yielded plenty of dirty laundry about larcenous Polish monks, was intuitively certain that he was on to something. There had to be something here, he felt, it all fit together too well, he couldn't have been misinformed. Besides, the details fit his notion of a master plan of response, the cover-up mechanism of the American bishops. Sherwood pounded away relentlessly, invoking the good cop/bad cop antiphonation that had served him well in other circumstances. Bernardin, as he would with the *Sun-Times* reporters much later, stood firm with the truth as he knew it.

For the archbishop, however, the meeting was yet another bizarre incident in a long episode that was trying for both him and for the American church. He heard Sherwood out, realizing that the journalist did not, in fact, have a story but was attempting, with all his skill, to get Bernardin to produce one for him. In the end, however, as in many other burdensome meetings, Bernardin's patience served him well. Truth was easier to remember than the tangled rumors and hypotheses the reporter related. It was not pleasant to deal with an experienced and highly motivated Pulitzer Prize winner but, as he had vowed in his private meditation, Bernardin faced the complex accusations with equanimity and the confidence born of his understanding that he was speaking the truth. He closed the door of the motel room more at peace with himself. The ghost of the Greeley papers had broken into his life and he had withstood the specter as effectively as possible. Inside the room, Sherwood poured himself a drink. "God damn it," he said of the meeting later, "I didn't get a thing out of him!"

Bernardin returned to his office, mulling a new insight about the media. While he valued his relationship with many writers and journalists, he now understood that, when some reporters were hunting for confirmation of stories whose angles they were sure of in advance, it did little good for the honest person to try to explain the complexities of the matter. All that crack reporters were concerned about, as in the bishops' attitudes toward Carter and Ford in 1976, was that distilled element that was truly new, at that time, whether the prelates endorsed the Republican over the Democrat on the basis of their relative positions on abortion. Explanations and distinctions were of no avail when such a sharpened journalistic point was in focus. While Bernardin had spent his life trying to elucidate ecclesiastical events for the press, he had now come to appreciate that such efforts could also seem to be self-justifications in which journalists had little interest. If the matter were serious, the most prudent course was to say as little as possible beyond the essential truth. Anything a person added by way of illustration or clarification only led to another news story, and further explanations led to still more stories; it resembled feeding oxygen to a fire. If you denied oxygen to the fire, it would go out by itself. He would not forget that in the years ahead.

Sherwood continued to search out sources to confirm his story. By the middle of September, he was again circulating in Chicago, suggesting to various interested parties that he could produce materials, meaning the Greeley tapes and papers, that would show that Cody was the innocent victim of a plot. "There are people in this town," he told this biographer on September 17, "who are willing to kill for this stuff. Don Reuben, for example, he'd love to get this stuff. It would take Cody off the hook." Reuben was then Cardinal Cody's lawyer. Sherwood also said that he was looking through the books of various Catholic agencies, such as the Church Extension Society, whose headquarters were in Chicago, to try to find evidence about Cody's financial dealings. He repeated his as yet unsubstantiated theory about the early warning cover-up system of the American bishops. When told that the bishops, like most executives, were hardly so far-sighted, planful, or paranoid to devise such an arrangement, that they improvised like everybody else when a big problem hit, that they were about as prepared for trouble as the military at Pearl Harbor, he bit his lower lip, shook his head. "God damn," he whispered, "I know I'm right...."

Years later, he explained the conclusion that he had reached by the fall of 1980 and had transmitted to his editors in Washington, D.C. "I wanted to put major emphasis on the fact that this was all an internecine Vatican plot, a byzantine effort to try to tip over a guy who was a senior churchman [Cody] in the country whom they didn't know how to deal with, and the Vatican's use of various people—the apostolic delegate [Jadot] in Washington to use this good-guy bishop in Cincinnati [Bernardin] to use a renegade priest [Greeley] to use a news service [Gannett] in Washington to use the Chicago press . . .'' He also claimed that he had earlier given Father Greeley this interpretation. ''It devastated Greeley,'' Sherwood claimed, ''Really brought him to his knees. After that he got really pissed.''

But as the autumn turned into one of the mildest winters that Chicago had experienced in years, the derring-do activities of Sherwood also calmed down. His editors had not bought his complex tale and he had dabbled with other stories, promising to monitor the Chicago church while he covered the local elections and hunted for connections that he had been reliably informed about between mass murderer John Wayne Gacey and the son of a prominent Chicagoan. ''They say,'' he confided, ''that he'll go at you with a knife if you ask questions.'' Father Greeley was delighted when the Literary Guild chose his forthcoming novel, *The Cardinal Sins,* as one of their spring selections. Cardinal Cody continued as Chicago's archbishop, his hospital visits occurring more regularly, his determination to remain in office deepening as the darkness of winter closed in on the city. The surface seemed calm, as the land does, rutted and reshaped, after an earthquake. The aftershocks would not be felt for over a year.

Archbishop Bernardin, having put the summer's flurry of dangerous excitement behind him, plunged back into his own work. The bishops remained judiciously quiet during the campaign between Jimmy Carter and Ronald Reagan that fall. Reagan, his strategy shaped by the same James Baker who had guided Ford in 1976, used his pro-life stand to appeal to one of the groups the Republicans had long targeted as necessary for victory, the working class Catholics who had once given unswerving loyalty to the Democratic party. On other matters, as the bishops well knew as they gathered for their November 1980 meeting in Washington, D.C., the Reagan agenda, especially on social issues, differed greatly from their own.

Near the conclusion of their gathering, the bishops voted to go forward with proposals for two pastoral letters. The development of the second of these, on the economy, was given to Archbishop Rembert Weakland of Milwaukee to oversee. The first, on nuclear war, was entrusted to Archbishop Joseph L. Bernardin of Cincinnati. Reagan, Baker, and the entire administration would have ample reason to remember their names well during their years in office. For the first time in memory, the Catholic bishops, once thought dependably loyal to such strong anti-Communist administrations as Reagan's, would begin to examine the morality of the country's posture of defense and the economic system that undergirded it.

XV

Standing in the cabinet room, the just inaugurated President smiled as he viewed the newly hung picture of Calvin Coolidge, the Republican 30th president. He intended to make his own the dour looking Yankee's famous statement that the "business of America is business." The eighties would be given over to a revitalization of the nation's capitalist instincts and a deregulation of government restraints on business activity. High on Ronald Reagan's agenda was a rebuilding of American defensive power as a validation of one of his and the era's ironic acts of faith, that only a country strong enough to destroy the world could save it and its own self-esteem at the same time. The president who had endorsed the pro-life movement also wanted to expand the country's capacity to make war. His Catholic constituents, first capitalized on as an influential voting bloc by Richard M. Nixon but courted even more successfully by him, would, Reagan was sure, approve of his muscular patriotism.

Reagan, who had been raised in the Protestant sect of his mother while his brother had been raised in the Catholic faith of his father, had appointed Catholics to important positions in the new administration: Alexander Haig, whose brother was a Jesuit, as Secretary of State, John Lehmann to head the Navy Department, and William Clark, a former seminarian, as National Security Adviser. The military services included Catholics in the highest ranks of command, Admiral James Watkins of the Navy and General Paul X. Kelley of the Marine Corps. Edward Hickey was a traditional Catholic with major responsibilities on the Secret Service detail. General Vernon Walters, a State Department appointee who would later become ambassador to the United Nations, exhibited an old-fashioned archbishop's convictions and demeanor in his dedication to the service of the republic.

Strongly influential think tanks in Washington, such as the Heritage Foundation, counted many Catholics in their leadership. Michael Novak, the gentleman philosopher whose writings offered an extensive apologia for Catholic support of capitalism, served at the American Enterprise Institute. Faith Whittlesley headed an office that maintained channels with religious groups and a Catholic who had formerly been with the United States Information Agency, Bob Reilly, was assigned to serve as liaison with the nation's Catholic community. American Catholics, it was thought by the shrewd Reagan handlers, including chief of staff James Baker who had watched approvingly as the bishops were backed into a pseudo-endorsement of Gerald Ford in 1976, were under respectful but good control as the new administration settled into the tasks of governing.

Not the least of the long-term informal relationships of the White House under both Democrats and Republicans was that with the man who served as cardinal-archbishop of New York. Although that archdiocese was not the largest in the country, it was considered the most influential in many areas, including the political, and, for that reason, the sitting president reflexively cultivated a friendship with that city's archbishop. This was a ''special relationship,'' as America's with Great Britain was, a public way of acknowledging the Catholic presence in America without genuflecting to it. Francis Cardinal Spellman had embodied what the government longed for in the nation's foremost Catholic prelate: A robust anti-Communism coupled with a devotion to the military services that inspired well-publicized Christmas visits to war zones to celebrate masses on Jeep hoods and beneath the looming guns of battleships.

Spellman, as head of the military ordinariate, in effect the canonical territory of the world-wide armed forces, had been, in his sturdy if sometimes sentimental celebrations of the heroic goodness of

American fighting men and their leaders' motives, an enormous asset to the government. Presidential contenders were naive if they thought they could skip the Al Smith dinner, hosted by the New York archbishop, and not lose an important political opportunity to demonstrate their affection for the nation's Catholics.

Cordial relations had continued, after Spellman's death late in 1967, with his successor, the gentle and popular Terence Cooke, to whose installation in April 1968, President Lyndon Johnson had come, and with whom Presidents Nixon, Ford, and Carter had preserved a politically advantageous kinship. Cooke had inherited Spellman's responsibilities for the American military and he had chosen, as his vicar for this, former chief of Navy chaplains, John J. O'Connor, who, having watched men die in Vietnam, had written a book defending the American involvement in that war. O'Connor, an auxiliary bishop of New York, had been appointed in the month of Reagan's election by the then president of the American bishops, John Roach of Minneapolis–St. Paul, as a member of the committee, to be chaired by Archbishop Bernardin, that would examine the issue of nuclear war. O'Connor, a highly intelligent man who was already being spoken of as a possible future archbishop of Philadelphia, was perceived as a counterweight to another bishop on the committee, the peace activist Thomas Gumbleton, an auxiliary of Detroit. The two other bishops, George Fulcher of Columbus, Ohio, and Daniel P. Reilly, of Norwich, Connecticut, were considered moderates.

These preparations for pastoral letters on nuclear war and the economy were not at all what government officials expected or wanted from the Catholic bishops. They had already expressed some irritation at the way the bishops seemed to be supporting movements in Central and South America that the Republican leaders would have preferred to suppress. Reagan, and his many Catholic appointees and loyalists, were hardly enthusiastic about the bishops' examining and possibly criticizing their developing policies; they certainly did not want Catholic prelates attempting to foreclose their options to begin military actions against successful Marxist regimes in the necklace of countries that stretched between Mexico and the South American landmass. The bishops, as the Reagan theoreticians viewed the matter, were not only stepping out of their pulpits but out of the role they were expected to fulfill in supporting counterinsurgency moves against Marxist-inspired governments in the Third World.

The Reagan administraton had also heard of the "theology of liberation" that had been developed by Catholic theologians in Latin America. That, too, smacked to the newly installed Republicans of leftist ideology and needed to be resisted more vigorously by the leaders of the American church. The bishops, however, seemed to be tolerant, if not encouraging, of "liberation theology," accepting its aspiration to free poverty stricken peoples for lives in which they could better realize the basic human and theological goals of existence. The worst case scenario for the Reagan administration, however, was that the American bishops, in studying the morality of nuclear war, might involve themselves in matters about national defense that they did not and could never fully understand. Let them, as many traditional Catholics also felt, pray for peace inside their cathedrals and let us take care of the business of the real world.

Archbishop Bernardin was well aware of these reactions and of the pressures that the government was prepared to exert on him and his committee as they began their task. Now, however, at the beginning of a new decade the moment had come, in Bernardin's judgment, to employ the form of the pastoral letter as an expression of the moral convictions of the newly consolidated conference of bishops. The bishops, had, after all, been issuing pastoral letters for almost two hundred years. Such missives provided the ideal mode for them to speak collegially on their own terms and in their own pastoral language to the American culture about serious matters. Bernardin had reflected long and hard on the lessons of the 1976 campaign and on the frustration that the prelates had experienced in their efforts to articulate their pro-life position in its true complexity. Even then reporters were interested primarily in the condensation of conflict that a generation later came to be called sound bites.

The 1976 experience convinced Bernardin that the conference had to establish its own forum for its collective deliberation on current moral and ethical issues. The proposed pastoral letters offered the bishops the ideal medium for this ongoing reflection and leadership. Bernardin was also convinced that collegial process, with meetings long enough to test even his own fabled capacity for listening patiently remained the ideal vehicle to gain the serious attention of America's buzzing, distractable, sensation devouring culture. Collegial procedures would also promote maximum involvement, a wide and necessary sharing of views from interested persons, Catholic and non-Catholic, on issues, nuclear war and the economy, that the popes themselves had underscored for decades as among the gravest matters confronting the human race.

Ten years before, the peace movement had been led by poetic outriders, such as the Berrigan brothers, the priests Philip and Daniel, who had fashioned dramatic protests as exercises of civil disobedience against the Vietnam war and the arms race. Along with many others, they had endured indictments, trials, and prison terms as a result. Had he not been forced from office, Richard M. Nixon, as the writer Jimmy Breslin then observed, would "have put the entire peace movement behind bars." That era's peace activists, often as ragged as the hippies of an earlier time, seemed to stand on the far shore of Catholicism, exiles from the institution that had dissented cautiously, if at all, from government foreign and defense policies during that period. When the priestly garbed Berrigans burned draft records, they had offered a startling contrast to the nation's finely tailored bishops who seemed to preside over Catholicism from behind gleaming executive desks. At one point during that tumultuous era, a New York magazine editor proposed that an invitation be sent to a Catholic bishop, with a guarantee of anonymity, to write an article condemning the arms race. But the project seemed so far-fetched that it was dropped.

As the beaming Reagan entered the White House, however, the bishops had already agreed to examine the morality of nuclear war in a series of open, collegial discussions, that, although far different in their symbolism from pouring animal blood on nuclear submarines, bestowed a new and invigorating validation on the purposeful examination of American strategic defense policy. This opportunity had not come into being accidentally. It was the recognition of an effective collaborative pastoral option that would never have come into being had Cardinal Dearden not envisioned a restructured, cooperative conference of bishops. Bernardin had shepherded that conference from its infancy through its uncertain adolescence, strengthening it by encouraging the appointment of a generation of younger bishops whose outlook had been formed by the second Vatican Council. Both the personnel and the processes were therefore available to initiate what would amount to a public meditation on the legitimacy and use of nuclear weapons. No issue seemed more urgent to the Cincinnati archbishop as he planned the first meeting of his committee. Nor was he surprised to hear a Reagan administration official quoted as saying, "These damn Catholics are causing us trouble everywhere."

Bernardin's balanced ticket of a committee gathered for the first time in July 1981. Its members quickly agreed that their main concern in developing the draft for the pastoral letter was to maintain and strengthen their position as moral leaders. Although the war seasoned chaplain, Bishop John O'Connor, seemed the opposite of the peace march veteran, Bishop Thomas Gumbleton, they shared much in common with each other and with Bernardin and the other bishop committee members. They understood the demands that the church made on them to support the moral reflections of the popes and a willingness to work long and hard with that virtue as about their only reward. Well practiced in the ascetic postponement of gratification, innured to at least a measure of public misunderstanding no matter what they did, these five prelates unselfconsciously manifested the obsessive dedication that would bind their collaborative efforts together.

Under Bernardin's characteristically mild but pointed coordination, the five bishops also decided to avail themselves of as much technical data as possible and to schedule a number of hearings at which experts, Catholic and non-Catholic, would be asked to testify. About 35 of these authorities, including former Defense Secretaries James Schlesinger and Harold Brown as well as the then holder of that office, Caspar Weinberger, would give their views before the committee finished its work. During the year of labor that stretched before them, the bishops would also solicit comments and criticisms from many other individuals and group representatives, including philosophers, a variety of activists, theologians, educators, and interested citizens. Bishops O'Connor and Gumbleton would be lobbied heavily by those who knew and respected them in the armed forces and peace organizations. The bishops would be assisted by the brilliant Father J. Bryan Hehir, who had led the seminarian strikers in Boston a dozen years before and who served now on the bishops' conference Washington staff. Other members of that same staff would also be deeply involved in gathering resource materials and helping the bishops reach their goal of a preliminary draft by July 1982.

Bernardin found himself, therefore, at that magnetic central point that attracted every interested or affected force, some threatening and some benign, including the increasingly anxious Reagan administration, as his commission began perhaps the most sensitive undertaking in the history of American Catholicism. The bishops soon found, along with the rest of American air travelers, that their plane trips to their meetings were often delayed because of the traffic holds that became routine that summer after President Reagan's firing of the striking air traffic controllers. That union breaking move, paired with the president's intention to further ease the regulatory supervision of big business, revealed clearly that the Republican administration was hardly implementing the papal encyclicals on labor in its domestic policies.

As they proceeded with their work, and as Archbishop Weakland's separate committee pursued its study of the economy, Bernardin and his brother bishops felt the pull of an unexpected but unavoidable destiny, that of standing as critics of an administration that had expected them to be allies. National Security Adviser William Clark, known as "Mister Catholic," was annoyed at what he considered the bishops' presumptions. His attitude, even in social encounters with bishops at various Washington functions, was one of undisguised irritation with their study of the nation's nuclear arms policies. "He used rudeness," one bishop later said, "as a form of intimidation."

If this were not ominous enough, Carlton Sherwood, reveling in what he described to others as a new assignment to investigate supposed irregularities at the U.S. Naval Academy at Annapolis, was also trying to monitor developments in the Justice Department in nearby Washington. He had heard that a federal grand jury had been looking into John Cardinal Cody's suspected use of tax free church funds for personal purposes and had finally served a subpoena whose issuance had been delayed during the Carter administration. Some had questioned whether the timing of such an unprecedented action was related to the bishops' work on the pastoral letters on nuclear war and the economy. Sherwood believed, although he was never able to verify it, that papers had been served on Cody by a federal marshal while the prelate was standing in a church sacristy waiting for a liturgical procession to begin.

The *Sun-Times,* its reporters' documented research on Cody and his clear but not fully explained financial aid to the Wilson family already in type, had also heard of the subpoena. The editors had been frustrated several times in trying to set a date for their story. It had been postponed once when Reagan had been shot at the end of March 1981, and again at midsummer when the wedding of Prince Charles overshadowed all other news and in its resonations of royal romance provided uncomfortable associations with Cody's princely status in the church. The service of the papers on Cody had, in fact, been the outcome of an investigation that had no relationship to or dependence on Father Greeley's campaign against his cardinal archbishop or the investigative work of Sherwood or the *Sun-Times.*

The federal investigation had been prompted from within Cody's own administration through questions brought to the office of the United States Attorney for the Northern District of Illinois. Reliable sources indicate that an employee who, at the request of a member of the Wilson family, reluctantly inspected the transfers of money in Cody's account, became so troubled in conscience by the seeming conflicts he thereby uncovered that he ultimately sought advice from federal authorities about the matter. The investigation was based on these reports rather than on the rumors that had been shopped around for years. Confirmation of the delivery of the subpoena triggered the publication of the *Sun-Times* story and the explosion of publicity that followed. Its shock waves would ultimately dislodge excerpts from what came to be called the "Greeley papers" and, just as he was embarking on the most challenging task of his career with the nuclear pastoral letter, threaten Bernardin's reputation and potential ecclesiastical future.

Sherwood planned to return to Chicago early in September to pursue the lead about the subpoena. He learned that Father Greeley was leaving shortly on a tour to promote *The Cardinal Sins*. The novel had already sold well through the summer, abetted by the priest's appearance on television shows and statements in magazine interviews through which he defended what many critics deemed his "steamy" fiction and continued his attacks on Cody, describing his archbishop as a "monster" and "the most evil man" he had ever known. The Gannett reporter continued to be frustrated in his efforts to confirm the issuance of the Cody subpoena. His inquiries of Jeremy Margolis, then assistant U.S. attorney, yielded him no comment but an appointment for Thursday, September 10. Sherwood experienced a familiar surge of excitement. He was, he felt, closing in on his long sought story at last.

Before he could reach Chicago, however, the *Sun-Times*, in possession of sure knowledge of the service of the papers on Cody, was preparing to publish its story. According to John Conroy's reconstruction of events, at "2:15 p.m., on Wednesday, September 9, Roy Larson called the cardinal to get his side of the story. The cardinal was at a bishops' meeting in Mundelein and declined to be interviewed, saying, 'I don't need any chance for rebuttal.' " The *Sun-Times* submitted questions to Peter Foote, the archdiocesan spokesman, about Cody's finances, his relationship with Helen Wilson, and whether he would cooperate with the reported federal inquiry. At 8:00 p.m., Foote responded that he doubted that any reply would be made. In the *Sun-Times* composing room, the next day's edition of the paper, containing a five-page first installment on its Cody investigation, headed for its press run. Word began to spread throughout the city late that evening that the long rumored expose of Cody would be on everyone's doorstep the next morning. When Sherwood heard by phone of the imminent publication of the

Sun-Times story, he telephoned his Gannett editors, asking to file at least a brief story that night but his request was refused.

The headline of the Chicago *Sun-Times* for Sept. 10, 1981, in letters, large and dark as death itself, read *"Federal Grand Jury Probes Cardinal Cody Use of Church Funds—Investigation Centered on Gifts to a Friend."* The initial story claimed that the grand jury was investigating whether the cardinal had illegally diverted "as much as $1 million" in tax-exempt church funds to Mrs. Wilson, that Cody had not responded to federal subpoenas but according to public records had indeed provided the money for Mrs. Wilson's home in Boca Raton. It also showed that Mrs. Wilson's personal wealth had grown, without substantial income of her own, to about $1 million and that she and the cardinal, although raised together, were not blood relatives.

Subsequent installments told of David Wilson's having received at least $150,000 in commissions on insurance premiums purchased by the Chicago archdiocese and of Helen Wilson's being the beneficiary of a $100,000 insurance policy on Cody's life that had been issued almost 30 years before. It was as if from Lake Michigan a towering seiche wave had broken and rushed across the city. Chicago, accustomed to tales of low and high cunning, home of every brutal sensation from Al Capone's beer wars through the explosive Democratic convention of 1968, was stunned anew by this story, which, although long rumored, seemed more stark, more unsettling when seen in print. The fine autumnal, beginning-again mood of early September seemed soured by the grimness of the tale.

A cynical Chicago lawyer once offered novelist Saul Bellow a distinction that matched the city's general lack of subtlety by saying, "Morals is sex, ethics is money." These were the double pulses of the *Sun-Times* series that quickly became a national and international sensation. Cody loomed out of a photograph behind Dan Rather's shoulder on that Thursday's CBS Evening News as the television journalist, like anchormen throughout the country, recounted the accusations pending against the prince of the church. The aura of possibly illicit sex between the cardinal and his alleged cousin outshone the financial core of the story and reporters were dispatched to Chicago from the major newspapers of the country.

After consulting governmental officials and members of congress, Cody's lawyers, Don Reuben and James Seritella, were reported to have advised him "to stonewall" the federal investigation they termed an outrageous breach of the separation of church and state. Helen Wilson, Chicago lawyer Leonard Ring at her side, clutched a silver rosary and wept as she gave various interviews saying that the paper made her feel "like a tramp," and recalling her childhood days with the man she called "Jack." Every Sunday, she said, "we'd go to our grandmother's house and play church."

There was something outlandish, repulsive, comical, and yet oddly touching about the Cody revelations. Autocratic, removed, high-handed and arbitrary as he had seemed to many, the possibility that he felt tenderness at some layer of his heart seemed a homely and not wholly unattractive flaw in Cody. He was quickly and loudly defended by offended Chicagoans, many of whom felt that the federal investigation had been an insult to Catholics, even to those who did not particularly like Cody. "The city," as one corporate lawyer observed, "is filled with far worse corruption than this. The judges would be better off looking at themselves."

Still, the siege had begun and, although the redoubtable Cody braved the questions of reporters shouted to him at public functions, defending himself by charging anti-Catholicism as the motive for the attacks against him, he seemed frail and diminished. As he would tell Father Timothy Lyne, rector of Holy Name Cathedral, before mounting the pulpit for Christmas mass three months later, "This is my last hurrah." His reputation was, for all practical purposes, in shambles, and, although he would hang on stubbornly, realizing that Roman authorities, no matter how displeased, would not act against him lest it seem they were reacting to the journalistic revelations, Cody would be seen less frequently after the December celebration of his 50th ordination anniversary.

As the storm broke, Carlton Sherwood arrived in Chicago where reporters were gathering for several days of follow-up investigative work that recreated the frenzied and antic mood of Hecht and MacArthur's famous Chicago set play, *The Front Page.* The sales of Father Greeley's novel, *The Cardinal Sins,* had boomed under the surge of publicity. Sherwood located him by phone in a New York hotel and, in an account of his conversation with the priest given immediately afterward, claimed that Greeley was delighted that the scandal had broken just as he had expected. He would lie low, however, and let it continue to build up, for it was all good for book sales. According to Sherwood, Greeley proposed to step forward and take credit for the archbishop's downfall which, once again, he considered imminent. That, he told Sherwood, would spur the sales even more.

Reporters stalked the city, many of them trying to locate *Notre Dame Magazine* editor James Winters at his parents' home or at his apartment in South Bend, Indiana. Rumors had begun to circulate that Winters had submitted a long article to editor John Fink of *Chicago Magazine* which contained large sections of quotations from Greeley's tapes that, like an undetonated World War II bomb, had lain just beneath the surface of events for a year. Sherwood told other reporter friends that he had seen a draft of the material, that it told of a conspiracy, planned by Greeley but joined by Archbishop Bernardin of Cincinnati, to overthrow Cody. Among those to whom Sherwood confided this story was Rob Warden, the intense editor of the periodical *Chicago Lawyer* who was ever alert for conspiracy themes. He called Winters, asking if he would let him print the story that *Chicago Magazine,* on its lawyer's advice, had declined to publish. Winters refused.

By September 17, the *New York Times* sent reporter William Schmidt to South Bend to interview Winters about his material. The varied efforts to get possession, in part or in whole, of the Greeley papers soon came to the attention of Greeley's lawyer, Patrick O'Brien. The priest, by then in England on his way to the island of Corfu, issued a statement through O'Brien, absolving himself of any involvement in Cody's decline and fall, and claiming that his private diaries had been ''stolen'' from his ''sealed archives.'' Besides, the diaries were only late night musings, Greeley said, fantasies projected after too much pasta and wine. The priest had not expected the material to be resurrected and, according to Sherwood, who talked to him regularly by trans-Atlantic phone during this period, feared, as he had the year before, the consequences of their becoming public.

But matters had gone too far and the reporters who clogged the city knew that Cody's haunch was turning slowly on the spit of events and everybody wanted some piece of it. The highly competitive journalists were intoxicated by the drifting fumes and the situation was soon too complex and unpredictable for those gathered to control their enthusiasm for what one of them called "the biggest thing since Capone." As a Chicago psychiatrist observed at the time, the city was "filled with a paranoid spirit" that would howl until it had satisfied its deepest demonic longings.

As the fury built up, Archbishop Joseph L. Bernardin carried out his official duties in Cincinnati while working conscientiously on the initial development of the pastoral letter on nuclear armaments. Occasionally, a priest friend from Chicago would call to tell him of the wild stories that were circulating in the clerical culture of the archdiocese. Bernardin pushed away the distractions, having no idea that, without any actual involvement, he had been cast in a leading role in the story that was about to break. Once again, the papers that Father Greeley had described as his "fantasies" were about to be disinterred by the storm whirling above the debris of Cody's reputation. Like a midwestern tornado, it might move at any moment, jaggedly and destructively, toward Cincinnati.

XVI

During that last full week of September the world tilted back through the invisible boundary of the autumn solstice and in Chicago the darkness began to overtake the light. The hardened old city became as jittery as the rustling tree leaves in the suddenly windy and cooler air. Cardinal Cody began telling people that yes, he had a separate fund under his control but it was used to help alcoholic priests and to funnel money to priests behind the iron curtain, what was wrong with that? The lean, black haired, mildly befuddled looking Marshall Field IV, the owner of the *Sun-Times* who had been married in Holy Name Cathedral, responded to surfacing questions about the largely circumstantial nature of his paper's expose of Cody. He was not worried, he said, the paper had plenty of documentation and, if Cody attacked them, they would counterattack. Across the city, the enterprising, kinetic Warden, having learned of the existence of the Winters materials during a long night of bonhomie with out-of-town journalists, set about acquiring them for the *Chicago Lawyer.*

One account of how he accomplished this suggests that the stymied Sherwood, anxious to bleed out some support for his own theory about the ecclesiastical conspiracy to use the press to do its dirty work against Cody, read it to Warden in segments over the telephone. By Tuesday, Warden began freely telling other Chicago journalists that he would soon have 15,000 or 20,000 words from the Greeley transcripts that outlined "a plot to topple Cody" and that

Archbishop Bernardin "was apparently deeply involved in it." The atmosphere in his office turned circus-like as reporters dropped in to sample, as if they were hors d'oeuvres at the mad hatter's cocktail party, bits and pieces of what he planned to publish in the next issue of his newspaper. "Listen to this," he told this writer by phone, "Greeley tried to get Father Hesburgh of Notre Dame into the conspiracy. He asked him, 'Ted, do you want to get in on fixing the next papal election?' " The enthused Warden, sure that he was countering the *Sun-Times* revelations, was in no mood for tempered reflection about Father Greeley's statement that these were "fantasies." It all seemed too good not to be true. During that turbulent week Warden called Archbishop Bernardin's office in Cincinnati and asked to "speak to him about Deep Purple."

Archbishop Bernardin had mixed feelings when he was told of the call. On the one hand, it was clear to him that the bizarre material from Greeley's archives would soon be out in the open where it could be evaluated for what it was. On the other hand, that his own name had been used so frequently and arbitrarily in the fanciful scenario about having him made archbishop of Chicago so that he could leak consistory information placed him in a difficult, if not impossible, position. Even to tell the truth—that he had no knowledge of the extraordinary strategies that Greeley had dreamed out loud five years before—lent a spurious credibility to the affair. To deny its outlandish particulars would entangle him in endless coils of flypaper, and the more vigorously he attempted to shake himself free the more surely something would stick to him.

That Bernardin was innocent of any involvement in such papal conclave machinations was, however, well known to Roman authorities. For almost fifteen years, curial officials had dealt with him in various capacities, including his presidency of the American bishops, his membership on Roman congregations, and his participation in synodal meetings. Vatican leaders appreciated Bernardin's dutifulness and his discretion as well as his consistency in fulfilling the ideal of being a churchman in the traditional sense. That was why he had been entrusted with so many delicate assignments over the years. The same officials were also well acquainted with Father Greeley, who liked to describe himself as a "loudmouth Irish priest." Recently, the Vatican had received almost as many complaints about Greeley as it had about his nemesis, Cardinal Cody.

Personally, Bernardin had already been investigated carefully when it was generally thought Rome was planning to make him coadjutor archbishop of Chicago in order to relieve the crisis with Cody in the late seventies. That, however, was before the sputtering fuse-like sequence of events—including the deaths of Pope Paul VI and Pope John Paul I—touched off the explosives that blew a hole in their plans through which the aged but nimble Cody had quickly stepped. Bernardin surveyed the situation, not sparing himself in his evaluation: His career was on the line. No great institution, especially the Roman Catholic Church, could promote even its most excellent man if he continued, even accidentally, to be splashed with too much public mud. How, Bernardin must have wondered, could this unexpected trial have come about? And what could he do, other than diligently go about his business, to endure it successfully? As this seemingly random ordeal intensified, Bernardin, who was not heard to complain even by those working closely with him at the time, quietly realized that, although he could not control events around him, he could master himself, implementing the lessons he had learned in 1976, with the self-restraint that had been the hallmark of his personal and public life. He would do that for the good of the church and to defend his own integrity. If anything further went wrong, it would not be because of anything Bernardin would do or say. His best defense lay in being himself.

Perhaps the most important understanding Bernardin had gleaned from the bishops' problems in dealing with the media in 1976 was that a news story needed a new twist or a further development to stay alive. Often people complicated their own problems by trying to explain wild accusations, or clarify their motivations, thus adding fresh elements that not only expanded the story they were trying to reinterpret but guaranteed its survival. Such well intentioned efforts often involved the person in repeating the very accusations whose falsity he was trying to illustrate. With the media one was well advised to follow the scriptural admonition to be as wise as a serpent and guileless as a dove.

Bernardin was, as he understood about himself, an explainer by nature and had always tried to make himself completely available to the press. Now, however, as the air became saturated with madness again, he would take a different but very simple stand. Father Greeley had described his potentially dangerous transcripts as "fantasy." Bernardin would not criticize the priest or step into the minefield of contorted facts, such as his presence half a world a way in Cincinnati when Deep Purple was supposed to be Greeley's mole gathering secrets inside the papal conclave. Questioned by reporters, Bernardin would simply agree with Greeley that his transcripts were indeed fantasies and let it go at that.

The storm growled mightily the next Saturday when the Sunday, Sept. 27, 1981, edition of the *Chicago Tribune* hit the streets. The *Tribune's* story, which would, in excerpted form, be reprinted in other newspapers from coast to coast, featured a picture of Archbishop Bernardin and the headline, *The Plot to Get Cody*. Father Greeley's ruminations on getting rid of Cody and replacing him with Bernardin were quoted extensively. The sensational impact was well summed up by novelist John Gregory Dunne after he read it on Sunday morning in the *Los Angeles Times*. "La shit," the chronicler of the Catholic culture said, "has hit la fan."

Cardinal Cody took some comfort in the revelations that, in effect, portrayed him more as a victim than a tyrant and cast suspicion on his possible successor, Bernardin, and doubt on the judgment of his foremost priest critic, Greeley. He talked to Bernardin by telephone that weekend, assuring him that he understood the falsity of the accusations, that he knew Bernardin had nothing to do with them. Then, however, after conferring with his lawyers, he ordered his diocesan newspaper editor, Ed Wall, to send releases on the so-called revelations to every Catholic paper in Ohio. The decision was an attempt to bolster Cody's position by letting Bernardin feel the heat of the controversy in his own backyard.

The archbishop of Cincinnati was immediately swamped with calls from reporters asking for his comments. Scheduled for a mass in Dayton the next day, Bernardin understood that he would be surrounded by reporters and cameras. He issued a simple statement to the press, "Father Greeley has said that these are fantasies and that is what they are." This terse denial was carried in many of the Sunday newspapers and on the television news. It was the only public statement Bernardin would ever make about the matter. In Dayton the next day, he would avoid reporters, going against his friendly instincts toward the press as well as his own inclinations to explain matters in detail. His simple statement would have to speak for his own integrity as well as that of the church. In fact, his surgical approach, which avoided repeating the plot charges as well as adding new fuel to the original fire, worked exactly as he had hoped. By Monday the focus of the media had slipped back to Cardinal Cody and to Father Greeley himself.

Those close to Archbishop Bernardin during the ensuing months observed a man who plunged back into his work without a backward or sideward glance. He was absorbed with the development of the pastoral letter on nuclear weapons and was scheduled to travel to Rome on business and then to visit his relatives in Northern Italy before returning to Cincinnati at the end of October. If he remained intensely aware of the charges being lobbed back and forth like mortar shells across no man's land, he gave little evidence of it in his demeanor.

Greeley, keeping in touch with developments by telephone from the Hilton Hotel on Corfu, made efforts to lessen the impact of the revelations through statements issued by his lawyer. He complained of feeling "psychologically raped" by the Notre Dame editor Winters whom he publicly charged with having stolen his sealed papers. This accusation would eventually lead Greeley into a complicated tangle of lawsuits. Meanwhile, he talked to Sherwood of the otherwise satisfactory outcomes of the blow-up: Things had worked out much as he had hoped, his book, *The Cardinal Sins,* was selling wildly because of the incident and he was, he claimed, already "working on my second million." The priest would reappear to reap the other harvests of his newfound celebrity after things cooled down.

While Greeley continued his vacation and Bernardin pursued his duties with a Trappist's determined reserve, rumors swept the American Catholic landscape about the possible destruction of Bernardin's career by the unseemly publicity that had flowed from the publication of the Greeley papers. At a pre-football game president's luncheon at Notre Dame that October, Father Theodore Hesburgh interrupted a chat with novelist Norman Mailer to respond to some concerned clergy who wondered if anything could be done to support Archbishop Bernardin's reputation against the damage that Greeley might have done to it. One of them noted that in Greeley's novel, *The Cardinal Sins,* the real villain was not the character loosely based on Cody but rather the sibling figure, the man who in the book became archbishop of Chicago despite his polymorphous perverse sexual activity. "Perhaps," that priest said to the university president, "Father Greeley's target was Bernardin, the sibling figure—they're the same age and Joe is scheduled for the job Andy has always wanted—maybe he unconsciously wanted to prevent that all along." Father Hesburgh shook his head grimly. "I don't know about that," he said softly, "Andy's always been a loose cannon. I don't think anybody takes him seriously now. But I do know that if anybody tries to help Bernardin now, they'll make things worse. In my judgment, Joe will get through this okay. He can stand on his own reputation."

Bernardin had vowed self-control during this time and, despite the mounting rumors, the man who conscientiously kept his promises to others intended to keep this one to himself. Rome, insiders averred, was completely satisfied with the way the archbishop of Cincinnati had conducted himself throughout the season's difficult weeks. In fact, as Father Hesburgh had predicted, Bernardin's integrity spoke well in the self-imposed silence he observed as the fall slipped quickly toward winter. When Bernardin met with reporters in Rome near the end of October, he was not even asked about the incident that had glowed with white heat in everyone's consciousness just a month before.

The inglorious episode was not, however, quite finished. Carlton Sherwood, patting an empty briefcase that he claimed contained proof of Cardinal Cody's bribing his way out of trouble with the Vatican with a $500,000 check, accepted an assignment from editors at the *New York Times Magazine* to do a piece on the Greeley–Cody relationship. He also signed a book contract, promising to tell the whole story of Chicago church scandals between its covers. In one of the double agent roles that Sherwood relished, he was back in touch with the priest writer shortly after Greeley returned to the United States in the third week of October. Greeley, as Sherwood later related to John Conroy, had already embraced the Gannett investigator's conspiracy theory. "After that," Sherwood said of the priest, "he got really pissed...Greeley was being used, we were all being used. I was being used to get the *Sun-Times* on the story, Greeley was being used by Bernardin and the Vatican to get me or somebody else on the story to get the *Sun-Times* on the story." Sherwood and the priest would, as November collapsed into December, cooperate in what the reporter described as a "mutually manipulative" manner in a strenuous effort to prove this theory. What Sherwood desperately needed was the non-existent "dossier," or supposed official report on a Vatican investigation of Cody. Greeley, according to Sherwood, wanted a way to blame somebody else for the untoward events for which his papers had been the scenario.

But, as in previous months. Sherwood had no luck in unearthing the document. Greeley, the Gannett reporter said at the time, had grown increasingly bitter at Bernardin for what he somehow construed as the archbishop's ongoing betrayal of him. Everything was really Bernardin's fault because of the way the prelate had seemed to befriend him when he was really monitoring him. Twice, invoking other Chicagoans as intermediaries, Greeley sent peculiar messages to Bernardin, half threatening him, half denouncing him as only "marginally better than Cody." Bernardin could only save himself, he intimated, through cooperating with Sherwood who had the goods on the archbishop from the interview in the summer of 1980. Cooperate, Greeley suggested, and Sherwood would now give him what the priest called "source protection." Otherwise, the truth about the Cincinnati archbishop's conspiracy to use the press would come out. "Don't ever threaten me again," Greeley wrote in this message from mid-December, "Pass that up as high as it has to go. Ask, don't threaten. . . . Don't call me or write me. The less I have to do with you the better."

Bernardin made no response to Sherwood's requests or Greeley's unusual communications. "That pissed Greeley off even more," Sherwood reported at the time, explaining that the priest wanted him to write the article for the *New York Times Magazine* as a vindication of his own position. "He gave me a copy of Jadot's letter in French to him and he promised me all his inside sources," the Gannett investigator said wearily as Christmas drew closer, "but there weren't any really, just one lawyer who had lots of gossip and not much more." As the holidays passed, he became convinced that most of the tales he had heard, such as that of the half million dollar check Cody had supposedly handed Pope Paul VI in order to buy more time for himself, were somebody's wishful thinking. Sherwood lost interest and late in January 1982 the editors of the *New York Times Magazine* officially dropped the project. Sherwood's proposed book, promised for 1983, was ultimately cancelled for nondelivery of a manuscript.

The enfeebled Cardinal Cody sat at the center of a slightly forced celebration of his fiftieth anniversary as a priest in December 1981 and, save for his "last hurrah" at midnight mass a few weeks later was barely seen in public again before his death in the early hours of April 25, 1982. Rome, it was reliably reported, had reopened its scrutiny of every possible candidate to succeed Cody. In the light of the tumult that had been set off in Chicago, the examination had to be achingly thorough and exacting. The man who succeeded Cody would have to have a personality and a record that could successfully stand up to an investigation worthy of the KGB. His character had to be as deep and as sound as his devotion to the church.

Just after the Fourth of July, Archbishop Bernardin travelled quietly to Rome at the summons of the pope. Pope John Paul II received him a day later and told him that Bernardin was his choice to become the new archbishop of Chicago. On Saturday morning, July 10, 1982, the appointment was officially announced from Rome. One long chapter in Bernardin's life, and in the history of Chicago, had come to a close. Another one would open when he was officially installed on the feast of St. Louis, August 25.

XVII

B ernardin, covered as if he were a rock star or roy-
alty by the media, managed a smooth transition to
Chicago. He skillfully kept the mayor, Jane Byrne,
at a gentlemanly distance as he arrived. The coquettish mayor, running behind in the early polls regarding her bid for the Democratic re-
nomination in the primary that would come six months later,
attempted to make the most of her role as official host for the new
archbishop's arrival. Bernardin was gracious but he was cautious
about being photographed with her or with any other politician or
business leader who might want to use such a picture for a public relations advantage in the heavily Catholic city. He tasted one of the
ironies of Chicago life when, after the exclusive dinner of welcome
hosted by Mayor Byrne at the Drake Hotel, he discovered that the
expensive commemorative cups were engraved in honor of Archbishop Louis Bernardin.

In his first words as archbishop from the cathedral pulpit on the
day of his installation, Bernardin staked out a position of civic independence through asking a series of rhetorical questions that were,
in fact, already well formed in the ever calculating heads of the dignitaries looking up expectantly at him from the crowded pews. Appraisal was everything in Chicago, from the now gone stockyards to
the then booming trading pits, yes, Chicagoans liked to fix costs and
gains early. Would the new archbishop favor LaSalle Street, Bernardin queried, City Hall, or some other power center in Chicago? He

asked but did not answer the questions that concerned those spread before him. Diplomatically but clearly, Bernardin's initial statements defined himself as a man declaring his friendly independence, a religious leader who would not allow the power of his spiritual office to be co-opted by any of these power centers.

He had already visited Cardinal Cody's now secure crypt in the tomb of the Chicago archbishops in a western suburban cemetery. By not avoiding Cody's ghost, Bernardin quickly overtook it with what people perceived as his own direct and accessible presence. Although his being named a cardinal just a few months later completed the difficult task of transforming Cody into memory, Bernardin had, merely by being himself, taken many steps in that direction by the end of the year.

One of the most significant of these was his intuitive decision to allow the team of reporters from the *Sun-Times* to interview him late one evening deep in December. Roy Larson, whom Bernardin had spotted covering a dinner welcoming the new archbishop, was asked by the prelate to invite his fellow reporters, Gene Mustain, and William Griffin to meet him afterwards in his North Side residence. Bernardin had prepared a report for release on December 17 announcing the appointment of a special audit committee for the archdiocese as well as a report on his own review of allegations of financial misconduct on the part of his predecessor. His conclusion, buttressed by the accounting firm of Peat, Markwick, Mitchell & Company, was that, on the basis of available records and interviews, "it has been estimated that the Cardinal had spendable personal receipts of approximately $38,000 per year . . . the available data indicate that his total personal expenditures did not exceed the total estimated personal receipts." Allowing that "Cardinal Cody did not always follow preferred accounting procedures" which "resulted in some confusion in the records," Bernardin judged that these were "the result of a failure to attend to detail and the pressing demands of an extraordinarily busy schedule." In a gentlemanly but clear voice, Bernardin observed that "I now bring this matter to a close."

The reporters, feeling that Cody's shade might still be inhabiting the venerable residence, were eager to question Bernardin. Despite

Marshall Field IV's assertions the year before, the paper did not have any conclusive documentation, at least in publishable form, of financial misconduct on Cody's part. Bernardin allowed them to quiz him intensively for more than two hours, their aggressive manner sometimes testing his own fabled patience so severely that he had to remind them that he was not the one on trial. But he also understood by their manner that they had no more information of their own to substantiate their stories about Cody.

At the end of the long trying evening, however, the journalists became reluctantly convinced that Bernardin was telling them everything he knew. That, as a matter of fact, was not much. Cody had intermingled some monies but not in any way that seemed criminal or that exceeded his authority as the corporation sole of the archdiocese. If other evidence existed, it had not yet been discovered but, from what Bernardin himself had seen, there was nothing he could tell the reporters to augment their story.

He spoke, as they knew, only about the records available to him. That obviously did not include any material that may have been removed from the files before his arrival. Nor was there information about funds Cody might have amassed by inheritance or investment before he came to Chicago in 1965. Cody, in fact, turned out to have been a shrewd chooser of stocks for the archdiocesan portfolio. In an ironic footnote to his career, these investments appreciated substantially in value in the stock market rally that began in the summer after his death. Still, his methods remain cloaked in some mystery.

As the investigators grimly descended the old fashioned staircase, Bernardin realized that although the evening had been an ordeal, his hunch, the sweet inheritance of his Italian genes, had been proved correct. He had put the *Sun-Times* investigation behind him for good. A few weeks later he was named a prince of the church and within a short time the image of the jowled and troubled Cody yielded, when Chicagoans talked about "the cardinal," to that of the lean, brown eyed, gently smiling Bernardin.

If his successful dealing with the skeptical reporters was rooted in the deepest layers of his Mediterranean sensibility, Bernardin's eager immersion in the details of his new responsibilities was powered by the other side of his personality, his almost infinite capacity for taking pains as well as finding delight in administrative tasks. The chore of familiarizing himself with the archdiocese was formidable. It necessarily involved paper work, numberless individual and group meetings as well as travel around the archdiocese. Nonetheless, Bernardin saved a measure of his attention for his ongoing work of chairing the preparation of the pastoral letter on nuclear arms. His becoming archbishop of Chicago and a cardinal underscored the prominence of this project, making it even more difficult for the Reagan administration to dismiss or to deride its intentions.

Despite his long days and frequent travels, Bernardin was also working, with the assistance of Father J. Bryan Hehir of the Washington staff on an idea that he had been mulling for years. He wanted to develop the strong pro-life position that the bishops had taken shortly after the *Roe v. Wade* Supreme Court decision. He was fully committed to the program that the bishops had adopted and which Terence Cardinal Cooke of New York had chaired for several years. Even before Bernardin had become president of the bishops in 1974, however, he had been thinking about the political and theological vulnerability of the church to the charge that it was really interested only in the single issue of banning abortion. That easy accusation, a ''one issue'' program, lent itself to easy caricature as well as a glib and demeaning media translation of the church's broader concerns and intentions.

Bernardin was convinced that, if the pro-life agenda was to move forward successfully, the other threats to the supreme value of life had to be linked in solid and informed fashion to the central task of opposing abortion. A believing Catholic, in Bernardin's judgment, must promote life organically, preserving and enhancing its profound significance positively and defending it against all negative threats to its sacred character. Otherwise, the pro-life movement might seem distorted and could come under the control of the extreme right wing of anti-abortionist activists. That would cripple its political appeal in the struggle for a constitutional amendment to overturn *Roe v. Wade*. In addition, the task of raising the consciousness of the country about the values of life depended on an intelligent broadening and deepening of the basic philosophical and theological foundations of the pro-life position.

The first version of the pastoral letter on nuclear arms had been completed in June 1982, just before Bernardin's appointment as archbishop of Chicago. It had been circulated for comments to the nation's 280 Catholic bishops and to 150 individuals. At the same time, this draft, still perceived by the bishops' committee as "in process," was sent to the Vatican and to a number of the bishops of Western Europe who were also preparing letters on the subject. Bernardin, patron of collegiality, understood these moves as important steps in implementing that procedure fully. He also understood the necessity for sensitive ecclesiastical diplomacy in soliciting comments from European church leaders. They, after all, lived on the front lines, where the land bore the scars of the century's wars and their message of remembered carnage. They viewed the geopolitical realities of the continent from a different angle of vision than did the Americans.

Some church officials in Rome, Bernardin also appreciated, were hesitant about endorsing the work of the American bishops for another reason. These Roman prelates assented to the notion of collegiality but they were made uneasy by the typically pragmatic way in which the American church had so vigorously and promptly institutionalized it. This rapid and efficient development of the national conference in the United States seemed classically American and lacking in the amorphous subtlety they savored. It smacked of Dodsworth, of the ambitious thirteen colonies, of a superchurch in the superpower, able to afford the self-confidence that seemed to well out of its democratic presence.

Bernardin did not dismiss this as European crankiness but viewed it as the understandable reaction of countries with very different traditions and national experience from those of the United States. The best approach, again typically American and classically Bernardin, was to deal with the matter straightforwardly and openly, letting everyone participate in the discussion. At the same time, he recognized the importance of preserving the American identity of the pastoral document. Equally significant, in his judgment, was the vindication, through this experience, of the sound theological structure of the national conference itself. It was precisely because the conference had achieved notable maturity that some Romans worried about its getting out of their control, of its becoming a threat to their conception of central church authority. This would be a constant problem, Bernardin grasped, for there were certain Romans who, despite Vatican II's justification of them, did not want such national conferences to become independent. Neither, of course, did Bernardin, for whom preserving the theological integrity of the American conference in loyal union with Rome would be a preoccupation, if not a calling, for the rest of the decade.

By the time the summer of his installation and adjustment to Chicago began, seven hundred pages of reactions had come to Bernardin's committee. Its members met for three days to review these and to decide that it would not be prudent to rush a second draft into circulation to their brother bishops. Neither would they force a vote on the interim document at the meeting of the bishops in November. The issues, the five bishops concluded, were too complex, many revisions were yet required, and the time extension could only benefit the process out of which the letter was to take its shape. This added interval would permit the committee to educate the people about the core issues of the proposed document: Questions about the morality of first-strike use of nuclear weapons, the need for a halt to the development of nuclear arms, and a careful examination of the government's stated targeting policy in regard to civilian populations.

Even more delicate was an inquiry into the traditional "just war" theory that the Catholic Church had taught since the time of St. Augustine in the fifth century. Could that position, often invoked in history, which held that Christians could engage in war in certain circumstances, be maintained in the starkly transformed world of nuclear weapons? Could the moral imagination make room for these instruments of warfare in any conceivable situation? The "just war" theory seemed to many Catholics an article from their catechism, one that embossed the proud record of Catholic patriotism in the defense of the republic. What would any change mean for the thousands of Catholics who were serving nobly and conscientiously in the armed forces or who were working in defense industries? To reexamine this time honored teaching would, at the very least, trouble the conscience of every Catholic who had accepted and structured the world according to its prescriptions.

The sensitivity of such an undertaking argued for more time and even wider consultation. This would allow Catholics to study and mediate on the applicability of the "just war" proposition in the nuclear age. From serious reflection, heartfelt and carefully thought out statements would be added to the ongoing dialogue. Long before purified of any naivete about any White House's tactics in trying to make the best for itself of any positions adopted by the bishops, Bernardin and his colleagues also felt that an extended period of debate and discussion would bring their document-in-process to the serious attention of the Reagan administration.

The same James Baker who had watched as the bishops had inadvertently been manipulated by the Ford White House was now Reagan's chief of staff. He would surely be alert to the dangers of the Republican president's suddenly coming into conflict in the middle of his first term with the leaders of the largest religious grouping in the country. The stakes were not small for, just the year before, Reagan had committed the country to the largest military build-up ever undertaken in peacetime. The plans had included the building of 100 B-1 bombers, 100 MX missiles, and, in a dramatic if unintentional metaphor for the depersonalized terrors of the era, the production of the neutron bomb which killed human beings but did not destroy buildings.

By the second week of October, a second draft had been completed and distributed to all the bishops and was discussed on the floor of the Washington, D.C., meeting in November. The strongest voice of opposition came from Archbishop Philip Hannan of New Orleans who had served as a paratroop chaplain in World War II. During his many years as an auxiliary bishop of Washington, D.C., he had been known as one of the most ardent of the cold warriors who had supported for a generation a strong moral and military defense against communism. The battle experienced Hannan apologized as he rose to his feet. He did not, he said softly, wish to hurt anybody's feelings but he felt that the entire document should be scrapped and that a statement of Pope John Paul II on disarmament be adopted instead. "Nuclear arms," he said, rehearsing a favored Reagan theme, "by their very existence have preserved peace in Europe for 30 years." The letter should be abandoned, he concluded, because "there's no unanimity among the bishops or the people on this issue." A strong if expected stand, everyone judged, by a man with the impeccable credentials of having lived in the inferno of battle itself.

Terence Cardinal Cooke, the self-effacing archbishop of New York who oversaw the military ordinariate, had previously raised questions about whether the document was sensitive enough to the loss of freedom in totalitarian nations and to the dedicated work of Catholics in the armed services. Other bishops, including the equally mild but outspoken anti-war activist, Raymond Hunthausen of Seattle, rose to defend the work in progress. He was joined by one of the nation's most skilled prelates, Archbishop John Quinn of San Francisco, a leader who, perhaps more than any other member of the hierarchy, shared Bernardin's awareness of nuance and timing in dealing with ecclesiastical realities. Although the outspoken Bishop Joseph McNicholas of Springfield, Illinois, who matched his conservative reputation by wearing the high roman collar popular in the thirties, suggested that the letter should give more support to the nation's traditions and contain more "flag waving," the suggestions by other bishops centered mostly on the use of scripture and moral reasoning to buttress the document's conclusions.

While Bernardin sat impassively at his desk in the Capital Hilton ballroom listening to the bishops' discussion proceed pretty much as he had anticipated, National Security Adviser William Clark was making a preemptive strike on the still unfinished pastoral in behalf of the Reagan administration. The administration had, only a few weeks before, revealed a budget deficit of $110 billion, a substantial portion of which was related to the defense build-up. In addition, the Nov. 2, 1982 elections had seen the Democrats win 75 percent of the governors' races and 60 percent of the congressional seats. Clark felt that it was already past the time to contest the bishops' on what might, if unchecked, cause unnecessary problems for the president.

Clark, his expression gloomy as an old pastor's watching people come late for mass, distributed to the press a seven-page letter addressed to Bernardin. The archbishop of Chicago was not, however, afforded the courtesy of seeing the letter before it was given to the media. Reagan aides believed that embarrassing opponents was an acceptable element in their no nonsense, semi-macho style. Clark's critique of the bishops' work made headlines across the country. How, the reporters were eager to know, would Bernardin and his colleagues respond to this assault on their labors? It was clear to the journalists that Clark's letter was an undisguised attempt to influence public opinion against the bishops as well as the deliberations of the bishops themselves. Bernardin remained calm as the giant glistening eye of the inquiring media once more focused on him. The bishops, he announced calmly, would accept Mr. Clark's letter as one more contribution to its work of gathering opinion and criticism.

"We were not intimidated," Bernardin said in response to reporters' questions about the incident. What then, the journalists continued, did the bishops feel about the president's judgment, from which he did not exempt the bishops, that advocates of a nuclear freeze were unwitting agents of the Kremlin? Bernardin smiled, absolving Reagan of any bad intention. "I don't," he added, "worry about things like that. It's inevitable when you discuss matters of this kind. . .there is going to be a great deal of feeling. It makes the process a little more interesting." Well, how did the bishops feel about charges that they had misread the administration's disarmament negotiations in Geneva? Bernardin paused, and, as *Washington Post* columnist Mary McGrory noted, replied dryly, "We will see who is misreading whom in due course."

The manner in which nuclear deterrence was dealt with in the letter's conclusion did not please all the bishops. While it matched the opinion of Pope John Paul II that it was morally acceptable to possess nuclear weapons as a step toward disarmament, its phrasing and the balance of the array of supporting arguments deserved further study and modification. The underlying question that troubled many bishops and other observers centered on the moral authority of the letter. Was it to be considered simply a series of questions raised by the bishops to underscore their moral concerns, or was it to possess substantial authority that bound Catholics to its judgments? Clearly this epistemological problem had to be resolved prudently and effectively. Bernardin knew the question had to be dealt with, but for the moment he was quietly pleased with the fact that the question of war and peace had been raised so clearly in the consciousness of American Catholics. The letter remained a document in progress, however, and another round of comments was solicited in mid-December so that a third draft could be prepared late in the winter. Close to four hundred pages of additional observations were received.

Meanwhile, the draft had evoked the European reactions Bernardin's committee had solicited. In January 1983, to provide a forum for an exchange between the French, West German, other European conferences such as England, Belgium, and Italy, and the American bishops, the Vatican Secretariat of State convened a meeting in Rome. The American delegation headed by Bernardin, who had just been named a cardinal, also included Archbishop John Roach, president of the bishops' conference. Not all the European conferences were as confident as the Americans of the wide collegial process before preparing their own letters and the Germans had dispensed with it altogether. The meeting was a careful exchange between the new and the old worlds, with Bernardin and Roach in the roles of Franklin and Jefferson, breathing the vigor of their freshly born nation, as they represented it, both in their personal styles and their methods, at the Parisian court. Rome, remembering the so-called heresy of "Americanism" from the beginning of the century, nodded toward but remained uneasy with the pragmatic democracy of the United States. That, of course, had for generations been one of Europe's problems with America.

Bernardin and Roach, having been told by the convenors of the Rome meeting to keep their discussions quiet, composed, on their return, a joint memorandum to guide the members of committee in their further refinement of the letter. They were, therefore, surprised early in March when the minutes of the Rome conference were distributed from the Vatican to all American bishops. Roach and Bernardin quickly released their own memo on the session and drew up an additional message to put that meeting into what they considered its true perspective.

What had motivated Roman officials to authorize what many observers considered at least an imprudent and at worst an unwarranted interference in the American process? One American bishop identified then Monsignor Jan Schotte, a close adviser to the pope who was later named an archbishop, as "the number one source of opposition" to the work of the American bishops. The obvious intent of the premature release of the information, like that of the Reagan administration, seemed to be to influence the bishops and the vote they were to take in May on the final draft of the letter. Rumors were also floated suggesting that the pope himself was not entirely pleased with the U.S. pastoral. These developments, at a crucial moment in the committee's work, injected a note of unneeded tension and drama into its otherwise totally absorbing and dutiful labors.

In addition, government aides began, in a way that suggested that their asides were not accidental, to chide the bishops in offhand comments to reporters. So, too, a group of Catholic professors also began to criticize the bishops' work, warning that it would compromise their efforts to speak authoritatively on other issues. Another higher level of criticism, developed principally by theologian J. Brian Benestad of the University of Scranton, centered on what he considered the bishops' misemphasis on the use of policy statements over individual moral and spiritual development in order to effect social transformations. In a letter dated Jan. 15, 1983, Clark advised the bishops that their second draft misrepresented the government's targeting policy. The United States did not, he claimed, target civilian populations.

Bernardin and his collaborators requested evidence to substantiate Clark's assertion in order to incorporate it into their ongoing work. Once again the process itself served well by making room for even another governmental accusation without disrupting its continuity or deflecting its purpose. Bernardin's committee, in receiving Clark's newest critique, announced that it reserved the right to judge the targeting issue according to the traditional principle of proportionality, that is, weighing whether the destruction of military targets could be justified if, as an inevitable result, large numbers of noncombatants would be killed.

In the final draft, the Bernardin committee not only incorporated factual material from government sources but also amplified the letter's theological and scriptural argumentation and its statements about the totalitarian nature of communist rule. The ultimate version of the letter was intended to examine the moral implication of the threat of nuclear war and to constitute as full and fair a presentation of the American church's thinking as possible. The bishop collaborators also dealt with the question of the moral authority that they wished the letter to have. They further clarified the distinction they had already made for themselves between general moral principles and general church teaching on the one hand, and the practical application of these principles and teaching in specific situations on the other. Their sentiment was that one did not attach the most compelling authority of the church to practical moral judgments that could be approached by people of good will from very different viewpoints. This distinction, respecting the consciences of sincere believers, would be worked carefully into the document's final draft.

In mid-March Bernardin convened his committee one last time at the International Inn in Washington, D.C. Even Bernardin's moderate optimism was tested on that long night when it appeared that the letter might, a little more than a month before the scheduled final vote, founder on differences that, like the restless dead, kept rising from their mist-laden graves. Bishop O'Connor, genuinely anguished, wondered whether the letter could ever properly acknowledge the American Catholic tradition of patriotism. Bernardin, the patient seeker of agreements, began to doubt, as the hours ground past, whether the committee would complete its work successfully. He had been through long sessions before, however, and firmly believed that the process would work if the committee members could continue to invest themselves in it. Its success also depended on his confreres' dutifulness and his own well known patience and stamina, his readiness to stick with a question as the clock chimed the night away, ever alert for the opening for compromise and agreement.

The five weary bishops worked together for nine hours, achieving what one participant later described as a "minor miracle" in completing the third version of the unprecedented pastoral. They would distribute the draft to the rest of the bishops in the first week of April and vote on it during the first week of May in Chicago. Well publicized modifications, such as transforming the call for a "halt" in the production of nuclear arms to a "curb," did not, in the committee's judgment, represent a surrender to any pressure from the government. They better illustrated, however, the exploratory nature of the document.

As presented, the letter's main conclusions were these:

- That nuclear war was a morally unacceptable means of resolving differences between nations.

- That "offensive war of any kind is not morally justified."

- That "the intentional killing of innocent civilians is always wrong."

- That "first-strike" attacks by nuclear weapons constitute an "unjustifiable moral risk."

- That the bishops support "immediate bilateral, verifiable agreement to curb the testing, production, and development of new nuclear weapons."

- That nuclear deterrence "is not an adequate strategy as a long-term basis for peace; it is a transitional strategy justifiable only in conjunction with a resolute determination to pursue arms control and disarmament."

- That a nation has the right to defend itself against "an unjust aggressor."

The bishops convened at the Palmer House in Chicago on May 2, 1983. A few blocks away in City Hall, white alderman Edward R. Vrdolyak was at the same hour challenging the new black mayor, Harold Washington, for effective control of the city council. This battle, which emphasized the racial divisions that were one of Bernardin's main concerns as Chicago's Catholic pastor, provided, in its rowdiness and incivility, an acidic flavored counterpoint to the polite and well ordered gathering of prelates half a mile away. Seated in the hotel ballroom at desks that made it resemble a large classroom, the

American bishops, decorous and earnest as the most dutiful pupils, set out to review their document and to discuss and vote on several hundred amendments that had arisen from within the episcopal membership.

Beneath the intense gaze of dozens of journalists perched on the balcony that encircled the old fashioned ballroom, the bishops proceeded systematically, doing in a sense what they did best, scrupulously reviewing the paperwork and voting according to the parliamentary procedure that guaranteed that the pastoral letter would truly be a function of their acting collegially as a national conference. For Bernardin, the successful passage of the letter was not only a triumph for his committee but for the organization to which he had given many years of his life.

Effective collegiality might sound romantic when described in popular journals but, in practice, its success was the fruit of arduous meetings, the review of hundreds of pages of testimony, and the study and restudy of several drafts of the proposed final work. The conference functioned according to the collaborative model in which Bernardin had placed so much faith. As he had hoped, the process outweighed the impact, one way or the other, of individual personalities. It had been able to absorb outside criticisms and pressures from places as different as the White House and the Vatican. The bishops felt that they had ample opportunity to express their own concerns and those of their people. The resulting letter, strongly applauded by all those interested in arms control and peace, proved to be an extraordinarily effective instrument for raising the consciousness of Catholics about the question of nuclear arms.

A later survey revealed that the process and the resulting pastoral letter had influenced the thinking of Catholics in a significant way. Bernardin himself received the 1983 Albert Einstein Peace Prize from Paul Warnke, chief United States negotiator at the SALT II talks in a Washington ceremony later in that year. As he accepted it, he understood that he was doing it in the name of the conference of bishops. He appreciated the irony of its being bestowed by a respected representative of the same government that continued to view the bishops' interests in national policy with suspicion. The new Cardinal archbishop of Chicago also understood that, at least in part, Cardinal Dearden's dream of a national conference that could meditate publicly relevant moral issues, which he himself had nurtured to maturity, had come fully of age at last.

All this was confirmed for him by the remark he heard as he left town. Republican administration members, reviewing the bishops' influence through this pastoral letter and their already well-established positions against government policy in Central America, were beginning to think that the bishops should be courted rather than ridiculed. "Take a bishop out to lunch" was becoming a popular saying among the powerful in the nation's capital.

XVIII

The last sweltering weeks of 1983's summer were slipping away like the calendar pages in thirties movies. So, too, unknown to most of his flock, was the life of the 62-year-old archbishop of New York, Terence Cardinal Cooke. In one of the most tumultuous cities in the world, Cooke, with a pale, full moon face that was a banner of his immigrant Irish lineage, had always projected an attractive inner serenity as well as the kindliness of a favorite confessor. Sophisticated Manhattan, easing toward the Labor Day weekend, was shocked to read in the Saturday edition of the *New York Times* that the cardinal had announced that the leukemia, which he had battled with drug therapy for twenty years, had raged out of control, that his illness was terminal.

In addition to his regular treatment, Cooke was cared for tenderly by his secretary, Father Edward O'Brien, in the small second floor bedroom of his Madison Avenue residence. President Ronald Reagan paid him a brief visit in the hushed old house that had witnessed so much American Catholic history and the people of New York grieved at the illness which, from all reports, Cooke bore with no complaints.

Cooke's imminent death was a further signal, however, about the changing nature of American Catholicism. Although he was relatively young, he was considered to be an extension of the influence of his predecessor, Francis Cardinal Spellman. The ringed hand he raised in blessing over the towers and tenements of New York was attached to an arm of Catholic power that stretched back half a century. Institutional Catholicism understood that as the beloved Cooke's pilgrimage neared its end so, too, a decade and a half after his death, Spellman's influence was finally disintegrating. Ever absorbed in speculation about archiepisopal appointments, the clerical culture of the church buzzed wildly about Cooke's possible successor, for this appointment would also tell which American archbishop now held the title of ecclesiastical prince maker. Before these gossipy exchanges had hit their stride, however, Providence, as darkly garbed as Fate, moved suddenly to expand and complicate the mystery of the ongoing transformation of the episcopal dominance in the American church.

The native of the Azores who had become the first non-Irish archbishop of Boston, Humberto Cardinal Medeiros, entered the hospital for emergency heart surgery and died there, a few weeks short of his 68th birthday, on September 17. Less than a year and a half after Cardinal Cody had taken his last labored breath, two more Cardinal archbishops of major American sees had also been fatally stricken. Boston and New York, as old as the country, steeped in the traditions and achievements of the immigrant church, were suddenly empty. With Bernardin in Chicago as the undisputed moderate leader of the American church, who would be chosen for these vacant archdioceses? And what would these pending assignments mean about the holders of power in institutional Catholicism? Such questions were high octane fuel for the now humming engines of the ecclesiastical rumor mill.

Three weeks after Cardinal Medeiros succumbed, exhausted, some said, by the burden of paying off Cardinal Cushing's debts, Cardinal Cooke died, a saint in the eyes of many because of his patient endurance of a wrenching illness, on October 6. Archbishop John Roach, president of the National Conference of Bishops, recognized that the church, especially since the Cody incident, would deliberate carefully before making appointments to such significant posts. He, however, was faced with a more practical difficulty because the respected Cooke had been chairman of the bishops' pro-life committee. Since the bishops' "Respect Life" program of activities was such a cornerstone of all their pastoral positions, including that of the just issued peace pastoral, Roach understood that he needed a man to replace Cooke who would be a credible leader, that is, someone who already enjoyed the confidence of his brother bishops and of the culture at large. He did not have the luxury of time because the bishops' annual meeting was only a few weeks off.

He called Cardinal Bernardin in Chicago. "Joe," he asked, "can you help us out?" He went on to explain what Bernardin already understood: The success of the "Respect Life" program depended on fresh dynamic leadership from a bishop whose authority to lead was already well established. "I'll accept if you understand," Bernardin responded, "how I believe we must approach this question at this time." The Cardinal archbishop of Chicago summarized his theological and political reflection of the last several years. He would, as his record clearly demonstrated, be as strong an opponent of abortion as Cardinal Cooke had been but he would add some other elements that he considered essential for the success of the church's crusade in behalf of the preservation and enhancement of life.

For years, Bernardin had been troubled by what appeared to be the isolation of the anti-abortion question from other pro-life issues. Not all pro-life matters were of equal importance, and each required its own moral analysis, Bernardin understood, but all were rooted in the same basic Catholic position about the sacredness of life. There had to be some linkage between these issues in order to reveal a consistent theological position. Bernardin had wrestled with these concepts even before the years of studying and applying them in the preparation of the pastoral letter on peace.

In addition, the pro-life activities of the bishops would founder if they could not be made more appealing to the vast array of priests and others who served in the front ranks of pastoral work. A more cohesive and consistent position that recognized a spectrum of pro-life issues, ranging from peace through capital punishment, would energize the priests, clergy, and laypeople in direct contact with the Catholic population in a positive way. Not only would this move gain greater support from Catholics and others but it would keep the pro-life movement from falling completely under the control of the right wing conservatives who were becoming its dominant sponsors. The latter, in the judgment of many, maintained a narrow focus that excluded linkage with any other issues, thus alienating large numbers of people who, although pro-life in their convictions, were convinced that the problem had to be placed in a richer context of moral concerns. Such people felt, for example, that you could not be against abortion without being against activities, some of them government sponsored, that endangered innocent civilians in the cause of destabilizing central American governments.

Roach appreciated and agreed with Bernardin's position. "I understand," he responded, "that we have to broaden our horizon." With that commitment of support, Bernardin accepted Roach's invitation to replace Cardinal Cooke on what the bishops viewed as one of their most significant committees. Bernardin, who had some five years before expressed his first vision of the linkage of pro-life issues before the convention of the Knights of Columbus, immediately contacted Father J. Bryan Hehir to explain the direction in which he hoped to lead this movement. Hehir, the priest intellectual who had made such a substantial contribution to the development of the pastoral letter on peace and who was also working with Archbishop Weakland on the forthcoming pastoral on the economy, immediately agreed to assist Bernardin in this new enterprise.

The thin, intense Hehir, his eyes bright beneath a Henry James brow fringed with hair as black as his clerical suit, was a soft-spoken, dedicated priest who, despite his intellectual interests and special assignment, lived in a parish where he could hear confessions and offer mass for the people. He would soon become the target for savage criticism from those who challenged the bishops' new public reflections on public policy issues. Some of these attacks arose from extremists on the right who characterized the bishops' position on peace as the fruit of burnt out leftist intellectual theory. Others, uncomfortable with the swift development of the conference as a national entity, would focus on Hehir and some of his colleagues as the staff gray eminences who manipulated the bishops' thinking from behind the scenes. Some critics, including Father Andrew Greeley, his own niche in the church still eluding him, attacked Hehir as a symbol of what he considered the intellectually bankrupt support people who were stealthily influencing policy development in the bishops conference. The peace pastoral, in Greeley's judgment, had been a weak document that, in effect, sold out the defense of Western Europe and made it vulnerable to Russian conquest.

Father Hehir, however, ignored such blasts, much as Bernardin himself had learned to do, as he joined the Chicago cardinal in the task of spelling out carefully and systematically his long hoped for braiding of the pro-life issues together. He proved an ideal working partner for Bernardin for their relationship was rooted in shared theological convictions as well as commitments both to the universal church and the conference of American bishops. This professionalism—with its concentrated blend of bureaucratic obsessiveness and searching theological reasoning—depended to some extent on Hehir's intuitive grasp of Bernardin's way of approaching problems. This intellectual sympathy undergirded their extensive collaboration on a series of public addresses that, in effect, changed the terms of the national dialogue on the pro-life program of the bishops.

Self-effacing although completely candid and forthcoming in his work with the bishops, Father Hehir would be defended vigorously by Bernardin. In a 1985 interview, the cardinal not only praised Hehir's dedication and pastoral zeal but also stated that, despite the noisy charges that had been leveled against the priest, none of the unfair criticism had ever been "substantiated." Still, Hehir, who would be publicly recognized by the MacArthur Foundation a few years later through an award in its celebrated fellows program, continued to serve the church silently, a prime example of one who understood, if he did not relish, the ironic Vatican saying that Bernardin had come to understand years before, "The Roman Catholic Church is never grateful."

After Roach's announcement of the Chicago archbishop's acceptance of the chair of the ad hoc pro-life committee at the November 1983 bishops' meeting, Bernardin spoke to his assembled confreres. He devoted the first portion of his remarks to the memory of Cardinal Cooke and his exemplary pastoral leadership. Then he turned to his long meditated vision of the opportunities that were open to the conference in expanding their lynch-pin issue of defending the life of the unborn by joining that to the defense of life wherever its value was threatened in the culture. The 250 voting bishops listened attentively, as Bernardin later recalled, and approved of his agenda. They did so, however, without emotional enthusiasm, as if they had not yet worked through the implications of Bernardin's proposals in their heads or their hearts. They were not diffident but neither did they send Bernardin forth on his mission with the enthusiasm of their convinced support.

Several months before this, Bernardin had agreed to deliver the Gannon lecture at Fordham University, named after a former president of that Jesuit institution, a New York landmark of Catholic education with campuses in the Bronx and in Manhattan. The cardinal decided that this talk, the original subject of which was the peace pastoral, would be a fitting opportunity, within the late Cardinal Cooke's own archdiocese, to begin his public reflections on the need for constructively joining the life issues together. Father Hehir, aware of the fact that Bernardin was about to make news by this fresh treatment of a pro-life position that had seemed until then a familiar one note melody, advised the *New York Times,* through its religion editor, Kenneth Briggs, of the potential significance of the event. He also supplied the paper with an advance text of Bernardin's talk which he was scheduled to deliver twice, one on each campus on Dec. 6, 1983.

Hehir's instincts had not misinformed him. The editors of the *Times* recognized immediately that a major shift was being introduced into the national debate about abortion. Much to Bernardin's surprise, the December 7 edition of the *Times* featured his talk on the front page and, implementing its tradition as a newspaper of record, published lengthy excerpts as well. Overnight Bernardin had transformed the perception of the Catholic Church's pro-life endeavor. The glaring light that had shone as if from a single source on the central issue of abortion was suddenly expanded by overlapping pools of illumination from the richness of the Catholic tradition.

Bernardin had succeeded in a three-fold manner: First, he had energized key personnel in the broader ranks of the church to rethink their positions and to regroup around a phalanx of questions in which the sanctity of life was at risk; secondly, he had disturbed the country's liberal left, that had confidently written off the church's anti-abortion stand, by connecting it to issues, such as capital punishment, which its members had long championed; thirdly, he had stimulated the militant right, which had ignored other life-related issues in order to emphasize an anti-abortion stand, to examine other categories in which they had previously evinced little or no interest and which they tended to disown as "soft" or "distracting."

Bernardin was surprised but gratified by the reception given to his talk by the country's leading newspaper. The reaction of the *Times* seemed to confirm a theme to which he had alluded in his address. Referring to the peace pastoral, whose full title was "The Challenge of Peace: God's promise and Our Response," Bernardin had carefully recapitulated the church's "role in helping to shape public policy," noting that its role was "at least as important in *defining* key questions in the public debate as in *deciding* such questions." The peace letter had been written, he noted, at a "new moment" in the nuclear age. He extended this "new moment," recognizing it as the opening in which to develop, define, and apply a consistent ethic of life to those issues that flowed naturally from the widely shared convictions about the indefensible moral character of nuclear war. "In an age when we *can* do almost anything," Bernardin asked, "how do we decide what we *ought* to do? The even more demanding question is: In a time when we can do anything technologically, how do we decide morally what we *never should do*?"

The lean, intense cardinal, a trace of South Carolina still softening the hardest of his consonants, continued, noting that "the spectrum of life cuts across the issues of genetics, abortion, capital punishment, modern warfare, and the care of the terminally ill. These are all distinct problems, enormously complicated, and deserving individual treatment. No single answer and no simple responses will solve them. My purpose, however, is to highlight the way in which we face new technological challenges in each one of these areas; this combination of challenges is what cries out for a consistent ethic of life."

The audience, largely composed of students and professors, grew silent, absorbed by this unique and somewhat unexpected presentation, for they were not being fed the mildly irrelevant pieties they sometimes associated with the remarks of visiting archbishops but carefully wrought convictions that spoke to their own deepest concerns. Bernardin explained the link between the Catholic attitude on war and that on abortion, for they were supported by the same basic principle that "prohibits the directly intended taking of innocent human life." That same principle was the foundation for the pastoral letter's condemnation of "directly intended attacks on civilian centers."

Bernardin paused, adjusted his glasses, sipped some water, continued in his Southern gentleman's tones, "The principle which structures both cases, war and abortion, needs to be upheld in both places. It cannot be successfully sustained on one count and simultaneously eroded in a similar situation. . . . Some see clearly the application of the principle to abortion but contend the bishops overstepped their bounds when they applied it to choices about national security. Others understand the power of the principle in the strategic debate, but find its application on abortion a violation of the realm of private choice."

He went on to insist that a concern for life cannot end with the successful birth of a child but must express itself in concern for the continuing quality of life. "Such a quality of life posture translates into specific political and economic positions on tax policy, employment generation, welfare policy, nutrition and feeding programs, and health care. Consistency means we cannot have it both ways. . . . Right to life and quality of life complement each other in domestic social policy." Such linkage, he observed, "has led the U.S. bishops not only to oppose the drive of the nuclear arms race, but to stand against the dynamic of a Central American policy which relies predominantly on the threat of the use of force, which is increasingly distancing itself from a concern for human rights in El Salvador and which fails to grasp the opportunity of a diplomatic solution to the Central American conflict." Bernardin concluded with a plan for careful development of the consistent ethic notion in a dialogue marked by listening and "civil courtesy" in a pluralistic society.

Bernardin's speech, stirring reactions across the land at a traditionally quiet year's end interval, angered the militant pro-lifers as much as it arrested the attention of a vast Catholic and non-Catholic middle and liberal left audience that had come close to writing off the anti-abortion movement as an emotionally grounded, intellectually somewhat disrespectful venue of advocacy. He had, in the judgment of many, set the American church on a revitalized course through a presentation that, aided by Bernardin's own modest and thoughtful manner, was, although he would disavow such a judgment, perhaps the most significant address given by any archbishop in the history of American Catholicism.

XIX

During the question period after the Fordham address, Bernardin had used the phrase "seamless garment" as a metaphor to suggest the interwoven pattern of moral questions that he had just placed on the agenda of American Catholicism. Although he never personally adopted these words in any formal way, they were picked up popularly and have continued to be used, almost as a synonym, for the consistent ethic of life. This shorthand usage was to be an ongoing source of mild frustration for Bernardin, an unnecessary loose thread promptly teased out of the fabric of his thought by those who found it easier to criticize the inadequate simile than the substance of his reasoning.

The "seamless garment" has been employed, often to considerable political and public relations advantage, by commentators on both sides of the ideological spectrum. Some charged Bernardin with backing away from and defiling the singular moral clarity of the anti-abortion stand that, as chairman of the bishops' committee, he should have bolstered unequivocally. Bernardin, such analysts harped, picking at the intrinsic vulnerability of the expression, was really "soft" on abortion and, if the trumpet sounded an uncertain note, who would arise to the battle? Hehir was also targeted, along with other members of the bishops' Washington staff, as a quasi-leftist infiltrator whose own watered down morality was being foisted on Catholics as the thought of the bishops themselves.

The tactic, which, for a time at least, threatened to obscure if not damage Bernardin's call for "civil courtesy" in the necessary dialogue of developing the consistent ethic of life, was also successful in blurring the discussion through reduction of its complexity to oversimplified but effective sloganeering. Thus, against the fiddling of the busy orchestra of derision that always accompanied their attacks, such extremists knowingly accused Bernardin of placing the provision of proper nutrition for babies on the same plane with the fight for the unborn. At the same time, critics from the left asserted that Bernardin's linking of the anti-abortion stand with that against nuclear war confused and encumbered the crusade against the arms race.

Bernardin, having spent his first Christmas as a cardinal in Chicago, had to face this criticism without a well-organized chorus of support from his fellow bishops. They were not opposed to the consistent ethic of life but, victims at times of the procedures that at other moments gave them strength, they lacked a ready forum in which to debate, qualify, or affirm the notion until their next regularly scheduled meeting. Some of them understood the weakness of the "seamless garment" figure of speech. A seamless garment, after all, implied a fabric of like quality and texture throughout. All its elements were implicitly equal. Bernardin acknowledged this and, as he planned follow up lectures during 1984, he intended not only to respond to the criticisms of his proposal-in-progress but to emphasize the use of the term "consistent ethic of life" which he judged flexible enough to accommodate subjects that were related if not morally equal to one another.

Meanwhile, he also had to deal with the archdiocese of Chicago, a vast, still energetic entity that was moving inexorably through necessary but painful post-conciliar changes. These were inevitable in any basically healthy diocese that wanted to flourish in the next century and Bernardin's objective, as usual, was to encourage wide debate and discussion on the issues that naturally emerged as the season of transformation moved on. Among the more pressing problems were the closing or consolidation of parishes and schools that could no longer justify their existence pastorally or financially. Still, such churches and schools were encrusted in sentiment thicker than that of the mortar of their venerable brick walls. They had sheltered generations of immigrants and their descendants. The structures held memories of struggle and growth, the histories of families, the symbols and consolations of the Catholic faith. Touch the buildings and one touched the souls of the remaining parishioners and others who had moved away whose identity was bound up with such schools and churches. Bernardin's practiced collegiality made room for extensive discussions and popular participation in decisions that were intrinsically difficult and, in some cases, heartbreakingly painful. He understood that it would be autocratic foolishness to attempt to impose decisions on his own, that the days when that was possible had been entombed with Cardinal Cody. Only the people, after long discussion—and sharp disagreement at times—could make choices about closing churches or combining schools so rich in remembrance.

The city was also riven with racial problems that had been accented by the so-called "council wars" that pitted white alderman Edward Vrdolyak and his followers against black Mayor Harold Washington and the aldermen who were loyal to him. Publicized across the nation, these battles quickly deepened the city's image as one divided racially and politically. The chronic problem had worsened under Mayor Jane Byrne, and had been badly exacerbated in the tumultuous primary election of February 1983, in which Washington emerged as the first black Democratic candidate for mayor of the city. In the ensuing months, the exchanges between Washington and Vrdolyak, which centered mostly on money and power, became so sharp that the *Wall Street Journal* referred to Chicago as "Beirut by the lake."

Bernardin, through the newly formed Metropolitan Council of Religious Leaders, offered to mediate the differences between the two political leaders and, while this was a healing public symbol, it led to no tangible results. Bernardin found the two leaders as emotionally pitted against each other in private as they were in public; the mayor and the alderman, in a lesson in the raw reality of Chicago politics, needed each other as political enemies to consolidate their own constituencies more than they needed to make peace with each other. They did not care it seemed, at their deepest level, what the cardinal and the other members of the council said or thought.

At this time, Bernardin, along with Archbishop Rembert Weakland of Milwaukee and Archbishop Raymond Hunthausen of Seattle, became targets of choice for a St. Paul based Catholic newspaper, *The Wanderer.* This weekly, which traced its origins back to a German language edition published for the immigrant Catholics who farmed the rich lands of the upper Midwest, had become the voice of those who wanted a return to unreconstructed pre-Vatican II Catholicism. Week after week it took boldly headlined issue with changes in the church and with leaders who seemed too liberal to its editors. The latter, led by Al Matt, Jr., a descendant of the journal's founder, strongly encouraged American Catholics to conduct massive letter writing campaigns to various Vatican officials to complain about what they perceived to be aberrations or failures in the moderately progressive Catholicism of which these three prelates were acknowledged leaders.

While some of these protests had a foundation in reality, most of them were based on wild rumors or distortions of facts that made the American church appear to Rome as an undisciplined and schismatic shambles. Such unverified assertions, if only because of their volume, came to have a cumulative effect in curial circles and, all out of proportion to the small number of writers beneath the avalanche of mail, indirectly to shape even the pope's impression of American Catholicism. As 1983 turned into 1984, the self-righteous critiques issuing from such sources as *The Wanderer* and *Catholics United for the Faith,* were enjoying a season of success in influencing Vatican judgments on Catholicism in the United States.

Bernardin's having been the chief architect of the peace pastoral as well as of the consistent ethic of life, made him a regular ecclesiastical whipping boy for the right wing complainants. Seattle's Raymond Hunthausen, a manly figure who, in his manner, reflected much of the outdoor directness of his Montana upbringing, was criticized because of his personal protests against nuclear arms and what some regarded as his forgiving pastoral style. Critics attacked his readiness to bend regulations in certain areas such as the ministry to homosexuals as evidence of a lack of doctrinal orthodoxy. Hunthausen, already under the shadow of an unprecedented Roman investigation rooted in the letters of extremists, had, before the bishops' pastoral on nuclear war, withheld the portion of his income tax that would go to the Reagan defense build-up and led a demonstration against the presence of a nuclear submarine in the Seattle harbor. Weakland was an object of scorn because of the unique intellectual leadership he provided to the American church, especially as chairman of the group working on the economic pastoral scheduled for release just after the November 1984 presidential elections.

Cardinal Bernardin, meanwhile, continued to prepare for the William Wade lecture that he would deliver at the Jesuit run St. Louis University on March 11 of the new year. He proposed to define the nature of the consistent ethic of life and to secure its roots more firmly in the Catholic theological tradition. He would say that the Catholic tradition "joins the humanity of the unborn infant and the humanity of the hungry; it calls for positive legal action to prevent the killing of the unborn or the aged and positive societal action to provide shelter for the homeless and education for the illiterate. The potential of the moral and social vision is appreciated in a new way when the *systemic* vision of Catholic ethics is seen as a background for the *specific* positions we take on a range of issues."

Bernardin would insist, "against those who fear otherwise," that the "systemic vision of a consistent ethic of life will not erode our crucial public opposition to the direction of the arms race; neither will it smother our persistent and necessary public opposition to abortion. . . . A consistent ethic of life does not equate the problem of taking life (e.g., through abortion and in war) with the problem of promoting human dignity (through humane programs of nutrition, health care, and housing). But a consistent ethic of life identifies both the protection of life and its promotion as moral questions. It argues for a continuum of life which must be sustained in the face of diverse and distinct threats. . . . It is not necessary or possible for every person to engage in each issue, but it is both possible and necessary for the Church as a whole to cultivate a conscious explicit connection among its several issues."

While Bernardin quietly revised his speech at his desk in the small office attached like a handle to the cup of his rooms in the archbishop's residence on Chicago's North Side, changes were taking place that would dramatically alter the landscape of American institutional Catholicism. On Jan. 24, 1984, Bishop Bernard Law of the diocese of Cape Girardeau-Springfield in Missouri was named to succeed Humberto Cardinal Medeiros of Boston. A week later, Bishop John J. O'Connor, former member of Bernardin's nuclear war pastoral committee who the previous June had become bishop of Scranton, Pennsylvania, was named to succeed Cardinal Cooke as archbishop of New York. Two cardinalatial sees had been filled within eight days by bishops who, although friendly with and admiring of Bernardin, owed their posts not to his influence or recommendation but to that of other very different figures in the American church. That each had Irish names suggested a revival of the classic mold of the American bishopric.

O'Connor, who employed his self-deprecating humor to charm the reporters who crowded his office in downtown Scranton for interviews immediately after his new assignment was announced, had been ordained a priest of the archdiocese of Philadelphia in 1945. Seven years later, he had accepted a request that he become a naval chaplain and had put aside his love of being a parish priest to begin a career that would last 25 years. He served in war zones and at the Naval Academy at Annapolis and eventually achieved the distinguished rank of admiral and became chief of chaplains. After he retired in 1979, he postponed his wishes to become a pastor in order to serve as Cardinal Cooke's bishop for the Military Ordinariate. His remarkable record of accomplishment and his readiness to do what the church asked of him were characteristics he shared in common with Bernardin.

They were also the qualities that had made him in the early eighties the clerical rumor mill's odds on favorite to succeed Cardinal Krol as archbishop of Philadelphia when, in a few years, Krol reached the retirement age of 75. Suddenly, however, and apparently at the suggestion of Krol, O'Connor had been designated for New York. Conservative American Catholics, of whom Krol was the hierarchical patron, rejoiced at the naming of O'Connor who seemed to them the straightforward, no nonsense kind of leader who would never waver in his enunciation of pure Catholic doctrine. As Monsignor John Tracy Ellis noted of the papal approval of the new archbishop of New York, ''The pope is very fond of O'Connor. Of course he is. Don't you think they're two of a kind?''

Church observers counted the appointment as a fresh assertion by Pope John Paul II of traditional Catholicism's vigor as well as a signal of the kind of uncompromising prelate he wished to place in the major archdioceses of the world. Although Krol himself owed his ascendancy, as did Bernardin, to the Cleveland connection, that is, the late Archbishop Hoban's influence on Vatican Secretary of State, Amleto Cardinal Cicognani, they now represented lines that diverged from that common source. Bernardin symbolized the collegial progressivism of his mentors, former Clevelanders Hallinan and Dearden, while Krol, the surprising mixture of old-fashioned individualism and anti-nuclear war modernity, was traditional in his views on piety, church discipline, and the right of the bishop to make decisions without a lot of consultation beforehand. Krol's influence was thought to have been decisive in the choice of a successor for Cardinal Dearden of Detroit who had taken early retirement in fear that his impaired health would be an impediment to the church. It did not seem accidental that the Polish pope, quite possibly at the urging of the Polish Cardinal archbishop of Philadelphia, selected an obscure bishop of Polish descent, Edmund Szoka of the rural diocese of Gaylord, Michigan, for the post in Detroit.

Bernard Law, barely 50, had risen through the ranks of the hierarchy by another route. Raised in an army family and educated at Harvard, the handsome, prematurely gray Law had served in Mississippi during the difficult years of the great struggle to realize equality between the races. He had succeeded to a small Missouri diocese that was by no means obscure in the power structure of the church. John Cardinal Carberry, the retired archbishop of St. Louis who had begun his career as a jovial but scrupulous assayer of canon law requirements in Brooklyn, had been the patron of Monsignor William Baum, one of the scholars who had worked on the bishops' study of the priesthood some fifteen years before. Baum's first assignment after becoming a bishop was to Cape Girardeau-Springfield in Missouri.

Within a few years, he was promoted to Washington, D.C., became a cardinal and was later transferred to Rome as head of the Vatican's education department. Baum, in private one of the few bishops with a keen knowledge of modern fiction as well as of classical music and opera, became in turn a patron of Law who had followed him into the largely rural diocese in the foothills of the Ozarks. In Rome, Baum had, through his championing of orthodoxy, earned the confidence of the pope and had become, as Law and O'Connor would shortly, a major mediator of American church policy.

Law also had powerful allies within Opus Dei, the somewhat mysterious association of clergy and laity that promoted a vigorous traditional Catholicism through what was, for all practical purposes, a secret organization. Opus Dei was so well thought of by John Paul II that he granted it a special extra-territorial status that allowed it to operate as its own diocese. He also allowed its members, against the advice of his counselors, to build their own seminary in the Monte Mario section of Rome. As members of an independent prelature, as it was technically called, its adherents were practically independent of other church structures. Law was closely associated with this network and one of its members flew with him on his first inspection trip of his new diocese.

The new archbishop of Boston, already acclaimed for his ecumenical work as well as for his outspoken stands against racism, and his missionary work, was ambitious, it was said, for greater national recognition and for imbuing the American church with a greater respect for the spirit and traditions that had caused it to flourish before Vatican II. Law was also considered a bearer of the pre-collegial instincts of being a bishop. His first love was not that of the national conference but of the identity of the bishop as an independent authority within his own diocese who did not need to collaborate with his brother bishops before acting in certain situations. This personalization of his role would lead him in 1989, for example, to develop a close individual relationship with President George Bush whom he would be able to contact directly on his own at any time.

Neither Law nor O'Connor approached matters with the studied subtlety of Bernardin. O'Connor took New York by storm, playing skillfully to the crowds that loved it as he displayed a New York Mets' baseball cap at his installation mass on March 19, entertaining the vast congregation by interspersing his comments with humorous asides and calling a young altar boy named John J. O'Connor up into the pulpit with him. On his way out of St. Patrick's Cathedral, Law, who would be formally invested five days later in Boston, was heard to say to a fellow bishop, "At my installation my talk will have a deeper theological character." It was clear by Easter that two distinct new voices had been added to the American church.

Bernardin sympathized with O'Connor who, just as he arrived in New York, was editorially criticized by the *New York Times* for having made a statement in which he compared the death of the unborn through abortion to the Holocaust. O'Connor's would be an uncompromising voice endorsing the pro-life position. His stance was viewed in manic, pluralistic, sophisticated Manhattan as that of a man who had not heard the news yet. He seemed to lack the modern moral nuance and social understanding that motivated many public figures to view the situation with a tolerance for, if not an approval of, abortion. One of these was the Catholic governor of New York, Mario Cuomo, who felt that as a governmental official he could not impose his Catholic convictions on citizens who did not share them or his religious faith. His position, which would also be voiced by the Catholic congresswoman, Geraldine Ferraro, who would be Walter Mondale's vice-presidential running mate that year, was that a Catholic holding elective office might oppose abortion personally but was bound to uphold the law of the land that, since *Roe v. Wade,* permitted the procedure.

On a lightning filled night at the University of Notre Dame in early September 1984, Cuomo would articulate his position carefully in the glare of the television lights that symbolized the intensity of the media coverage of his remarks. He quoted with admiration Bernardin's consistent ethic of life theology, using it as a framework on which to construct his case. The Chicago archbishop, wary of having his still developing thought distorted even slightly before it was mature enough to be adopted by all the bishops as the foundation of their pro-life efforts, did not want to become involved in the debate between the governor and the archbishop of New York. The tone of that estrangement became clear the next year when Bishop Joseph O'Keefe, New York's vicar general, referred to the Notre Dame speech as "the encyclical by Mario."

Bernardin identified a basic disagreement with the New York governor that could be distinguished from Cuomo's increasingly personalized clash with Archbishop O'Connor. The Chicago archbishop felt that the bishops had to stand together collegially on their basic pro-life position. He suggested that the New York governor had not defined the terms of the question as the bishops had. They agreed with Cuomo that abortion was a public policy question but they differed with him because they also viewed it as a human rights issue. There were difficulties with such positions in a pluralistic society but Bernardin held that the state had a responsibility to respect and insure the preservation of human rights, seeking remedies for abuses when they were identified. Emphasizing the need for a better definition of terms, Bernardin pleaded for a dialogue that would contribute to "clarity, not passion" in the debate.

Bernardin's diplomatic skills were under severe test during that long season of electioneering. He wanted to protect the integrity of the bishops' pro-life position even as he broadened its base in the consistent ethic of life theology. He well knew that men familiar from the 1976 campaign, including the enigmatically smiling, ubiquitous James Baker, were involved in Reagan's 1984 run and that, especially after the challenge the bishops had thrown down to them in their nuclear war pastoral, they would not be averse to winning a few points at the expense of the Catholic hierarchy. Reagan had wrapped the pro-life mantle around his shoulders, and his supporters were delighted when O'Connor publicly criticized Ferraro for her Cuomo-like stand on abortion. Cardinal Bernardin offered an example of principled restraint; by his actions and his words he signalled that the bishops should not back away from their position but that they should be very wary of being drawn into partisan politics in ways that might compromise the pro-life goals they wanted to achieve.

This was very different from retiring from the fray, as many people, Catholics among them, wanted the bishops to do in terms of their efforts to affect public policy. While he and O'Connor and Law shared the same convictions about abortion, Bernardin's systematic approach, relying on careful theological reasoning as well as the proper definition of terms, was a classic example of his reflective, nonimpulsive emphasis on process over personality. The new archbishops of New York and Boston, perhaps true to their Irish heritage, had initiated highly personalized terms of service in which their individual statements and actions tended to overshadow the collaborative function of the National Conference of Catholic Bishops. Bernardin's task was to support his archiepiscopal brothers, soon to join him in the College of Cardinals, but to secure the conference as an ongoing structure for the collegial development of theological positions, moral stands, and public policy recommendations. That would become an increasingly important aspect of his role as a centrist leader of the American church for the rest of the decade.

XX

In the Sept. 30, 1984, *New York Times Magazine,* a lead article on Democratic vice-presidential candidate Geraldine Ferraro contained a vivid campaign anecdote. Reporter Jane Perlez described Congresswoman Ferraro's holding "an impromptu news conference to defend herself against the onslaught of the Archbishop of New York, John J. O'Connor, who on three successive days had criticized her for her position on abortion." A recent half hour phone conversation between the two principals had not resolved their differences. Standing in a hangar waiting for repairs to be finished on her plane, she addressed the issue, "her manner . . . ," as the reporter described it, "firm, her words precise, almost curt." Ferraro, accenting the distinction Governor Cuomo had already made, said, "I am opposed to abortion as a Catholic. I also feel very, very strongly about the separation of church and state."

Cardinal Bernardin realized that O'Connor's position, like Law's in Boston, was difficult because each was constantly being asked, if not badgered, by reporters in informal settings for comments which were then magnified enormously in newspapers and on television. The media were interested in the conflictual aspects of the relationship between Catholic bishops and Catholic officials. This inevitable bias made more difficult the calm development of thought on the role of Catholics in government in a pluralistic republic. Bernardin decided that the time was right for another talk in which he could restate the

Catholic teaching on abortion, offer support for his brother archbishops, and extend the boundaries of the dialogue about the distinction between private and public moral positions. Bernardin also appreciated Cuomo's contention that what was required to deal with the problem was "education" rather than "politics" or "legislation." The parameters of that education, in what many observers judged to be a subtle reestablishment of his leadership in a suddenly diversified hierarchy, was what he intended to focus on in an address to be given at the Jesuit Woodstock Center at Georgetown University in Washington, D.C.

On Oct. 25, 1984, Bernardin, building on his earlier reflections on the consistent ethic of life, delivered this major talk under a title that reflected the trying season almost exactly, "Religion and Politics: Stating The Principles and Sharpening The Issues." It was not until page 17 of his 24-page address that Bernardin, having established his foundation in the works of the late Jesuit theologian John Courtney Murray, reached the heart of his concerns. "The phrase 'public morality'," he said in his gentle, mediator's tones, "is at the center of the debate on religion and politics, but it is not a concept that is well understood.... The problem is partially due to the collapsing of two distinct questions into one argument. One question is how—in the objective order of law and policy—we determine which issues are *public* moral questions and which are best defined as *private* moral questions."

He paused, surveyed his attentive audience briefly, continued, "A second question is the following: How, in the face of an issue of public morality, should a public official relate personal convictions about religion and moral truths to the fulfillment of public duty?" Having earlier restated the church's position on abortion as a human rights issue, he linked the much needed transformation of public consciousness about such a subject in an analogy between prohibition as a failed articulation of public moralizing and civil rights as a successful expression of that same dimension of judgment. "Today," he said, "we have a public consensus which clearly defines civil rights as issues of public morality, and the decision to drink alcoholic beverages as clearly one of private morality."

After praising Archbishop O'Connor, he summarized the bishops' position that "abortion is without question an issue of public morality because the unborn child's right to life is at stake. . . . we see the abortion issue in the same category as civil rights questions. This is not sectarian theology, but sound public moral philosophy." Bernardin then quoted Bishop James Malone, new president of the American bishops, who 10 days before had said that "We realize that citizens and public officials may agree with our moral arguments while disagreeing with us and among themselves on the most effective legal and policy remedies." The Chicago cardinal went on to emphasize Malone's conclusion that, although the debate about workable responses should go forward, it "should not be about whether a response in the public order is needed."

Bernardin had skillfully fashioned an orthodox opening through which Catholic civic officials and their bishops could make safe passage as they explored the requirements of conscience in shaping public stands of constitutionally bound legislators on matters such as abortion. This prudently opened space would make room enough for analytic discussions of this achingly relevant subject. These should be characterized, Bernardin said, quoting Murray, "by civility." He wanted, he concluded, "candidates who are willing to say. 'The fact of 1.5 million abortions a year is unacceptable, and I will work for a change in the public policy which encourages or permits this practice.' " While stating the ultimate goal, Bernardin urged an intensified research program to serve the ongoing process of dialogue. An as yet missing interval of steps had to be climbed before this ideal principle of action could be fully realized. The address relieved the immediate tensions of the 1984 campaign while it clarified the issues and proposed the means of seriously exploring and settling them in the future.

Those who could appreciate the finely balanced levels of Bernardin's performance understood how much he had, in his patented manner, achieved. The drama of his presentation arose from the studied lack of drama with which its carefully reasoned arguments were offered. The last thing Bernardin wanted the presentation to be was excessively histrionic. It was instead an informed, theologically based call to the depths of the contemporary Catholic imagination. He thus healed the flaring irritation caused by candidates and archbishops unnecessarily bruising each other in conflicts that were often debates by reporters who intuitively understood them as a major story. Bernardin thereby supported the bishops, gave Catholic officials a breathing space, and allowed the church to be present in national life in a more restrained and balanced manner. After reading an advance copy, Archbishop O'Connor told Bernardin that he could put his own signature to it.

Bernardin had extended his refections on the consistent ethic of life and charted a course for reflecting on and resolving the challenge of forging public responses based on internal moral convictions about issues that needed development—slow, measured, difficult—but development nonetheless. In an American church in which there had been much speculation about whether Bernardin would be overshadowed by the new personalities in major sees such as Detroit, Boston, and New York, it was also clear that, as a by-product of the evening, he had increased his credibility at the very center of the American hierarchy. When he gave his first report as chairman of the bishops prolife committee at the November 1984 meeting of the bishops, he received a standing ovation from his brother prelates, a strong validation of the expanded thrust he had given to their most significant program by his linkage of issues through the consistent ethic of life.

That busy autumn had also seen him make an important comment on the Vatican document on Liberation Theology which many had interpreted as a wholesale condemnation of the Latin American thinkers who had developed it. Bernardin realized that the severest critics of this theological reflection were, like Michael Novak, the scholarly resident fellow at the American Enterprise Institute, strong supporters of Reagan's economic and Central American policies. They had already been busily criticizing Archbishop Weakland as he put the finishing touches on the pastoral letter on the economy. Bernardin's brief comments, classic in their sheathing of a sharp bladed defense in a smooth orthodox scabbard, upheld the church's right to expect its theologians to support magisterial teachings while vindicating the integrity and freedom of the Latin American scholars to reflect on the realities of life in their own countries. In the midst of these weighty issues in which he was playing a nonstop significant role, he was also made aware of a minor but persistent irritation in Chicago.

Father Greeley, according to friends in touch with him at the time, was eager to have Bernardin's seal of approval for his novels. The priest was not happy that what he argued to be stories of God were perceived widely as "steamy" mixtures, popular for the same reason Cecil B DeMille's movies were: They lavishly combined sex and religion. While complaints came in to Bernardin from all sides about Greeley, there was certainly nothing in his erotically counterpointed stories to warrant any ecclesiastical penalty, even though the priest, just before *The Cardinal Sins* was published, had dramatically forecast an effort to take away his roman collar, a move, he wrote in his columns, that he would reject. That had not occurred and now Bernardin had other, far more significant matters on his mind.

While he was comforted by many who enjoyed his work, Greeley was disturbed by analyses of his fiction such as that that appeared in *Forum,* a magazine of the *Penthouse* empire of Bob Guccione. In an article titled "The Phallic Priest," he was described as "the Harold Robbins of the Catholic Church" who had undergone "a literary sex change." Attacking Greeley's frequent comparison of himself to the writers of the bible who told similar stories of human problems, the *Forum* writer offered examples of what he considered the "whacko art" of the priest's "violent pornography." In an example of his contention of Greeley's "unseemly reliance on the darker side of sex," the concluding paragraphs of the priest's *Happy Are The Meek* were quoted: "I twisted one of her beautiful breasts viciously. Lisa's attempt to shriek with pain was only a faint whimper. 'And let me tell you the ending first. After everything else is over, and after I've had all the fun I possibly can with you'—I held up the cosh—'I'm going to smash your brains out!' " The *Forum* writer concluded, "Sounds very new testament to me." Such sado-masochism under the guise of religion disturbed many people, including some church officials, but others felt that, if these were lapses of taste and judgment that proved that Greeley was not Henry James, critics would deal with them. They were hardly matters worthy of being publicly condemned by any archbishop, much less Bernardin who was so deeply involved in the most pressing moral issues of the age.

Bernardin respected the canonical status that had been granted to Greeley by previous archbishops of Chicago. The priest had been freed from parish and administrative assignments, as several other diocesan priests had been, to pursue special work. Father Greeley continued to talk and write about the official frustration of his desires to be a parish priest in his native city but, as Dan Herr, one of his principal confidants, had often said of such claims, "The last thing Andrew really wants is a regular assignment. He would die if they gave him one."

But Greeley, restless if prosperous, had one clear objective. He eagerly pursued, often by convincing other priests to speak in his behalf, the public endorsement of the most influential churchman in the United States, Joseph Cardinal Bernardin. When the cardinal neither censured nor approved of him, Greeley began to criticize him, using familiar strategies, first attacking what he considered the archbishop's inadequate staff, and then suggesting that Bernardin, far from being a saviour for Chicago, was going to destroy what Greeley conceived of as the past glory of the archdiocese. In May 1984, Bernardin had called Greeley as a sign of his own good will to congratulate him on his 30th ordination anniversary. He was surprised that the priest later distorted the content of the conversation in writing and speaking of it, saying of this and another contact with a diocesan official that the church would only accept him if he did public penance for the novels he wrote. No such condition, according to those who had contact with him at the time, was ever mentioned to him.

But the priest, described by close friends like Herr as a "genius" at manipulating others to get what he wanted, continued his campaign, similar in its charges to the one he had waged against Cody, trying to force the cardinal to engage with him. Greeley would, a few years later in his autobiography, offer the following carefully phrased provocation, "It is not unlikely, in my judgment, that sexuality, indeed perverse sexuality, will be to the Bernardin archdiocese of Chicago what financial corruption was to the Cody archdiocese of

Chicago. I hasten to add that I do not question the Cardinal's own sexual orientation. (Some who do not know him but are aware of the prevalence of it in Chicago do have their doubts.)'' (*Confessions of A Parish Priest*, Pocket Books, 1987, p. 131.)

Bernardin had, by this time, become well known and highly respected by Chicagoans, indeed by Americans of every religion, and such critiques by Father Greeley, whatever their motivation, began to seem self-serving and somewhat petty. In November 1984, as Archbishop Weakland successfully launched the pastoral letter on the economy at the bishops' meeting, Bernardin was far too absorbed in national and international church matters to be drawn into any contrived arguments with a priest who relished his own controversial reputation.

XXI

I f Bernardin was increasingly conscious of the presence of two new leaders, each highly intelligent and energetic, in the national landscape of American Catholicism, his well honed instincts told him that he served the church best by remaining himself rather than changing in any way to match the more colorful public styles of his still somewhat unseasoned confreres. He had a long range view of goals for American Catholicism that could only be attained, as he understood the church and the culture in which it found itself, by a combination of committing his energies without hesitation to the Holy See while also committing himself in the same way to the healthy growth of the post-conciliar American Catholic church.

The church might profit in many ways from the presence of Cardinal archbishops, such as Law and O'Connor, who emphasized personalized apostolates that seemed to make them stand aside from and, at times, loom larger than the national conference. Bernardin would be happy to endorse the good that such leaders could do. Still, in his own vision, the church of the future that was still being born would best be nurtured through increased collegiality. American Catholicism would thrive only as its bishops worked together, incorporating believers at every level in the ongoing dialogue of the faithful without whom the church would be an empty administrative shell. His continuing role would test all his reservoirs of prudence and judgment as well as his fabled sense of balance. Bernardin was not known to drop his manuscript or his composure on his way to the microphone. He thought often of what he had learned from Hallinan and Dearden, Irishmen different in temperament from those now on the scene, the patient, far-seeing leaders under whom he had apprenticed. They never panicked, they kept faith with their vision, that is what he would do, too.

Cardinal Bernardin had much to meditate on as he rose every morning at 5:30. O'Connor and Law were excellent men but many commentators on American Catholicism were beginning to describe their enthusiasm for their new roles as a kind of impulsiveness of the spirit, well-motivated but sometimes easily misunderstood. O'Connor, of course, stood, like the biblical children, at the very heart of the unforgiving blast furnace of New York. He was not allowing Catholicism to be compromised in public affairs and, stunned as even the great and powerful are when they meet a true believer, influential New Yorkers were beginning to realize that attention had to be paid to their new archbishop. "The Catholic Church," O'Connor observed in the midst of one of his skirmishes with the city over his insistence that the church would not compromise its teaching just to get municipal contracts, "like China, is a sleeping giant just waking up."

The archbishop of Chicago sympathized with O'Connor and was glad to join him when he could, as in their testifying together before Congress against the deployment of the MX missile. They quietly but quickly developed an understanding working relationship. One of the burdens they would shoulder together within a few years was, in fact, a problem that, if not well handled, could divide and dispirit American Catholicism with explosive force. That was the still ongoing investigation of the administrative and pastoral practices of Raymond Hunthausen, archbishop of Seattle.

Educated American Catholics, mostly moderate in their theological views, constituted a unique phenomenon. Despite the old hierarchical model that no longer commanded their immediate response, their disagreements in conscience over such issues as birth control, and their memories of church life and schooling that were sometimes as tinctured by misgiving as joy, they had great affection for their church. Such Catholics, even those who did not practice regularly, found that it was difficult, if not impossible, to shake off their deeply ingrained religious identity. They might argue with the church or its representatives but something of its sacramental life and its residual moral power still affected them. As writer Jimmy Breslin put it, "Nobody ever really leaves the Catholic Church."

Those Catholics still strongly affiliated with the church often described it as a home. Bernardin, like many others, spoke of the church as a family in which it was not strange to find misunderstandings and disagreements that could be borne successfully because of the larger prevailing sense of comfort and the true bonds of affection that were mysterious but real virtues of the church. Catholics who worked hard for their beliefs remained its core strength. These were the very ones who were already greatly distressed by the theological investigation of moral theologian Charles Curran at the Catholic University of America. Curran had his right to teach theology—his license, in effect—removed because of what the Congregation for the Doctrine of the Faith, headed by Joseph Cardinal Ratzinger, judged to be his unacceptable dissent from church teaching on birth control and homosexuality and other related issues. If the ongoing examination of Hunthausen, who was perceived nationally as a brave pastoral figure, should be mismanaged, the results could generate enormous disaffection among the very Catholics the church in the United States could hardly lose without feeling drastic long-term effects. The resulting schism might be silent but it would be severely damaging to the church.

Complaints against Hunthausen's administration of the archdiocese of Seattle had come to Rome in the bundles of letters inspired by publications such as the *Wanderer.* Cardinal Ratzinger was a noted theologian before he became prefect of the department that, once termed the Holy Office, examined issues involving orthodoxy throughout the world. In an unusual move, Ratzinger's congregation and that in charge of bishops, obviously with the approval of the pope, had authorized official visitations of two American dioceses, Hunthausen's Seattle and Walter Sullivan's Arlington, Virginia. Archbishop James Hickey, Baum's successor in Washington, D.C., who had once been rector of the North American College in Rome, had carried out the visitation of Hunthausen's diocese during the first week of November 1983. The mere publication of the information that two well-regarded bishops who shared, among other common pastoral concerns, commitments against nuclear arms and a readiness to provide pastoral service to homosexuals, shocked and disturbed Catholics who grouped themselves at the moderate center of the church.

Ratzinger would send a long letter to Hunthausen on Sept. 30, 1985, revealing what proved eventually to be only a portion of the actions he had recommended against the Seattle archbishop. The tone of Ratzinger's missive was evenhanded and fraternal. He dismissed extremists, presumably the *Wanderer* inspired letter writers, "who are wholly lacking in a spirit of cooperation and seek to destroy or suppress whatever is not to their liking." Ratzinger commended Hunthausen for his reputation as a compassionate pastor but went on to cite several specific areas in which he felt, on the basis of what he termed Hickey's "exhaustively documented" report, corrective action should be taken. After the entire story of the Vatican's actions against Hunthausen broke a year later, *Wanderer* publisher Al Matt, Jr., spoke as proudly as a bounty hunter might of a notable kill. "If it hadn't been for the voice and clamor of faithful Catholic lay people," he claimed, "nothing would have happened."

"It appears," Ratzinger wrote, "that there has been a rather widespread practice of admitting divorced persons to a subsequent church marriage without prior review of your Tribunal, or even after they have received a negative sentence. . . . At the present time, steps need to be taken to ensure that your Metropolitan Tribunal. . . conforms with all the prescriptions of the revised Code of the Church's public law." Ratzinger held the same supervisor of orthodoxy pitch throughout the six-page letter, enumerating further concerns about the need to teach more clearly the nature of the church as well as the character of the sacraments and the need to keep the laity in their proper roles in relationship to the priest. Several times, Ratzinger referred to what he called "flawed" notions about the human person that he perceived as having crept into pastoral practice in

Seattle. He was also at pains to suggest that the consciences of Catholics needed to be formed in relationship to the teachings of the church.

The prefect also commented on Hunthausen's "steps to correct the practice of contraceptive sterilization which had been followed in local Catholic hospitals," and reinforced church regulations about the time for first confession, the abuse of employing general absolution rather than individual confession when it was not permitted, and a certain excessive flexibility in liturgical matters. In his penultimate item, he referred to the "current politicization" of the question of women in the church and reminded Hunthausen that the church had already spoken definitively, as he put it, on excluding them from the priesthood. The last lengthy paragraph discussed ministry to homosexuals. Ratzinger wrote of "the teaching of the Magisterium concerning the intrinsic evil of homosexual activity" and criticized "the ill-advised welcome of a pro-homosexual group to your cathedral, as well as events subsequent to the Apostolic Visitation, [that] have served to make the Church's position appear to be ambiguous in this delicate but important issue."

The full impact of this embarrassing reprimand would not be felt by the Catholic community at large until September 1986, when Hunthausen would reveal that he had, in fact, been relieved of his authority in five areas of church administration and that these were being transferred to Bishop Donald Wuerl, a native of Pittsburgh who had worked for many years as an official in Rome. Few issues in contemporary Catholic experience seemed so to dramatize the operational tension that existed between mainstream Catholicism and what many observers described as an effort on the part of certain Romans to impose a "restoration" of the monarchical model of canonical governance on the church.

Not only did the unparalleled penalties levied against Hunthausen seem to humiliate a widely admired figure but they also struck at the hearts of centrist Catholics who felt that they, too, had been shamed by this untoward action. Bernardin, who had made several efforts to mediate the dispute between Rome and Seattle in the year before Bishop Wuerl's assumption of the major portion of Hunthausen's authority became public, well understood the explosive potential of the matter. The Seattle controversy was not only injuring Hunthausen but also the great body of moderate Catholics, confusing and demoralizing them. If it were not resolved satisfactorily, many of them might be permanently alienated from the official church.

As the last weeks of August slipped away, Bernardin was keenly aware that the divisive potential of the Seattle problem would soon be realized. Across the country, American Catholics would express unparalleled distress when they learned that Hunthausen's powers had been handed over to Bishop Wuerl. As he gazed from the office window of his residence at the crowds gathering for picnics in Lincoln Park, Bernardin wondered what else he could possibly do to alleviate the pain that would settle into the bones of American Catholicism when on the day after Labor Day, they read of what they would construe as Hunthausen's punishment. He had travelled to Seattle during the previous year more than once and, in March, felt that a satisfactory resolution was within an inch of being attained.

But, despite the age of mass communication, ambiguities and misunderstandings rose out of the messages being transmitted between Rome and the misty city in the Pacific Northwest. Archbishop Hunthausen had been reluctant to accept compromises that seemed unfair and unjust to him and to his people. His priests and the members of his flock had already been stung by the intimations that they had failed the church when their consciences convinced them that they had acted in the spirit of Vatican II. The very idea of an investigation had saddened them, had dug ferociously into their souls.

There were two sides, Bernardin understood, to any matter in which human beings were involved. In Seattle, despite warm hearts and good will, gentle people had, in certain circumstances, gone beyond the regulations of the church. Ratzinger was not the ogre that many unhappy persons, desperate for a villain, made of him. It was his responsibility, after all, to oversee just such situations; he could not fulfill his office if he ignored problems. Still, many of Bernardin's brother bishops were incensed at the manner in which Murphy's Law seemed to operate, making the situation worse at each succeeding step for just about everybody, Hunthausen, Bishop Wuerl, the papal nuncio, and themselves.

One bishop observed that appointing Bishop Wuerl was "the worst ecclesiology I've seen in my life. It is evidence of ineptness on the part of the Holy See. Putting another bishop in to take over a man's power has never worked in other situations where it has been tried. What this represents is a failure of the central authority of the church." Other bishops worried that the entire hierarchy, as had occurred the year before in Brazil, was under seeming examination for its orthodoxy and its loyalty to the Holy See. Which one of us, they wondered, will Rome go after next? And for what reason? Had the extremist letter writers sold their hysterical exaggerations about American Catholicism to some Roman officials?

Perhaps that explained the comments Cardinal Ratzinger made two years before in an interview published in the Italian monthly, *Jesus,* in which he had said of the United States, "Many Catholics choose to dissent from the church teaching authority rather than dissent from the secular values promoted by their wealthy nation." Some in the Vatican still viewed Western European bishops as visionaries while they looked on American prelates as builders and managers. It was clear that some officials were falsely worried that the national conference might overshadow the individual rights of bishops. Clearly, the Hunthausen affair carried the seeds of further estrangement and misunderstanding. Nobody wanted that outcome.

Bernardin, picking up a folder of notes and letters from his desk before leaving for the diocesan offices on East Superior Street, believed that there was still enough room on both sides for continuing discussions. The last sands were cascading into the lower part of time's glass. One could only watch them tumble silently away, knowing that the pressures would multiply when the matter became public, and that, as a result, a man closing his hand at the last moment for resolution of the problem might grasp empty air. As he descended the old fashioned oak staircase he was aware that more than Seattle's future might be at stake. The collegial process was being tested as was, to some extent, the integrity and maturity of the National Conference of Catholic Bishops. What would the conference's future be like if it could not effectively manage a problem that should be handled within its confines? Would Roman interventions, made hazardous by inevitable cultural clashes and communication problems, become more common, undermining the conference structure?

In a sense, he felt that his life's work, dedicated to the universal and the local church, was being examined. The American bishops were in the process of dealing successfully with Vatican investigations of American seminaries and religious life. Those analyses had provoked grave concerns when they were announced but once the bishops, particularly Archbishop Quinn of San Francisco, began reviewing matters with Rome, a more restrained and helpful vocabulary had been developed that had changed the situation from negative to positive. The American bishops had also managed their way successfully through the minefields of government opposition and media overkill with two major public statements in the pastoral letters on nuclear war and the economy. The soundness of their collaborative process had been proved many times. Its most difficult trial was already underway in Seattle. Before he addressed that, however, there was another matter that required his attention.

A simple and clear response was essential to Father Greeley's proposal to make a gift of $1 million to Chicago's Catholic schools. Although Bernardin did not doubt Greeley's well known generosity and understood that no conditions were placed on the gift, the invisible strings on this proposal were easy to discern. Father Greeley was making what he felt was an offer that nobody could refuse. If the archbishop accepted money that had been earned through novels that had, among other things, savaged his predecessor and attacked him as well, Bernardin would be indirectly approving of them, granting the *imprimatur* that Greeley wanted for himself. Such a public endorsement would redeem Greeley from the widespread criticisms that he was a purveyor of sado-masochistic themes rigged up in ecclesiastical settings. Such approbation would be equivalent to the cardinal's imprinting his ring in a waxen seal on his novels. Some observed that the proposed gift was well-timed for the publicity that would accompany its acceptance would come out just as the priest's autobiography appeared in hardback.

The main work of Bernardin's life as a priest and bishop—the continuing growth of American Catholicism mediated by a national conference of bishops working collegially—was in danger of being destroyed by the Hunthausen affair. If the conference splintered, the collaborative process inspired by Vatican II would be damaged, probably beyond repair. The instrument that made slow but healthy growth possible for the church in the United States would be surrendered like a defeated general's sword. The American church might well lose its sense of being a family that could move forward despite obstacles. Its members would surely not find domination by individual episcopal personalities an appealing substitute for true collaboration between bishops and laypeople. Dearden's vision of an authentically collegial church would be but a memory. These were the matters to which Bernardin had to devote all his energies of mind and spirit.

Although he was still not heard, even by his closest associates, to make a harsh comment about Father Greeley, Bernardin's mind was made up about the proposed gift. He refused it, okaying an archdiocesan statement that read simply: ''We appreciate the impulse behind the gift, but regret that we are unable to accept it at this time. Reasons for declining this gift are a private matter between a bishop and one of his priests. As a matter of policy, we don't comment on such matters.'' It never made another statement on the matter. Although Father Greeley reacted with his usual flourish and gave an account in the paperback edition of his autobiography that did not match Bernardin's experience of the exchange, the decision had other unforeseen effects. Those voices, official and unofficial, that had clamored for some canonical penalty for the priest writer were suddenly stilled. It was as if Father Greeley's position and his relationship with Bernardin had finally been put into a clear perspective.

XXII ━━━━━━━━━━━━━━━━━━━━━

A merica's Catholic bishops felt the Hunthausen case pressing down on them as if a massive low had settled over Washington, D.C., as they unpacked their bags at the Capital Hilton on Nov. 9, 1986. The newspapers and television had, over the past two months, amply reported what had come to be called the "Seattle situation." Thousands of Catholics in that archdiocese that spread from the Canadian border to the Columbia River had carried lighted candles in marches of support for their 65-year-old archbishop in a mood less of defiance of Vatican orders than of sadness over what they perceived as their unjust character. Religion writers such as the highly esteemed Bruce Buursma of the *Chicago Tribune* would speculate about whether "the theologically moderate consensus...shaped by key leaders such as Chicago's Joseph Cardinal Bernardin, has begun to erode in the emergence of a vocal and growing faction of conservative prelates."

As the bishops settled in, they found that the day's *New York Times Magazine* featured the distinguished Catholic theologian, Father David Tracy of the University of Chicago, as its cover story. His reflections on Roman efforts to reduce the faith to concrete statements that also destroyed their essential mystery struck home to many bishops who were concerned about the way some Vatican officials were energetically trying to implement a restoration as fated to ultimate failure as that attempted for the monarchy in nineteenth century France. They also found in their mailboxes copies of the *Na-*

tional Catholic Reporter with a front page opinion piece that seemed to express the dismay of centrist Catholics that, in the Hunthausen matter, the punishment had exceeded the crime, and that the archbishop was being humiliated and emasculated publicly. It concluded that "orthodoxy and good order have not been vindicated as much as a powerful instinct to force others into submission has been satisfied." The inner discomfort of many of their people—as if they were being violated by such investigations—was shared by a substantial number of bishops.

Bernardin understood that the meeting, to which Hunthausen was journeying determined to ask his brother bishops to help him regain his full rights, would be the decade's most severe test of the conference's continuing visability. Not only would the Hunthausen case be explored in executive session but the archbishop of Boston, Bernard Law, now a cardinal, was said to be seeking an active elective post in the conference. So, too, were other American churchmen, such as Bishop Anthony Bevilacqua of Pittsburgh who would succeed Cardinal Krol in Philadelphia the next year, and Archbishop Roger Mahony of Los Angeles, sure to be a cardinal, who were identified as members of the newly developing bloc, styled by journalists as "conservative." The moment had arrived, in the midst of heightened Roman expectations and tension over Seattle, for these bishops to make their bids for the elective offices that would put them in virtual control of the national conference.

Bernardin's style of leadership of the pro-life committee had been strongly validated at the annual meeting just a year before when the bishops had given almost unanimous support to his updated pastoral plan for their "Respect Life" program. The victory was of no small consequence for it meant that the bishops had stretched and pulled at the fibers of the consistent ethic of life position and found it very much to their liking. The language of the consistent ethic was therefore incorporated into the bishops' program definition of their pro-life activities. Almost singlehandedly, Bernardin, with the help of Father Hehir, had introduced this vocabulary linking moral and ethical life issues into the ongoing national dialogue on the issue.

The Chicago cardinal, furrowing his brow in answer to a reporter's question in the hotel lobby, had learned long before never to enter a crisis unprepared. While under severe attack for his "seamless garment" approach, especially by right wing extremists such as Chicago's Joseph Scheidler, he had sent his series of talks on the subject to Joseph Cardinal Ratzinger, asking the prefect of the Congregation of the Doctrine of the Faith to review them theologically. Six months later, he had received a two-page letter from the German theologian-official saying that Bernardin was on target in the development of his arguments. Ratzinger had included a few suggestions "to enrich" the argument. While Ratzinger's response had been a personal one, Bernardin had been pleased with this further affirmation. Bernardin had been sure of his ground when he had presented his report on pro-life activities the year before.

This year, however, contingencies rode in the melancholy November wind. Archbishop Hunthausen wanted the support of his fellow bishops and, while many were sympathetic to him, they could not take any public stand that seemed to challenge the very church authority that they were dedicated to uphold. Still, the pastoral consequences of permitting misunderstandings and the complications of communication between European officials, trained in nuance and diplomatic suggestion, and plain spoken Americans, to shake the conference and unsettle Catholics were very real. Bernardin wanted to avoid dramatic confrontation with any Vatican office. That might be emotionally satisfying for many frustrated bishops and Catholics but it would only harm the prospects of a just long range settlement. In the heady atmosphere of this meeting, it seemed truly impossible to predict the outcome.

Bernardin knew that he would have serious challenges to his moderate and well balanced leadership in the years ahead. Late the next summer, for example, Pope John Paul II would arrive for his second visit. It would take him in the eye of the fall hurricane season that became an uncomfortably appropriate symbol for his pilgrimage, across the south and west of the United States. Nor was it a secret that many critics of Bernardin's approach, were already warning the pope of the disordered and undisciplined condition of Catholicism in what many Europeans still construed imaginatively as the uncultured "new world." At the Synod of Bishops that would occur in Rome shortly after the pope's return in late September 1987, Bernardin would have to deal with what amounted to a deliberate effort on the part of some synodal members to adopt positions that would have aided their cause by reinstituting outdated clerical domination over lay Catholics.

The Chicago cardinal, paired with Milwaukee's Archbishop Weakland, would choose at the synod a strategy of damage control, avoiding conflicts that would have lessened their credibility and working for texts that would allow plenty of room for progressive development. "Bernardin and Weakland," a participant would observe immediately afterward, "may not have won everything they wanted but they saw to it that not much was lost either. The synod would have been much worse in its outcomes without them."

That October meeting, made noteworthy by the distribution, against the rules of the synod, of a right wing Catholic journal critical of Bernardin and Weakland on the chairs of all delegates, would indeed press Bernardin to dig deep within his soul for the reserves needed to preserve the concept of the church as a People of God according to the theology of Vatican II. His sense of the conciliar documents was that, momentous as they were, they had necessarily been compromises forged to make the transition that Pope John XXIII's *aggiornamento* required. The restorationists were attempting to use the older aspects of them to justify a return of the church to the nineteenth century at the very moment that it was challenged to prepare for the twenty-first. Bernardin's diplomatic efforts would be directed toward keeping the doors of St. Peter's open to the future.

The pope's pre-synodal American visit, despite the rainstorms that interfered with the liturgical celebrations at certain stops, would be far less a visitation by a justly wrathful father than many American critics supposed. Bernardin, along with Weakland, Archbishop John Quinn of San Francisco and Archbishop Daniel Pilarczyk of Cincinnati, would give the main addresses in behalf of the American hierarchy at a closed meeting with the pope in Los Angeles in mid-September.

Bernardin's address would be a subtle evocation of Catholicism rooted in American traditions, stressing the people's affection for and unity with the Holy See and asking persuasively for a "discernment of what will enhance unity." He would urge that room be provided for continuing organic growth for American Catholicism based on collegial forums for the careful application of theological principles to personal and public life. American Catholicism, he would suggest, was learning to balance its own heritage of democracy with the revered traditions of the church. Bernardin would skillfully support a healthy dialogue that would prevent the extreme left or right from dictating the eccelesial agenda, thus allowing Americans to reaffirm in their own true voice their identity as "Roman" Catholics.

Thus, Bernardin's and the other presentations by men as moderate and collegial as he, would be considered important factors in shifting the pope's view of American Catholicism. Having visited places as varied in countryside and customs as Bernardin's home city of Columbia, South Carolina, and both Los Angeles and San Francisco, the pope would feel the unmistakable vitality of the nation's Catholics. On returning to Rome, John Paul II would tell associates that "I had been misinformed about Catholicism in the United States."

That kind of favorable outcome was, however, far from predictable as Bernardin, stepping into the elevator with a grave visaged Cardinal O'Connor, searched his mind for a strategy that would accomplish several goals in one initiative. The bishops had to support the Holy See, that was obvious, but they also had to offer some fraternal support to Archbishop Hunthausen in a fashion that would make it possible for him to cooperate in some manner with the Holy See. They also wanted to respond pastorally to the demoralization that was spreading like a hideous dye through mainstream Catholicism. The bishops would face an internal examination of their goals that would constitute a further test of Bernardin and everything he had believed in and worked for during his 34 years as a priest and 20 years as a bishop. It was not melodramatic for those watching the elevator doors glide shut to judge that the future of American Catholicism depended on what men like Bernardin and O'Connor were able to accomplish during the next 48 hours.

The events of the past few weeks had roiled rather than calmed the waters. The papal nuncio, Archbishop Laghi, had apparently been instructed by the Roman officials who were handling the Hunthausen matter, Bernard Cardinal Gantin and Joseph Cardinal Ratzinger, to issue a chronology of the events involving the investigation of the Seattle archbishop. Hunthausen had protested to Bishop James Malone, president of the American bishops, that his rebuttal should also be distributed. Eventually, after consideration by the bishops' executive committee, Malone, adopting the role of the conveyor rather than the advocate, had distributed both versions to the American bishops. Naturally, this increased the attention and vigilance of the media throughout the country. What could be better for an editor's disposition than a face-off between the American bishops and the Vatican in the dead news hollow between elections and Thanksgiving?

The mailing of incompatible versions of prior negotiations had made the earth move under ecclesiastical structures on both sides of the Atlantic. Hunthausen had also disagreed with the interpretation of the incidents that had led to what he considered the administratively impossible situation of having a young bishop, Donald Wuerl, trying to run the archdiocese of Seattle with him as if they were a team in a three-legged race. It wasn't working, Hunthausen insisted, and it never would. Most bishops agreed with him, at least in the quiet chambers of their own souls. It was not Wuerl's fault. Despite good intentions on the part of those who authored it, the plan was objectively unworkable.

Bishop Wuerl, carrying out a difficult assignment as churchmen were expected to, was hardly a popular figure among many of the priests or people of Seattle. He might have authority technically but he did not possess it personally and his duty had turned into a chilly semi-exile. Archbishop Laghi found himself in an uncomfortable position as he attempted to represent the intentions and wishes of Rome in a dispute that was becoming more complex and more threatening to the good order of the church and the morale of Catholics with every passing day.

The priests of Seattle had been loyal in overwhelming numbers to their archbishop, feeling that if his humane pastoral approach violated some demands of Rome, they more than answered those of the hearts of spiritually anguished men and women. One diocesan official was quoted as being preoccupied with the "radical injustice" of the charges against Hunthausen. Many bishops felt that Hunthausen, in his big-hearted attitude toward divorced Catholics and homosexuals, was doing no more than they themselves had done for years. Hunthausen's acceptance of the Catholic homosexual organization *Dignity* was cited by some insiders as the pill that Rome, which had recently described homosexuals as possessing an objectively disordered condition, could not and would not swallow. Officials had been quietly pressuring bishops to drop their sponsorship of chapters of *Dignity* throughout the country because it had advocated positions opposed to church training on homosexual behavior. That Hunthausen had permitted its members the use of his cathedral was something that was more offensive in Rome than his strong activism in the cause of peace.

The matter had taken on a life of its own, Bernardin concluded ruefully, for he was convinced that with a little more give on Hunthausen's part, the plan, though faulty, might have worked. Hunthausen in recent weeks had interpreted Roman responses as suggestions that he should resign. This, in turn, upset his closest aides who, in their loyalty to him, were not disposed to further compromise with the Holy See. Bernardin saw no other route at the moment but compromise. The American bishops were trying to remain neutral but they could hardly refuse to listen to Hunthausen in what, in effect, was a painful moment of truth for all of them. Neither, as Bernardin well knew, could they publicly reject actions already taken by the Holy See. This was an interval for patience, for the calming of the seas if not their biblical parting, so that men of good will could at least hear each other if not make passage through divinely tunneled waters.

Bernardin had already expressed his feelings about the problems in Seattle in his column in the Chicago Catholic newspaper. After reviewing and attempting to make Roman procedures understandable if not wholly acceptable to his people, he had suggested that "in a more tranquil climate, a constructive dialogue can begin that will help to move everyone beyond the present impasse." He had acknowledged how "the Seattle situation has adversely affected morale both here in Chicago and elsewhere," and concluded, "I want you to know that it has been a difficult time for me as well. It is difficult for all of us to live with the tensions of our age."

The Cardinal archbishop of Chicago was not alone in his emotions or in his soul searching for a political solution to the deeply troubling predicament. In conferences in their hotel rooms and leaning across their meeting tables before the sessions were gaveled to order under the ballroom chandeliers, the American bishops, whether thought to be moderates or conservatives, shared their concerns with each other. As Bernardin reflected in a conversation with a colleague at the time, "We have to try to look at this objectively. There have been some violations of church teaching and discipline and misunderstandings in Seattle. The way the public evidence is mounting up, it looks worse for the Vatican than it should. In such situations, I always try to deal with the truth and look for a core of hope, something near the central meaning of the story. We bishops have to work through a process that will both deal with our feelings and come to the truth, and then move toward a statement that will honor that truth."

What he had in mind—along with many other bishops—was the drafting of a statement that would support the pope and yet contain an element that might yet uncover hope in the pain, sharp as that of shattered bones, at the deepest root of the story. Hunthausen himself was described as doing remarkably well under the pressures, as if what some considered his mixture of holy simplicity and Dutch stubbornness was buoying him up as he sought to regain his full authority and reestablish his full unity with Rome. He was not interested in leading a schism or causing more suffering, he just wanted fair treatment on what he perceived as the face value of the things that had happened and words that had been said. Mainstream Catholics, as the bishops well knew, were looking forward, their confidence marbled with worry, to Hunthausen's private address to his brother prelates.

Meanwhile, Bernardin received another strong affirmation of his leadership of the bishops' pro-life program when the conference changed its status from an *ad hoc* to a standing committee and gave him a remarkable 215 votes in electing him to a three-year term as its first chairman. On Wednesday, the bishops debated the wording of the statement that had been drafted as their response to the Hunthausen situation. Five hours of anguished but almost courtly debate took place. The first version, which had strongly supported the Vatican action with the phrase that the decision was "just and reasonable," was modified considerably. The prelates, instead of indiscriminately embracing the Roman intervention, said mildly that the decision "deserves our respect and confidence."

While thus affirming curial procedures, they then added the sought for "new element" by offering their services to assist in the final resolution of what at the moment appeared to be a deteriorating stand-off between Rome and Archbishop Hunthausen. This seedling of a notion was far greater than the sheaf of the statement for it made provision for a Bernardin specialty, that familiar opening in the heavy curtain of loyalty to Rome through which men of good will could pass together. This was viewed as the best chance for a settlement that would bring healing rather than greater disruption to the American church.

Commentators on all sides agreed that the November 1986 annual meeting was of the "watershed" variety in refining the relationship between American Catholicism and the offices of the church in Rome. If the bishops were successful in accomplishing their aim of an honorable agreement that would restore not only Hunthausen's authority but ongoing cooperation with curial administrators, the collegial character of the conference would be strengthened. It would stand soundly on its own but as a structure whose meaning derived only from its close union with the Holy See. Everything depended on how Rome would respond to their offer.

The bishops did not wait long to find out. Before the month ended, further discussions were held at the Archbishop Laghi's Washington residence between him and leading American bishops, including Bernardin. In January, Cardinal Gantin replied in a letter to Archbishop Laghi, assuring him of the Holy See's receptivity to the American offer. A special commission was to be set up and, while technically this group was called into existence by Rome and would work under the authority of the Holy See, its formation was spiritually a victory for the American conference. The Apostolic Commission, as it was called, would be expected to mediate the problems in Seattle. Cardinal O'Connor of New York was to be a member, as was Archbishop John Quinn of San Francisco. Its chairperson was to be Joseph Cardinal Bernardin of Chicago, the senior in cardinalatial appointment. As a witty priest observer of the American church noted at the time, "When there's real trouble, you put your best pitcher in the game."

The November 1986 meeting, which had been anticipated as the occasion when the newly deployed flank of strict constructionist bishops would assert their leadership, turned out to be a massive endorsement of the moderate centrism of Bernardin and the more than two hundred bishops who found him the most credible of the major figures in the conference. Not only had Bernardin's approach to pro-life matters been strongly validated but in a series of other elections, conservative candidates such as Bishop Bevilacqua, soon to be transferred from Pittsburgh to Philadelphia, was defeated by a more moderate but orthodox archbishop, Theodore McCarrick of Newark, New Jersey.

In what was ultimately an unfortunate and unplanned embarrassment for the Cardinal archbishop of Boston, Bernard Law lost in a series of contests. He was understandably devastated by the fact that, in seeking to be chosen first delegate to the 1987 synod, he was beaten by Bernardin by a two to one margin. Weakland easily defeated him for the second position and, in painful if ironic political denouement, Law lost out for both first and second alternate positions to relatively unknown bishops. He would joke about it with Irish humor later, but Cardinal Law had learned something about the steady, consistent leadership that the great body of bishops found trustworthy. Genuine authority in the national conference was not something claimed but a mysterious quality that was earned, as with Bernardin and Weakland, over a long number of years.

The Apostolic Commission was charged with making an "assessment" of the Seattle situation. The members were not, therefore, to seek testimony but to review all the pertinent materials, confer with the principals, and to reach a "common sense" judgment on how the matter could be harmoniously resolved. Bernardin had good relationships with both Cardinal O'Connor and Archbishop Quinn and they undertook their commission immediately, meeting on Feb. 10, 1987, in Dallas, Texas, with Archbishop Hunthausen and Bishop Wuerl. The pro-nuncio, Archbishop Laghi, attended the morning session but he was not present as the commission members met separately in the afternoon and evening with Hunthausen and Wuerl.

On March 6 and 7, the commission gathered at a seminary near San Francisco to meet with the eight bishops of the ecclesiastical provinces of Seattle and Portland. Eight priest consultors and four priest administrators of Seattle also joined them for discussions. At weekly intervals throughout the month, the commission members met with other relevant priests and bishops, including Archbishop Hickey of Washington and Archbishop Francis Hurley of Anchorage, Alaska. As April deepened into the fullness of spring, Bernardin, O'Connor, and Quinn continued their mission, using conference calls, letters, another direct meeting with Hunthausen, and spending a great deal of time reviewing all the pertinent documentation. But as May drew closer, and they were ready to make their recommendations to the Holy See based on what they had presumed was Hunthausen's willingness to cooperate, negotiations suddenly broke down.

Archbishop Hunthausen had hesitated about one of the commission's recommendations. Although they supported the transfer of Bishop Wuerl to another diocese and the restoration of Hunthausen's complete authority, they had also suggested, in view of what they felt were documented lapses in administrative controls, the appointment of a co-adjutor archbishop to assist Hunthausen. He would not accept the latter suggestion and, after several days in which no headway was made, even Bernardin felt that nothing more could be accomplished. Reluctantly, he and O'Connor and Quinn decided to release their report to the Holy See at the end of the first week in May.

They were saddened, after months of intense negotiations, to contemplate the unravelling of the entire process. The commission's inability to reach an acceptable settlement would stir up the widespread anguish that had been so evident in November. Not only would the central body of Catholics be demoralized about Hunthausen's fate but they would sense that, after all, collegiality had not produced the longed for solution. What measure of disaffection from the institutional church would then occur was anybody's guess. Bernardin was depressed but felt that the commission had foundered not on the rock of Peter in Rome but on the shoals of Seattle. Hunthausen was a wonderfully compassionate pastor but only he could make the move that would rescue the negotiations from public failure. It did not seem, as the date set for the release of their report approached, that further movement could take place.

While Bernardin prayed and went ahead with other pressing business in Chicago, other developments, possible only in a collegial structure, began to occur. Hunthausen, a deeply prayerful man, had lengthy discussions, not only with his associates and others, but, by telephone, with a sympathetic layman who understood how much was at risk, both for Hunthausen and the American church, if the archbishop did not accept the commission's recommendations which were largely in his favor. Hunthausen reflected with this friend about the spiritual realities of the situation and on the damage that his handling of the affair might do to himself and to the principle of collegiality.

The sensitive caller seemed to sense what was going on in Hunthausen's soul. The weary archbishop could not accept a judgment on his archdiocese but, seeing the matter with the eyes of faith, it became clear that something more was being asked of him personally.

He could only resolve this in terms of the gospels to which he had devoted his life, he could only say yes by making an act of faith. Hunthausen wanted, he told his caller, to pray over the matter. A short time later, the archbishop resolved his uncertainty. He called his friend back and said that he wanted to say yes to the Holy Father, he would meet the condition of accepting a co-adjutor archbishop.

On that evening, May 6, 1987 Hunthausen placed calls to Bernardin and Quinn, both of whom were out. He reached Cardinal O'Connor in New York and was overwhelmed by the latter's overjoyed reaction. "In my 41 years of being a priest," the New York cardinal told him, "I've never had a happier phone call than this." Hunthausen was touched, as he finally reached the other commission members, by their evident warmth and goodness. In the long months of negotiation, he had not fully realized how collegially committed these men had been to his welfare.

Bernardin was delighted but uneasy. He had been right up to the edge of a settlement several times before only to see it collapse mournfully at the last moment. In the human ups and downs of this highly emotional incident, Bernardin's Italian soul warned him, anything could still happen. And it did, a few days later when Hunthausen, reflecting on whether his acceptance of the recommendations might be seen as a betrayal of the people who believed in him, wrote a letter to the Holy See which seemed to be critical of the commission and to place himself again at odds with the settlement by demanding to speak directly to the pope himself. Bernardin shook his head in gentle exasperation after hearing of Rome's excited reaction to this latest development. "For months we didn't know whether we could deliver Seattle," he said softly to a friend, "and now we don't know whether we can deliver the Holy See."

On May 14, Hunthausen again conferred with many people and spent harrowing hours in prayer and reflection. He spoke once more to the man with whom he had explored the spiritual nature of what was happening to him the week before. At his advice, he rewrote the letter that he was preparing in response to Rome's demand that he clarify his position on five points. In addition to his accepting the conditions outlined in the commission report, Hunthausen had to understand that any meeting with the pope would not be for the purpose of rearguing the case, it would only be an opportunity for him to express his obedience to the Holy Father. As they talked, Hunthausen came to accept the notion that the experience could only be suffered, that it was *his* redemptive suffering. The Seattle archbishop, however, remained restive. The singular pain he was feeling was not completely cured by his deep realization of its nature. By noontime, however, Hunthausen had signed the required letter and sent it by express mail to Bernardin.

Now the burden fell on the shoulders of the Chicago archbishop who was flying to Rome with Archbishop Laghi and his fellow commission members to meet with Cardinals Gantin and Ratzinger in order to finalize the settlement. Good will existed on both sides but misunderstandings and communication difficulties had plagued the discussions from the very beginning. Bernardin and his colleagues spent an entire day reviewing the matter, by now as delicate and complex as resetting a leg that has been broken more than its share of times. He needed a last word from Hunthausen promising precise agreement before they met with the pope. If the archbishop could send it, Bernardin told a Seattle official by phone, "I think we can resolve the impasse." In Seattle, the pain had not lessened but Hunthausen sent a midnight telegram of reassurance to Bernardin.

Pope John Paul II, his eyes narrowed, his brow checkmarked with lines, listened carefully as the entire Hunthausen matter was reviewed. Bernardin concluded his summary of the situation, citing the archbishop's willingness to accept whichever co-adjutor archbishop the pope designated as well as the ongoing existence of the Apostolic Commission with whom he would meet on a quarterly basis to examine progress. Hunthausen would be fully restored and Bishop Wuerl would be given a new assignment. The church in Seattle would return to a normal state.

The pope looked from one commission member to another, pulled at his jaw as if well aware of the potential consequences of the matter before him. If that is the way you think this should be settled, his expression said, then that is what we will do.

On May 25, 1987, the ratification of the agreement was announced publicly. Thomas Murphy was named co-adjutor archbishop. The story appeared on the front page of the *New York Times* and on television newscasts throughout the United States. The Catholic people rejoiced at what was considered the healthy healing of the gravest crisis the American church had suffered since Vatican II. Not only was Hunthausen's authority returned to him but Bernardin's collegial approach was, despite the long and trying character of the process, clearly vindicated. While the commission was established by the Holy See and worked under its authority, the process was a collegial one that had been regularly used by the National Conference. Without it no "good services" of the American bishops could have been offered to Rome and no reopening of the negotiations might have been approved by Vatican officials. Nor would there have been breathing space in which the suffering Hunthausen could have reflected deeply on the redemptive meaning of his final acceptance of the settlement.

Cardinal Bernardin, along with his fellow commission members, Cardinal O'Connor and Archbishop Quinn, had demonstrated again that the bishops' conference was mature enough to resolve American problems in a way that revealed unquestioned loyalty to the Holy See and sensitivity to and the pastoral needs of Catholics in the United States. In short, a recapitulation in one situation of Bernardin's entire career.

XXIII ═══════════════

Almost two years later, in 1988, Bernardin was in Rome with the other bishops of his province for their *ad limina* (to the threshold) visits to the pope. By ancient practice, the bishops of the world came every five years for a formal review of their diocesan conditions with the pope himself. The journeys of the other American bishops, which had begun shortly after John Paul II's 1987 pilgrimage to the United States, had gone well. The bishops, initially somewhat nervous in view of the tension that had risen like summer heat from the Hunthausen affair and rumors that the pope was skeptical about the depth of American Catholicism, had been uniformly pleased with the warmth of the papal greeting for them. John Paul repeated warnings about such matters as the unwarranted use of general absolution instead of individual confession in his overall appraisals. In the main, however, his assessments were strikingly positive and he repeated to many of his American episcopal visitors his feeling that he had previously been misinformed about the condition of Catholicism in the United States.

The bishops were as pleased as they were when the principal gave them gold starred report cards back in Catholic school for they had accomplished what was expected of churchmen—they had been loyal to the pope and had won from him the paternal approval that, in their experience, was the most important of all Mother Church's signals of approbation. Such affirmation from the Holy Father not only encouraged the American bishops but motivated them to rededicate themselves to their episcopal labors. Many of them began to wonder whether there was any real need for the special "air clearing" meeting between delegates of the American bishops and the pope, which had initially been suggested in November 1986, when the steaming vat of the Hunthausen case had spilled onto the floor of the bishops' annual meeting. With the subsequent bittersweet but successful resolution of the Seattle situation and the pope's favorable impression of America the next fall, the urgency for such a gathering had faded.

Bernardin was among the last of the American prelates to visit Rome for this review of his stewardship in Chicago. As he waited to enter the papal office, he reflected on the events that had teemed around the healing of the wounds in the Seattle church. Chicago was not without its problems and, although he had proceeded there with the same measured pace and long-term view that he employed on national and international matters. Bernardin was keenly aware that many vigorous Catholics wanted him to address such difficulties as the increasing shortage of priests with dramatic proposals that might attract publicity but would never have a chance of success in Rome. He had learned from Cardinal Dearden that the best service one can give to the people is to plan for the future, to put into place those structures that would both bear the weight of a changed church in the next century and yet be supple enough to accommodate the men and women who wanted to play a greater part in it. Bernardin was criticized for not challenging outmoded Vatican attitudes but he was extraordinarily popular with Chicagoans. They saw him as he was, an able, good, and patient churchman, a pastoral administrator who would always opt for evolution, glacial though its steady pace might be, over revolution as a means of reforming the church.

Nineteen eighty-seven had ended on an off-key note when the statement, *The Many Faces of AIDS: A Gospel Response,* issued by the bishops' administrative board was publicly criticized by both Cardinals Law and O'Connor. The paper, in line with Bernardin's own archdiocesan pastoral letter on AIDS as a "human disease," spoke of the invitation "to walk with those who are suffering, to be compassionate toward those we might otherwise fear, to bring strength and courage both to those who face the prospect of dying as well as their loved ones."

Halfway through the 30-page paper, the paragraph that disturbed their eminences of Boston and New York appeared. In a discussion of educational policy in a pluralistic society, where not everyone went along with the Catholic ideal of sexual abstinence as a means of overcoming the disease, the document acknowledged that some "educational efforts . . . could include accurate information about prophylactic devices" if such efforts were grounded in an authentic vision of human sexuality. Such a vision was articulated in a previous paragraph, as follows: "Human sexuality, as we understand this gift from God, is to be genitally expressed only in a monogamous heterosexual relationship of lasting fidelity in marriage." This statement was nestled in *caveats* and supported by St. Thomas Aquinas's teaching about the preferability of the lesser of two evils in an extreme situation. "We are not," the paragraph continued, "promoting the use of prophylactics but merely providing information that is part of a factual picture."

Cardinal Law had immediately rejected the notion, adding the names of his auxiliary bishops to the statement he issued. Cardinal O'Connor, speaking to reporters after offering Sunday mass at St. Patrick's Cathedral, declared unambiguously, "I am shocked to hear this presented as the lesser of evils because that can be applied to many things." The New York archbishop, according to one of his theologians, meant that relativistic thinking could open the way for abortion or euthanasia as well. About 30 other bishops, including Archbishop Szoka of Detroit, joined in the protest. So, too, did Judie Brown, the conservative Catholic who headed the anti-abortion American Life League in Stafford, Virginia. The statement, prepared by a committee of bishops that included Bernardin, was, however, strongly praised by many organizations involved in AIDS education as helping Catholics to grasp the enormity of the public health problem caused by the unforgiving and unrelenting disease.

As Americans passed through the days of Christmas that led to the end of the year, Bernardin strongly defended the statement, noting that the selective quoting of a letter by Archbishop John May, president of the bishops, had led to greater confusion. Without Cardinal O'Connor's knowledge or approval, one of the New York archdi-ocesan press officers had used excerpts from May's letter to contend that the bishops were retreating from their position and that the pa-per would be withdrawn. The *New York Times* had based a front page story on this interpretation and, within a few days, it appeared that not only the statement but the process by which it was developed as well as the cohesiveness of the bishops' conference were once again under threat. Supported by Bernardin, Archbishop May declared that the paper had not been withdrawn, that it remained in place as a statement of the conference, but that he would allow further discus-sion of it at the bishops' meeting scheduled for June 1988, at Colle-geville, Minnesota. In what its editor, Thomas Fox, described as the "firestorm" precipitated by the criticisms of the mention of con-doms, the *National Catholic Reporter* posed the question of "whether the bishops' conference is becoming unraveled."

Bernardin focused first on the principles of moral theology in which the statement had been anchored and which served as the guides for the conference policy. These must, he felt, be kept in proper perspective and, while he was convinced that the document could only benefit from a healthy review, he also argued successfully for keeping the paper, as he said, "in place" and not to give any in-correct idea that it had been withdrawn. His objective was, of course, to preserve the proper functioning of the conference as a whole, to draw on its collegial possibilities, and to safeguard it from having its deliberations overturned by individual criticisms made outside the channels of normal conference communication. Once again, as the Collegeville meeting approached, Bernardin was facing the challenge of preserving the integrity and prestige of the National Conference of Catholic Bishops.

Bernardin's work was cut out for him as the bishops gathered in the great abbey of St. John's set in the gently rolling fields, already gilded with rolling seas of wheat, in Northern Minnesota. The Bene-dictine monastery and college had been a vital factor in preserving the faith of immigrant Catholic farmers and of educating the genera-tions that came after them. Former Senator Eugene McCarthy had studied briefly for the priesthood there and, from a cramped office high above the campus, the celebrated Catholic novelist, J.F. Powers, presided as author-in-residence. The prelates gathered in a great symbol of American Catholicism's successful American adventure. Would these serious looking bishops, aware that some compromise had to be struck in order to preserve their conference, be able to reach one that would satisfy everyone?

They were by no means sure when the opening session came to order in the old fashioned gymnasium. Those concerned about the future of the conference as a collaborative group quickly concluded that the only man who could work them through the unpleasant impasse occasioned by the AIDS statement was Joseph Cardinal Bernardin of Chicago. Bernardin fully realized that his life work, as well as Dearden's vision, were once more at stake. He consulted with a number of other bishops, personally visited and listened to men with convictions on both sides of the matter during one long evening, and then spent the rest of the night writing the proposal he would present at an executive session of the bishops later that day, June 27. The greater good here, Bernardin realized, was the future welfare of the bishops' conference itself.

After reviewing the development of the original statement, Bernardin turned to the divisive repercussions that followed its issuance. "So," he said in his gentle voice, "the problem remains. And the division among ourselves, the teachers, is reflected among the people. In this instance it is not appropriate to count numbers, that is, how many are on each side. Rather, we must address and resolve the problem itself, whether real or perceived, whatever the cause, regardless of numbers. We cannot allow it to go on festering. Our unity must be restored so that we can get on with our business." He paused, looked up briefly at his intently listening brother bishops. "In a real sense," he continued, "that is the larger issue which is at stake."

He reviewed the calls for a withdrawal or a retraction of the document that had been made by some immediately after its issuance. That, he said, would be "imprudent, indeed, in my judgment, disastrous. Withdrawal could give the impression that the entire document is flawed and that the entire Administrative Board was in serious error." Bernardin raised the possibility of such an action causing a more intense debate and repeated his sense that the faithful were really not in doubt about what the bishops taught, in accord with church doctrine, about sexuality. He then came to the point that was also the solution of the problem. "I propose that, as a conference, we announce that we will issue another statement on AIDS." This, he said, would allow for the incorporation of new information, for the clarifications that "are needed to put to rest any doubts which might exist regarding the church's teaching...and how that teaching applies to the current crisis." He suggested that the second document, which should be developed with some consultation with Cardinal Ratzinger, use the first, which should retain its status and integrity, as "a stepping off point."

Bernardin surveyed the nearly three hundred bishops spread at tables before him. They knew, almost as well as he, that their future ability to function together depended on Bernardin's success in making this presentation. It was utterly silent in the old building as he concluded, "The solution I am proposing is not without its difficulties.... But no solution is perfect. Nevertheless, I offer this as the one which best addresses both the question of the document and that of our unity as a conference." After the strong applause that his presentation received, Cardinal Law rose to second the motion Bernardin had made on behalf of the task force. The Boston cardinal's action guaranteed that Bernardin's proposal would pass unanimously. Bernardin made his way out of the gym through a gauntlet of good wishes and congratulations from his confreres. Perhaps the phrase that underscored his achievement most appropriately was that from an old friend. "Joe," the bishop said, "you've saved the conference."

Bernardin sat across the desk from Pope John Paul II. They had reviewed all the matters connected with the archdiocese of Chicago. The pope looked down at the area of the Great Lakes on the map that he had spread across his desk, his eyes moving down and slowly across the path of the trips he had made to the United States. He was anxious to meet with the American bishops in March 1989 even though the seeming problems of communication between them and the Holy See, thanks to Bernardin and the collegial process he had so frequently defended, had now been largely resolved. Bernardin would, indeed, be named the co-moderator of that unusual gathering and would give the final 30 minute summary talk before John Paul II himself spoke. It would be a further signal that the National Conference was an effective working implementation of the collegial theology of Vatican II.

That was months off, however, and at the moment the 60-year-old Bernardin sat quietly with the pope. He would tell his auxiliary bishops later of watching John Paul slowly move his ringed hand across the map toward the Pacific Northwest. "Thank you," the pope said earnestly to Bernardin, "thank you for Seattle. That is an example of real collegiality, brother helping brother."

Perhaps no phrase could have summed up the meaning of Joseph L. Bernardin's career—and the long chapter in the life of American Catholicism he has influenced—quite as well. Bernardin left the audience feeling that he had only done his duty as a churchman, that despite the problems and misunderstandings and the tensions that might yet appear, he had done what the church he loved had asked of him. Then he heard his mother's voice out of the past. "Walk straight," she seemed to whisper again to the now slightly smiling Cardinal archbishop of Chicago as he moved down the inmost corridors of the Vatican, "and try not to look too pleased with yourself."

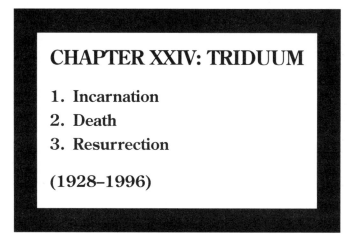

CHAPTER XXIV: TRIDUUM

1. Incarnation
2. Death
3. Resurrection

(1928–1996)

XXIV

Triduum

1. Incarnation

In late 1985, Cardinal Bernardin had asked two experts in mental health and the psychology of the clergy to prepare a proposal for additional research on what he judged to be a building crisis for the American Catholic Church: the incidence of pedophilia among priests. He was concerned about the implications of the mounting number of priests being accused of this offense and troubled by the anecdotal information about what some termed the "homosexualization" of the priesthood. He submitted the draft presentation to the National Conference of Bishops, hoping that it would serve as a basis for a collegial effort at developing a national policy on this sensitive but already highly publicized problem. It contained a request for $25,000 to initiate the research.

The incidence of sexual abuse of their charges by priests had been discussed in executive session at the meeting of the bishops in Collegeville, Minnesota, the previous June. The prelates understood that the once generous regard that was given to priests and other public officials discovered in compromised sexual situations by police and prosecutors had disappeared. Now priests were being arrested and tried for sex abuse, and dioceses and religious orders were being sued successfully for millions of dollars in damage awards.

It had been commonplace less than a generation earlier to grant societal cover to clergy and others to shield them and their professions from the scandalous sequelae of what were not regarded as felonies but as functions of the "weaknesses" or "illnesses" of the clergy. In pre-Vatican II Catholicism, Catholic priests enjoyed a unique status within their communities. They were highly regarded, largely on the basis of the esteem earned by priests who cared for immigrant Catholics in earlier generations. They were depicted in the movies by virile personalities, such as Spencer Tracy and Charles Bickford. They were forgiven easily because their basic manliness was thought secure and their trustworthiness absolute. Of priests who occasionally drank too much, a favorite forgiving phrase was "Father's sick again."

A routine aspect of such cultural subterfuge was to treat the priest and to ignore the impact of such sexual abuse on the victims. The latter, often underage boys when sexually assaulted, were sometimes burdened with intimations that they were somehow at fault and were frequently told not to talk about what had happened. Members of the clergy were usually sent for treatment in some discreet setting, such as the famed Seton Institute in Baltimore, Maryland, run by the Sisters of Charity and staffed by expert psychiatrists. The priests underwent evaluation and treatment on the campus-like facility in the same reserved manner afforded to congressmen and other high public officials. When they returned to their dioceses or religious orders, they were routinely reassigned to other parishes or schools where, a few months or years later, many of them reverted to abusing those in their charge.

The Cardinal Archbishop of Chicago felt that the bishops' policy of allowing each diocese to deal with the priest pedophilia problem in its own way was short-sighted and would result in confusion and delay in understanding and developing common guidelines for a problem he regarded as insidious. He did not wait long for a reply from the General Secretary of the Bishops' Conference, Monsignor Daniel Hoye. In a brief, carefully worded letter, Hoye said that, after discussing the idea with the committee responsible for priestly welfare and training, he had decided not to submit it to the bishops in general. Hoye did not think that the proposal would be adopted so he decided to return it to Bernardin.

Cardinal Bernardin was disappointed but not surprised by this bland negative response. The problem was no less threatening in its implications for the priesthood and the Church. These incidents now turned into large headlines, especially after the work of investigative reporter Jason Berry, a Catholic himself who typified a new generation's way of assessing and dealing with priests. The old protective screening had been torn away. The sympathy once dispensed uncritically to priests was now given to the victims. Priests and their sponsoring dioceses were to face the legal consequences of their actions. Despite an explosion of lawsuits, most bishops continued to deal with these incidents in an ad-hoc manner. They were criticized by some observers for acting like business executives instead of pastors and turning to lawyers and insurance companies for advice in handling these problems.

Bernardin understood that this scattershot approach would never be successful and would, in fact, make the Church appear to be just another big company, somewhat like Union Carbide after the deaths of thousands caused by leaking gas at one of its plants in India: a monolith seeking damage control rather than justice. Still, the problem was not easily understood and it would require a more careful examination of candidates for the priesthood as well as of seminaries and their programs of spiritual training. Although he again attempted to motivate the bishops to act as a group on this policy, his re-submission of a revised proposal was lost in the bureaucratic maw of the conference.

The problem, Bernardin felt, was devastating the morale of his best priests. Many felt uncomfortable being seen in their roman collars and, although it was a healthy response in their everyday parish work, many of them gave up hugging children for fear that even such natural acts would be misinterpreted as those of a prospective child molester. The Archdiocese of Chicago had not been immune to the problem that was so widespread that, when singer Michael Jackson was accused of sleeping with young boys, he was caricatured as a possible candidate for the priesthood.

If he could not move the bishops to develop guidelines, he would consult and draw up a manual of procedures to be followed in his own archdiocese. Bernardin understood that a set of protocols would not solve the deeper problem of why priests experienced such sexual conflicts, but he was confident that a systematic way of investigating charges against priests was a necessary first step to a serious and orderly approach to a situation that, for all concerned, was verging on the unmanageable.

A group working in collegial fashion was asked to discuss and propose a program for dealing with accusations of sex abuse by members of the clergy or any other employee of the archdiocese. A previous group had processed complaints but it was felt that a more public forum was urgent in order to make it clear that the archdiocese was not manipulating cases or merely shifting accused personnel to other assignments. Bernardin wanted everything in the open. The procedures were also to respect the rights of those who brought the accusations but also the rights of those who were accused. It was no secret that not every allegation was based on fact and not all of them could be regarded as of equal gravity.

These guidelines had a title that captured vintage Bernardin initiatives: Archdiocese of Chicago: Policies and Procedures to be Followed in Cases of Accusations of Sexual Abuse. The document was issued on February 1, 1993. It established a Fitness Review Board to which all accusations would be referred for an initial evaluation. This committee could also make decisions about when priests or other personnel should be removed or returned to their assignments.

Bernardin's work, as he had hoped, was quickly adopted by many other dioceses. It became the seedbed for the healthy growth of policies that guaranteed the rights of accusers and accused as proper investigations proceeded. On the day of their issuance, Bernardin phoned one of the experts he had consulted on the earlier frustrated research plan. The Cardinal seemed relieved and proud of the accomplishment, satisfied but still anxious to examine the roots of the problem. "For now," he said in the tones of a man who has just laid down a long borne burden, "these are real steps forward."

He did not realize that his own name would soon be submitted to the commission he had authorized to vet charges of sexual abuse.

It was a week before the November Bishops' Meeting in 1993. Cardinal Bernardin had been in New York City to give a talk to a group of pastoral ministers at Columbia University. He had stayed in the Madison Avenue residence of John Cardinal O'Connor. Over breakfast, O'Connor mentioned that a rumor was circulating that a high American churchman would soon be accused of sexually molesting someone.

Both prelates shook their heads. They had known the sorrow that flowed like a river through Santa Fe, New Mexico, eight months earlier when the popular archbishop Robert Sanchez had been forced to resign after his sexual relationships with a number of women had been revealed. People in varied circumstances were beginning, they claimed, to recover memories of earlier sexual abuse that had been long repressed because of the emotional trauma associated with the incidents. A woman had claimed to recover images of her father killing a child years before and he had been sent to prison on the basis of her testimony.

Who would it be now? Everybody was vulnerable to accusations and Bernardin himself, along with Archbishop John Roach, had been accused of participating in a macabre orgy by a troubled former seminarian in Winona, Minnesota. The bizarre tale had fragmented in its very narration. This new rumor said something more substantial was about to break.

Neither Cardinal had any idea as they shook hands and Cardinal Bernardin headed for the airport and home. He had a great deal of work to do before he left the next Sunday for Washington and the meeting with his fellow bishops. ✦

At the same time, a Ventnor, New Jersey, lawyer named Stephen Rubino had reached a decision. Daniel Pilarczyk, the archbishop of Cincinnati, had recently rebuffed him brusquely when the lawyer, who had made a reputation and a considerable amount of money by initiating suits against priests for sexual abuse, had proposed moves to settle a suit pending against Father Ellis Harsham, a priest who had served for a while at the Cincinnati seminary.

The plaintiff, Steven Cook, then 34 and seriously ill with AIDS, alleged that in 1992 he had recovered memories of Harsham's repeatedly abusing him while he was a seminarian almost 20 years before. While Archbishop Pilarczyk scoffed to associates at the idea that Rubino would file his case, Rubino would add Cardinal Bernardin's name to the lawsuit. Rubino had already secured a Cincinnati lawyer, Andrew S. Lipton, to sign and file the complaint for him in that jurisdiction. The formal papers would be served on Cardinal Bernardin on the following Friday, November 12, 1993.

Rubino was as sure of his position as Pilarczyk seemed to be of his. The aggressive New Jersey lawyer was well aware that he was filing the most explosive case of all the hundreds that had been detonated on the legal battle over priest sex abusers. This was a case that would bring him nationwide attention. He had guaranteed that in the final weeks of his case preparation. Valuing the media attention that the case would draw, he decided that he needed one clear voice at the outset, one powerful enough to convey his accusations unambivalently to the public.

He had agreed, therefore, to give CNN exclusive access to plaintiff Steven Cook, who was living in Philadelphia. They could interview him, see the evidence he intended to use, and, if his calculations were right, break the story on the very eve of the start of the Bishops' Meeting. CNN's producers had already prepared a special program on the problem of sexual abuse committed by priests. They had been in Chicago months before and had interviewed Cardinal Bernardin because of his leadership in drawing up guidelines regarding charges of sexual abuse against church personnel.

Now they could so prepare the program that he, the supposed searcher for right, would be seen as the accused author of wrong in an incident that rolled power, eroticism and ecclesiastical deceit into a sensational program that would air just as the bishops were unpacking their bags in Washington on the Sunday night, November 14, before they opened their meeting. The title of the program would be "Fall From Grace." CNN's promotional spots for this show would leave little doubt that it was a Prince of the Church who had taken the fall.

On Thursday, November 11, calls began to filter into the archdiocesan offices on Superior Street. What's this we hear about the Cardinal's being accused of sex abuse? Calls made to Archbishop Pilarczyk were greeted by a dismissal of even the possibility that any case would be filed involving Cardinal Bernardin. It was, Pilarczyk insisted, out of the question. Nonetheless, the rumors reached critical mass at mid-afternoon. Cardinal Bernardin asked the diocesan lawyer, John O'Malley, to come to his office to review the matter.

Despite the bluff assurances of Archbishop Pilarczyk, it gradually became clear to the Cardinal and to O'Malley that a case would be filed. Reporter Mary Ann Ahern managed to obtain fragments of the charges and to broadcast them on the local NBC television station. A tense excitement filled the city as the early November dark settled over it. The Cardinal, stunned by charges that were so potentially devastating to his pastoral trustworthiness, called her. The plaintiff's name was Steven Cook, she told him, he was an ex-seminarian, in his 30s, now suffering from AIDS. His lawyer's name was Rubino. They claimed to have pictures.

The Cardinal replaced the phone, turned in his chair towards the city he had come to love, even as it had come to love him. What was happening and how could this have come about? Steven Cook. He could not place him as a seminarian back in Cincinnati. If people believed this accusation against him, he reflected, how could they ever trust him as their spiritual leader? Yet, as he sat trying to sense God's purpose in allowing this to occur, he understood that the news — this false, still unseen but still crippling charge — was being broadcast throughout the world.

An aide came into his office with the information that Steven Cook had been a high school student at St. Gregory's seminary in

Cincinnati in the mid-70s. He was now dying of AIDS. The hard-to-ruffle John O'Malley suggested that, although it was clear that the accusation was false, the Cardinal should issue a statement about it. The Cardinal glanced at O'Malley. How, he wondered, can I issue a statement about a charge I have not seen from persons I do not know about something that never happened? He nodded, wrote, in his clear, manly penmanship in blue ink on a yellow legal pad, "While I have not seen the suit and I do not know the details of the allegation, there is one thing I do know, and I state categorically: I have never abused anyone in all my life, anywhere, any time, any place."

Later that evening, the Cardinal, now at the center of a news-seeking frenzy, talked to close priest associates and to old friends on the phone. Nobody who knew him believed the charges. Some worried that, despite his innocence, some faint film of accusation would never be completely washed away. Bernardin, who devoted the first hour of every day to prayer, searched deeply in his soul for strength and some understanding of what was happening. There seemed to be some evil in this, some calculated evil aimed at destroying his most valued possession, his reputation. How cruel if, as some said, the penalty for innocence would be the scar left by the sabre blow of the charge.

As he prayed, he quietly reaffirmed his trust in God. The truth, he remembered from the Gospels, will make you free. Yes, he thought, that is what I must rely on, that I must have faith in, truth that outlasts all lies and distortions. I must, he realized, put all my faith in the truth and I know that it will make me free.

The next morning, Cardinal Bernardin headed for his office past newspaper boxes through whose stained windows headlines seemed to throb and quaver with the lurid charges against him. He began to feel, as television anchor Bill Kurtis had suggested on the 10 o'clock news the night before, that some organized group had been involved in setting him up for these accusations. Still, one of the first things he would do was follow the procedures he had set up for handling allegations made against priests. He would refer these charges against himself to the review board immediately.

Three hour's drive away, in a 12,000 square foot mansion just outside Madison, Wisconsin, a balding, 58-year-old priest, Charles Fiore, was not displeased with the landslide of negative publicity set loose about Cardinal Bernardin the evening before. To Fiore, then a member about to be formally ejected from the Dominican Order, Bernardin symbolized everything that he saw as wrong with post-Vatican II Catholicism. He had shown little restraint in the attacks he had mounted against the Chicago Cardinal. Today, however, was a day that rewarded him. They got Bernardin at last, he might have mused, feeling, it would seem from his later comments, that Bernardin had at last been revealed as the "evil man" he felt him to be.

Fiore had styled himself a crusader against priest sex abusers. He had described himself to the *Milwaukee Sentinel* the year before as a "member of an informal investigative network…of physicians, lawyers, law enforcement personnel, parents and others (who)…follow up on reports of abusing priests." He had, as it turned out, been happy to consult with Stephen Rubino on the case of Father Ellis Harsham of Cincinnati.

Cincinnati, after all, was where Bernardin had once been archbishop. If Steven Cook could recover memories about Father Harsham, was it not possible that he could recall some about Bernardin as well? He gladly accepted what he termed the role of spiritual counselor to the young man. He was ill, after all, and had suffered much. Surely, he appeared to reckon, if Bernardin were as bad as he thought, then he could well have abused Cook during the same period.

The vigilante Fiore's meeting with the vigilant Rubino has been described as something like "the conjunction of a full moon with high tide." They seem to have brought a force out in each other. If Rubino had been reassured about Fiore's crusading zeal by others, Fiore was equally confident that Rubino would never file a case in which he lacked full confidence.

As Steven Cook would later recall, Father Fiore suggested strongly that Cardinal Bernardin might have been involved in abusing him back in the seminary. Cook still felt bitter about the

Church and, now dying, he felt that he might get some justice out of it. Fiore, who sent presents to Cook's mother, urged him to join Bernardin's name to the case. A month before the suit was filed, Cook was taken to a woman described as a hypnotist and, allegedly with her help, recovered what he termed a vivid memory of Father Harsham's leading him to Bernardin's room, the setting for the sexual abuse.

Cardinal Bernardin met with his regular cabinet of department heads and some other public relations counselors and related professionals. The complaint filed in the United States District Court, Southern District of Ohio, Western Division #0-1-93-0784, had finally been served and was being reviewed by the group. Such documents are adversarial by their nature but the aggressive tone of the language turned everybody solemn.

Paragraph 21 notes that beginning "in October, 1993, plaintiff began to recall sexual abuse committed against him by defendant Bernardin while plaintiff was a minor." The next paragraph says that the abuse "included kissing, fondling of the genitals and buttocks, culminating in Steven Cook's being sodomized." At this point, Bernardin interrupted the meeting. "That's where they've gone too far," he said, "Nobody who knows me will ever believe I did those things to anybody."

Bernardin had felt the outrageous margin of the accusations but how were they to be handled? He had a press conference scheduled for 1 p.m. The priest advisers, to a man, recommended, somewhat against the subtle but sophisticated strategies offered by others, that Bernardin should, as he usually could, trust his instincts in the matter.

The Cardinal went by himself to his office, looked down to see the media trucks swarming on Superior Street. He prayed and thought the entire matter over carefully. The public relations men had been through things like this many times. Perhaps he should follow their methods of deflecting this from himself. He prayed a few more minutes, reached for his phone and dialed an old friend. "I've been listening to a lot of advice this morning," he said calmly, "but I'm going to take charge of this thing myself. I'm not following any strategies. I'm just going to tell the truth and if some don't like it, they can go their own way."

Bernardin felt sure of himself now as he headed downstairs to meet the press. About 70 reporters were spread before him around the television cameras, tensed for one of the biggest stories of the year. The first questions came in like fastballs. But the Cardinal did not step back from the plate. Perhaps the calmest person in the room, he began to respond to each inquiry gently and fully. As his dignity and lack of defensiveness manifested themselves, the tension in the room relaxed. The harsh tones of doubt and accusation softened. The journalists, it would be written later, came to find a good story and found a good man instead. As slowly as the careful opening of an ancient chest, the mood was transformed from radical doubt to willing assent. This man, Joseph Cardinal Bernardin, was telling the truth.

The last question of the conference seemed as unfair as a foul in an already decided fight. A reporter just below the Cardinal in the front asked, "Are you sexually active?" Bernardin paused for just a moment in the room so suddenly hushed that not even the snap of a camera was heard. He replied gently, "I have always lived a chaste and celibate life." The transformation of the room's sentiment was complete. One veteran reporter turned and said, "I wish I could just take him in my arms and say, 'Don't worry, Cardinal. Everything is going to be all right.'"

During this same afternoon, CNN was showing excerpts of the exclusive interview that Rubino had granted the cable station with Steven Cook. Reporter Bonnie Anderson seemed to cluck sympathetically as she questioned Cook, who replied in bitter tones about his betrayal by his former archbishop. They were seen viewing the supposed pieces of evidence, a picture, an autographed bible, and a painting.

At the same time, WLS talk show hosts Ed Vrdolyak and Ty Wansley were speaking to a caller from near Madison, Wisconsin. Father Charles Fiore renewed his attacks on Cardinal Bernardin as an administrator, averred that he believed the charges against him, and suggested that he knew other damaging things about him as well. In an interview with Tom Roberts of Religious News Service a few days later, Fiore said of Bernardin, whom he considered disloyal to the Pope, "I have watched this man for years. I've seen his thumbprints all over the place."

Fiore's word was, however, doubted by many callers and, as the period of preparation for the possible trial, known as discovery, proceeded under the direction of O'Malley and James Serritella, the same transformation that occurred in the press conference was confirmed by reactions of Catholics of all ages and stations in Chicago. Still, the Cardinal felt the unjust and unprovoked attack keenly.

A few days later, he became convinced that this case had been contrived to harm his reputation. The instincts that served him so well at the initial press conference served him well at conferences he held in Washington, D.C., to which he traveled as scheduled for the Bishops' Meeting. Their standing ovation cheered him as did the hundreds of supportive letters that poured in. But, in the darkness of night, in the hours when the whole city was asleep, Bernardin found himself waking up wondering. The case was a clumsy mass of lies but would he have to enter a courtroom anyway and listen to all the charges hurled at him by a desperate attorney?

His concern shifted as he thought about Steven Cook. Surely, Bernardin felt, this lonely and seriously ill young man cannot have made up these accusations by himself. Suppose he is caught, differently than Bernardin, but on the same slowly turning spit of lies? How terrible for a young man, soon to die, to be used in this kind of deception. The Cardinal sat down at his desk and drew out a piece of paper.

Addressing the letter for Federal Express shipment to Cook's attorney, and enclosing a brief letter asking Rubino to transmit the letter to Cook, Bernardin wrote on November 20:

> Dear Steven,
>   Needless to say, I was shocked and hurt by the allegation you made against me. I was shocked because I have never abused anyone in my life.

But as I thought it over, I began to think that you must be suffering a great deal. The idea came to me yesterday morning that it would be a good thing if I visited with you personally. The purpose of the visit would be strictly pastoral — to show my concern for you and to pray with you.

If you are interested in such a visit, please let me know. I will come to you if you wish.

Sincerely yours in Christ,

Joseph Card. Bernardin
Archbishop of Chicago

It was only after the case collapsed for its lack of foundation and framework that Cardinal Bernardin learned that Rubino, against the rules, never gave the letter to Steven. The case was, however, collapsing rapidly even as the Cardinal wrote the letter. The fantasy of charges was approached by O'Malley and Serritella as if it were an old building that needed to be razed. It was obviously devoid of use but it was dangerous to tear it down. Demolition had to be done very carefully so that the relationship of the structural pieces was not compromised and to guarantee that it would not fall into meaningless rubble but be sorted, each brick tagged and carried away in an orderly manner. O'Malley agreed with Serritella's suggestion about how to deal with the opposing attorneys, "Let's reason with them, not against them."

Not one aspect of the charges manufactured against Cardinal Bernardin held up to the careful scrutiny that the period of discovery allows. The evidence, referred to complacently by CNN's Bonnie Anderson during her interview with Steven Cook, turned out to be nonexistent. The "picture" so sensationalized as to suggest a secret assignation, proved to be a group photo of an occasion at the seminary in which Bernardin could be seen on one side of the room and Cook, along with several other seminarians, at the other.

The autographed bible was, in fact, not autographed at all and was identified as a possession of a dead bishop of the Covington, Kentucky, diocese that lay just across the Ohio River. The picture was not a framed gift but a glossy sheaf such as those used in mailings for books or records.

The "hypnotist" was a young woman who took a few hours of courses and had no idea that her interview with Steven, to which she attached no clinical value, would be employed as proof against a man like Bernardin. She, too, seemed to be used by the plaintiff's lawyers. Andrew Lipton, the Cincinnati lawyer who signed off on the filing of the case, later admitted that he quickly became aware of the inadequacy of the case and, had Cook not recanted in March, 1994, he would have withdrawn from the proceedings.

Where, then, did the case come from if not from the unfortunate pairing of the lawyer Rubino with the self-appointed reformer priest, Charles Fiore? The latter, whose own checkered curriculum vitae soon came to light, was invited to give a deposition in which he could support the case against Bernardin as he had done so vigorously in its filing. Fiore, however, claimed that he had a heart attack and was hospitalized so that he could not appear to give testimony under oath. By mid-February, the structure of the case had been neatly demolished and piled up carefully to be taken away.

The case was dropped 108 days after it was initiated, on February 28, 1994. Steven Cook formally recanted a few days later. Once more, Cardinal Bernardin stepped before a battery of microphones. "Deo Gratias," he said, "Thanks be to God."

Cardinal Bernardin found that, perhaps because he had hidden nothing but had been completely honest, the truth made him free of even the residue that some feared might cling to him after the case was over. During the time of discovery, reporters scoured the country, talking to everybody he had ever known, to see if there was some flaw they could uncover, some indiscretion to bring forth. None was found and Bernardin, perhaps the most thoroughly scrutinized person in the country, also seemed the most trustworthy man as well. He was happy about all this but one pastoral mission remained for him to carry out.

Steven Cook was on his mind as he returned to his work as Archbishop of Chicago and as the natural leader of the country's

Catholic bishops. He realized that Bernard Cardinal Law of Boston and John Cardinal O'Connor of New York were favorites of Pope John Paul II and had enormous influence in Rome. Still, he persevered in his own patient way and felt that when a crisis loomed in Catholicism, it was he in whom his brother bishops invested their faith for its resolution. He had been in Rome for New Year's Day of 1994, in the middle of the case, and the Pope had invited him to be his only guest at dinner. The Holy Father offered him his complete support and had, for the first time in their long relationship, embraced Bernardin.

That great test, like a warship that had lacked an engine and a knowledgeable crew, now drifted almost out of sight behind him. Still, in his prayers and meditation, he thought of Steven Cook and his heart went out to him. At the same time, he intensified his own dedication to the work of the Church, giving up bank accounts and giving away the gifts of money he received, in order to be less attached to the things of this world. He was not denying the good of the world as much as trying, in a description of Christ by St. Paul, that he often meditated on, to "empty himself" in order to serve others better.

But Steven Cook still sat in his imagination, a young man, growing more ill every day in his lonely exile in Philadelphia. Through the help of Cincinnati priest, Father Philip Seher, who was pastor of the parish in which Steven's mother lived, Bernardin began gentle probes to see whether he could visit the young man. By late in the year, Steven had accepted the invitation for what Bernardin called a "reconciliation" and their meeting was set for December 30, 1994, at the Philadelphia archdiocesan seminary, St. Charles in the suburb of Overbrook.

Cardinal Bernardin was excited about the trip but uncertain about how he would be received. He had been told that Steven was very bitter about the Catholic Church and that his feelings about meeting Bernardin face to face were mixed at best. Bernardin, accompanied by a young priest friend, Father Scott Donahue, flew into Philadelphia on the penultimate day of the year, hired a car, and drove to the seminary grounds. Some snow remained along the edges of the roads and campus quadrangles. Nothing, Bernardin mused, is as forlorn as seminary grounds when the students are away.

They were welcomed by the rector at the main building and went upstairs to a spacious room, furnished like a parlor, to await Cook's arrival. The slightest creak sounded loud in the utterly silent room. Would Steven really come, Bernardin wondered, would he be up to the meeting that the Cardinal longed to have? A car was heard arriving below the windows as Steven Cook and his caregiver companion, Kevin, were ushered into the room. Steven, a handsome young man, according to Father Donahue, whose face was gaunt but not yet ravaged by his illness, sat stiffly on the same couch with the Cardinal.

The Cardinal began to speak softly, gently, as a priest might in a confessional. "I've come here, Steven, to put an end to everything we've been through. I know that there were many influences on you at the time but may I say that I have no ill feelings towards you, none at all. I just hoped that we could meet and perhaps pray together for your physical and spiritual well-being."

Cook hesitated, then began to speak, "I wanted to meet you, too, and apologize to you for all the embarrassment and hurt that I caused you a year ago." He wanted, he said, to tell Bernardin about his life, a bitterly remembered story of being seduced in the seminary by a faculty member and of how, when he told the authorities, they did not believe him. He had become estranged from the Church and often, when he was in a hotel room, he would throw the Gideon bible against the wall to express his anger with organized religion.

He explained his coming in contact with lawyer Stephen Rubino to file suit against the priest who had abused him in the seminary. He spoke of the intervention by phone of a Father Fiore who had urged him to remember if Bernardin had abused him and to include him in the suit, and of how he had tried by words and gifts to get Steven's mother to cooperate in the venture. Steven seemed confused and uncertain when he spoke of the alleged hypnotist and his supposed recovered memories of the Cardinal. His companion broke in to state that he had never trusted the lawyer or Fiore.

Bernardin gazed gently at Steven. "You know that I never abused you."

"I know," Steven replied, "Can you tell me that again?"

"I never abused you," Bernardin repeated, looking into Cook's eyes, "You know that, don't you?"

The young man nodded. "Yes, I know that and I want to apologize for saying that you did."

Bernardin accepted his apology and assured him of his concern and of his daily prayers for his well-being. "Would you like me to say Mass for you?"

Steven paused, "I'm not sure I want to have Mass. I've felt very alienated from God and the Church for a long time. Perhaps just a simple prayer would be more appropriate."

Bernardin wondered if the young man would welcome the gifts he removed from his briefcase. One was a bible that he had inscribed for him. "I do understand, and I won't be offended if you don't want to accept it." Steven's eyes welled with tears as he took the bible and pressed it to his heart.

Bernardin removed a century-old chalice from his case. "Steven, this is a gift from a man I don't even know. He asked me to use it to say Mass for you some day."

Steven smiled, "Please, let's celebrate Mass now."

The mood of the room was transformed by Steven's reply. It closed the ring on Bernardin's pilgrimage of forgiveness and reunion. Steven and Kevin accompanied the Cardinal and Father Donahue to the chapel. Kevin asked whether his being a non-Catholic ruled him out. The Cardinal waved him on and they grouped around the altar as the priest and the Cardinal celebrated the Mass for the Feast of the Holy Family. They embraced at the greeting of peace and, afterwards, the Cardinal anointed Steven with the sacrament of the sick.

The Cardinal then spoke softly in the chill, echoing chapel. "In every family there are times when there is hurt, anger, or alienation. But we cannot run away from our family. We have only one family and so, after every falling out, we must make every effort to be reconciled. So, too, the Church is our spiritual family. Once we become a member, we may be hurt or become alienated, but it is still our family. Since there is no other, we must work at reconciliation. And that is what we have been doing this afternoon."

Before he departed, Steven said, "A big burden has been lifted from me today. I feel healed and very much at peace." Although the Cardinal had agreed to keep the meeting secret, Stephen now changed his mind, asking Bernardin to tell his good story so others would know of it. Bernardin promised to do so in the Chicago diocesan newspaper, the *New World*. He did so a few weeks later.

Flying back to Chicago with Father Donahue that evening, Bernardin was overjoyed. Not only was the year ending but so, too, was the long pilgrimage that had begun fourteen months before when the accusation that he had abused Cook exploded like a long buried shell. A year before the Pope had embraced him and now he had embraced and forgiven his accuser. He was happy for Steven, happy that it was finally over. Now he could get back to work again.

2. Death

The next June swelled into fullness and the Cardinal seemed to enter a second spring of his own. He felt and looked fine and was pleased when, at the May 1995 Commencement Ceremony, the University of Notre Dame awarded him its Laetare Medal, presented every year to recognize a Catholic man or woman for his or her Christian example and service to the world and the Church. The Cardinal placed it, a medal suspended in a miniature bell jar, on the table next to the couch on which he habitually sat to read. Nobody would have guessed that within a month his own life would once again be suspended in a sphere in which time seemed to hold its breath.

On the second Monday of June, he presided at a ceremony at a local church. His master of ceremonies was Father Scott Donahue, who, with black-haired good looks, resembled the priests of an earlier era. When they returned to the residence, the Cardinal mentioned that he had noticed an odd thing. His urine had turned brown. It seemed peculiar but of no great consequence.

The young priest asked if the Cardinal had called Dr. Furey, his personal physician. No, Bernardin answered, slipping off his coat, there wasn't any urgency about it. But Father Donahue was not sure of that. He would not, he told the Cardinal, leave the residence and go home until he made a doctor's appointment.

Bernardin smiled. Donahue was one of a group of young priests whose talents the Cardinal had recognized and encouraged. There was something of himself in them, the kind of thing a father sees in his sons. He agreed to call Dr. Furey, who asked him to come in early the next morning for some tests.

Dr. Furey — tall, angular, gentle, as serious yet as filled with wonder as a dutiful little boy — examined the Cardinal, took some urine and blood samples and told him that he would be back in touch with him. The Cardinal, preoccupied about the day's schedule, returned to the archdiocesan offices to pursue it with the signature brand of concentration that would lead chief of staff Sister Mary Brian Costello to describe him as "Saint Joseph the Worker."

Shortly before five o'clock, the Cardinal was standing by the elevator when his secretary, Sister Ann, came down the hall after him. Dr. Furey was on the phone, would the Cardinal speak to him? Bernardin returned to his office and picked up his phone. Dr. Furey spoke almost as softly as the Cardinal himself. The tests revealed that the Cardinal had bilirubin in his urine. "Who is bilirubin," Bernardin asked good-naturedly, "and what is he doing in my urine?"

Dr. Furey did not laugh but asked when the Cardinal could get in to see him again. "Well, tomorrow is Wednesday," Bernardin replied, looking at his appointment book, "and I have to fly to Minneapolis." Thursday, then, Dr. Furey said evenly, there were some other tests he would like the Cardinal to undergo.

On Thursday, June 8, 1995, the further examinations revealed that the Cardinal, who felt that he had put the worst trials of his life behind him, was suffering from an aggressive form of pancreatic cancer, an insidious disease that enters the body as thieves do houses in the night. The damage is done before daylight arrives, the patient is already gravely ill when the symptoms that lead to the diagnosis reveal themselves.

"Am I in trouble?" the Cardinal had asked Dr. Furey when the testing was complete. The kindly physician might have been reading his own diagnosis, so wrenched was he as he nodded and told Bernardin that it was likely that this illness would eventually bring death to the archbishop.

The doctors scheduled a press conference for 3 p.m. on Friday, June 9. Chicago was stunned by the news that came, with the special poignancy of sadness garbed in beauty, on an afternoon filled with the promise of summer. The city seemed to stop in its tracks and people of every faith and occupation suddenly realized that, one sure step at a time, Cardinal Bernardin had entered deeply into their hearts.

Bernardin accepted the diagnosis in his classic fashion: He wanted to know everything about the disease, the Whipple procedure the surgeons intended to use, and the prospects for future work. His chances, the physicians told him, were one in four of living five more years. And, yes, he would return to a full schedule of work after recuperation and a period of vacation.

As the Cardinal was driven to Loyola University's Medical Center on Sunday, June 10, by his closest aide, Monsignor Kenneth Velo, he felt a deep twinge as he saw the words "Cancer Center" inscribed on the building to which he was going. Which was worse, reporters shouted as he walked towards the door, the accusation of sex abuse or the diagnosis of cancer? The accusation, he replied, "because I can accept illness as part of the human condition. The accusation, however, attacked my reputation, my trustworthiness. If that were to be destroyed, how could the people believe in me?"

Cardinal Bernardin was told that if his condition were grave the surgery would be very short. If the surgeons felt that they could operate successfully, the operation would last a long time. When he opened his eyes in the recovery room, Monsignor Velo smiled down on him, "It was a long surgery, Eminence, a long, long surgery."

Bernardin was the focus of the city's attention as he followed a normal post-operative course. He appeared thinner, subtracted somehow, but he smiled broadly when he returned to his residence on the edge of Lincoln Park. He began to receive visitors, to do some paper work at home, to grant some interviews, and to plan a visit to his relatives in Northern Italy.

The illness had shifted his focus slightly for now, after a generation and more of administration, he found, on his return to the hospital for chemotherapy, that illness had freed him to be a parish priest again. His parishioners were the other cancer patients and their families. Calls and requests piled up and he diligently tried to respond to each one of them, sometimes by a visit at the hospital, but most of the time by notes, letters, and telephone calls. Monsignor Velo helped him by making follow-up phone calls to those who had contacted the Cardinal. The prayer group, Bernardin's spiritual parish, quickly mounted in number, finally reaching 600. "I am never happier," he told a visitor, "than when people know me as a priest."

He would smile shyly, unself-consciously, when talking about unexpected outcomes of his illness. People had begun to seek him out just to touch him. "I thought they were trying to get my attention," he would say, shaking his head. "And I've been deluged with cancer cures. I thank everybody who sends one but I'm going to stick with my doctors."

One of the first people to write to him was Steven Cook. He, too, wanted to help. He understood, he wrote, and wanted to share what he had learned battling illness himself. "I've been dealing with my own mortality, chronic physical discomfort and the fear of the future (will it hurt? how long do I have? are there any good days left? etc.) for several years now and if there is *anything* I can do to give you comfort or support, I am ready, willing and able...."

Another autumn arrived and Bernardin had taken up a full schedule of work and ceremonies. Yet even here, just as he seemed to reach a clearing, a shadow fell across his recovery. Sharp pain invaded his legs, the effect, not of cancer, but of a new problem, spinal stenosis, in which the lower vertebrae tighten their grasp on the spinal cord. This condition was aggravated by osteoporosis, a bone disease complicated by the radiation treatments he had been undergoing. He soon found that, even in simple activities, such as reaching for something at his desk, he would fracture a bone.

As the year turned, he was wearing a back brace and using a cane for balance. One night in January as he climbed the stairs in his old-fashioned residence whose thick walls and heavy carpets swallowed even the hint of a sound, he fell. He had damaged another bone and it was agony to move even a few inches. With their doors shut, none of the priests who lived with him could hear his calls for help. He crawled, heaving himself up the steps against the surges of pain, and made his way along the floor to his rooms where he was able to reach a phone and call for help.

He was confined for several days after that accident and, although he rode the tide of his work successfully, he was faced with another decision. What could be done about his back? The evaluations proceeded across the spring and, as the summer of 1996 approached, he accepted the plan to undergo back surgery to relieve the stenosis on September 16.

Aware of the criticism he had received from some elements in the Church for championing, as best he could, the reforms of Vatican II, he reflected on the problem of dissension, sometimes bitter, within the American Catholic Church. Working with Father Philip Murnion of New York and a committee that included Roger Cardinal Mahony of Los Angeles, he developed an initiative that he termed Common Ground. It would provide a forum in which Catholics, much like members of a family, would be able to resolve their apparent differences through dialogues with each other.

Most of the disagreements were, as Bernardin recognized, on matters of discipline, such as the celibacy of the clergy, rather than doctrine, or the central teachings of the Church. If each side listened to the other, understanding would resolve difficulties. He unveiled this agenda in mid-August of 1996 in a statement entitled "Called to Be Catholic: Church in a Time of Peril."

In the first paragraph, he asked, "Will the Catholic Church in the United States enter the new millennium as a Church of promise or as a Church on the defensive?" He suggested that "American Catholics must reconstitute the conditions for addressing our differences constructively." That could only be achieved by seeking "a common ground centered on faith in Jesus, marked by accountability to the living Catholic tradition, and rule by a renewed spirit of civility, dialogue, generosity, and broad and serious consultation."

He unveiled this agenda on August 12. It was met, he was surprised to discover, by pointed dissent by some of his brother Cardinals, particularly Bernard Law of Boston, who immediately commented that Bernardin's suggestions "are not very helpful." He went on to say that "Dissent from revealed truth or the authoritative teaching of the Church cannot be 'dialogued' away." James Cardinal Hickey of Washington, D.C., claimed that the initiative "does not give the Magisterium (the teaching authority of the Church) its due."

That Bernardin's simple proposal for dialogue was criticized so promptly and in such an unprecedented public fashion by brother Cardinals as if he were leading a putsch against orthodoxy, suggested, to many observers, a surprising measure of defensiveness on their part. Chicago's Cardinal was accustomed to headwinds when setting sail on a new project but there was a sting in the critiques of brother Cardinals. Ordinarily, Cardinals, and other bishops, refrained from what the generally conservative Catholic commentator Russell Shaw described as "sharp public exchanges among leading members of the American hierarchy." What nerve had Bernardin hit with this mild plan for reconciliation within the Church?

Some friends told him what he already understood and accepted as a fact of high ecclesiastical life. Many church leaders were ever intent on being perceived as utterly loyal to what the Pope seemed to want. Pope John Paul II, many bishops judged, looked favorably on those who took uncompromising positions, even if the latter might be judged by theologians as at the extreme end of the orthodox spectrum. Even the discussion of the possibility of women priests, for example, would seem, to bishops with wetted fingers ever raised to test the drift of the papal wind, equivalent to heresy.

By this proposal, Cardinal Bernardin was following his reconciler's instincts, the mediator's work of his calling as a pastor, priest and bishop. That it prompted so many quick pledges of loyalty to the Holy See by others did not surprise but it did sadden him. "If there were a new Pope who seemed to them more flexible," he said wistfully to a friend, "they would come around on this right away."

He was never really surprised by people who acted in their own interest, just as he was never shocked by people who sinned after promising to pursue virtue. He had too much to do, he felt, and he would not be discouraged but would move ahead with the initiative. He was buoyed by the steadfast support that Roger Cardinal Mahony of Los Angeles offered him on Common Ground. Mahony was hardly an extremist, but as a commission member he had been subjected to grave pressure by other American Cardinals to turn against the project.

In the next week, the Cardinal was scheduled for a regular examination by his oncologist, Dr. Ellen Gaynor, a tall, intense nun physician who had a contagiously kind way of speaking and dealing with patients. Bernardin drew encouragement from these regular blood tests and MRIs, reporting the results publicly after each one of them. He had cheerfully but carefully answered inquiries over the past fourteen months by replying, "I'm cancer free."

He sensed immediately that something had changed radically when Dr. Gaynor said, after his MRI on August 28, "We'll have to talk about this." The cancer, she explained, to the Cardinal and Monsignor Velo, had returned. There were five spots on the liver, one of them two inches wide. The Cardinal remained, as usual, calm after an initial stab of terror. He wanted to know more. How much time did he have? A year, the doctor replied gently, and it might be good if he tried a new drug that showed some effectiveness in retarding such cancers. He agreed and returned to his residence, sorting and resorting his plans, taking the measure of this new adversary, rejecting self-pity, deciding how to make full use of the days he had left. As Monsignor Velo said later, "For the Eminence, being told he had a year to live meant at least 364 more days."

He called his sister Elaine that evening as well as some old friends. One of them sat with him the next morning as, in shirtsleeves at his study desk, he drafted, as usual, in blue ink on yellow legal paper the message he would read the next afternoon at a press conference at the archdiocesan headquarters. The Cardinal then read it aloud. "Is that okay?" he asked, the inevitable Bernardin question, always sending out feelers, asking for feedback in order to make any message as clear as possible. "Don't change a word," the friend replied softly.

The 1996 Democratic Convention was just concluding. It had been a week of blue skies and moderate temperatures, Chicago at its most benign for August. The local reporters, most of whom had been on extra assignments during the convention, were stirred out of efforts to catch up on their rest by the announcement that the Cardinal would have an important announcement on Friday afternoon, August 30, at 2 o'clock.

This was news they dreaded for the reporters who covered the Cardinal had come not just to respect but to revere him. At least two of them, Jay Levine of Channel 2 and Mary Ann Ahern of Channel 5, had the story early in the morning but held off until Bernardin could make the announcement himself. The other journalists sensed that this could mean only one thing as they hurried, as they had on that November day of false accusation less than three years before, to the archdiocesan headquarters. Once again, Superior Street was clogged with the satellite-topped panel trucks of the local television stations.

As he waited with a group of priests and other friends in his office, he opened the latest issue of *Origins*, a publication that carried documents of current Catholic interest. "Here," he said, pointing to the pages that fell open across his hand, "Archbishop John Quinn's talk at Oxford, raising the need for further church reform. It's followed by Rembert Weakland's comments. And, on the following pages, strong criticisms of him by Cardinal O'Connor." He paused as he rose to leave his office for the press conference. "And they say there's no dissension in the Church!"

In the hour before he had been at a meeting of the American Cardinals and other staffers held at O'Hare airport to discuss health care issues. Beforehand, and with the slightest sense of satisfaction that he was laying his aces atop the unfilled straights of his confreres, Bernardin had called his brother princes of the Church aside and given each of them a copy of the announcement he was planning to give within a few hours downtown.

The Cardinal, flanked by Monsignor Velo, his assistant bishops, and some old friends, entered the crowded room, adjusted his glasses and began to read, in the lilting cadences of the South that had never completely left his voice, to the hushed room.

"Since I was diagnosed as having pancreatic cancer last June and, later, various spinal difficulties, I have kept everyone fully apprised of my health. In keeping with that policy I come to you again today to give you an update."

Once again, Cardinal Bernardin was the calmest man in the room. He might have been reading a subcommittee report to a sea of black suited bishops.

"On Wednesday of this week, examinations conducted at Loyola Medical Center indicated that the cancer has returned, this time in the liver. I have been told that it is terminal and my life expectancy is one year or less. I will indeed begin a different form of chemotherapy entitled Gemzar. If successful, this therapy may increase my time somewhat but it will not effect a cure."

He explained that because of this the back surgery had been canceled and continued, "I have been assured that I still have some quality time left. My prayer is that I will use whatever time is left in a positive way, that is, a way that will be of benefit to the priests and people I have been called to serve, as well as my own spiritual well-being."

The Cardinal then spoke of his pastoral work over the last year with cancer patients and of how he had urged them to place themselves in the hands of the Lord. Some of his friends embraced each other while some journalists bit their lower lips against the tears that were pressing for release.

"I have personally always tried to do that," Bernardin went on, projecting a vulnerability that seemed sealed against assault by strengths that most of the reporters and others sensed but could not quite name. Guts, some thought. Faith, others judged, far livelier than their own.

"Now," the Cardinal continued softly, "I have done so with greater conviction and trust than ever before. While I know that, humanly speaking, I will have to deal with difficult moments, I can say in all sincerity that I am at peace." The room now ached with silence. "I consider this as God's special gift to me at this moment in my life.

"There is another thought I have shared with my friends who have cancer and I would like to share it with you; indeed it follows from what I have just said. We can look at death as an enemy or a friend. If we see it as an enemy, death causes anxiety and fear. We tend to go into a state of denial. But if we see it as a friend, our attitude is truly different. As a person of faith, I see death as a friend, as the transition from earthly life to life eternal.

"In the coming months I will continue to serve the archdiocese in the way I have in the past. I will keep a full schedule for as long as I can. Moreover, as appropriate, I will keep everyone informed of my health.

"In conclusion, I wish to speak two brief words. First, to my priests and people whom I love so much. Pray that I may continue to serve you and the broader Church with understanding, compassion and fidelity. Through our solidarity and mutual support and trust, may we give credible witness to God's love for all of us.

"My second word is to you, the members of the media. We have enjoyed a good professional relationship in the years I have been Archbishop of Chicago — and this will continue. Now I ask that you stand with me personally. Whatever your religious affiliation may be, I ask that you say a prayer for me. And, in return, I will pray for you and your loved ones."

The room was utterly silent as he reached inside his suit coat pocket and removed a prayer card that he always carried there. On it was printed a prayer, dear beyond all others to the Cardinal, that of St. Francis of Assisi. He concluded, in his gentle fluted tones, "Lord, make me an instrument of your peace...."

There was a silence for a fraction of a second, as there is after the sunset lowering of the flag, then the reporters began to ask questions. The first was telling, for it was a follow-up on the journalists' relationship with the Cardinal, a personal territory they hardly ever entered with other public figures. Why are you telling us this, they asked, almost in unison. Because you are part of my family, Bernardin answered with a smile, "and," he added, "if I didn't, you would find out anyway."

As the news conference came to a close, the huddled reporters broke into a round of applause that trailed the Cardinal as he left the room and returned to his office. There he sat and talked with some of his close friends. How had it gone, he wondered, in his classic post-event manner. Then he and Monsignor Velo left for home where more reporters were staked out to ask him the same questions all over again. But he smiled, paused, and answered them before climbing the steps and disappearing into the shadows cast by the port cochere.

Once again, Chicago erupted in shock and concern that their shepherd — their good shepherd — was faced with a death sentence just when it seemed to have been deferred. It did not seem fair that God should take him now before, as many expected, he might very well become the next Pope. But it was not for the smashed possibilities that people grieved anew. It was for this man who not only bore his crosses but seemed, out of the strength of his faith, to embrace them without self-pity and without fear.

The Cardinal was not wholly without fear, as he readily admitted to close friends. "Nobody can be without fear and be human. And nobody can be without doubt either. But, as I've told many very ill people who worry about their fears and doubts, these go along with faith, they do not contradict it. That we have doubts does not mean that we do not have faith."

Such was the subtext of many of his conversations and thoughts over the next weeks. He wanted to bring comfort, to share with others what he had learned through the experiences of the last three years. He decided to write a brief book while the light still lasted and, with the help of Father Al Spilly, whose translation of his thoughts he trusted implicitly, and young editor Jeremy Langford of the Loyola Press, who, earlier that year, had overseen the publication of a picture book, *This Man Bernardin*, he set out, in spare moments, to do so.

Still, as September began, autumn invaded the Archdiocese and the city as dye tinctures the purest stream, faintly at first, then unmistakably, and finally, overwhelmingly. Much like the reporters who crowded around him at his press conference — death-averse Boomers almost to a person — ordinary citizens found that the Cardinal's openness about his own death made it possible for them, many for the first time, to acknowledge and speak aloud about their own deaths.

So, too, in area hospitals, doctors, nurses and chaplains began to report that their seriously ill patients had taken enormous strength from the Cardinal's example. They were trying to face and deal with their own problems as directly and bravely as he. Cardinal Bernardin, still immersed in his work, being treated weekly with the experimental drug Gemzar, had, again unselfconsciously, begun another pastoral initiative, teaching Americans how to die.

He was identified in a meditation released by the Religious News Service as the nation's real answer to Dr. Jack Kevorkian, the advocate of assisted suicide. As autumn began to harvest the leaves from the trees whose season was almost over, Cardinal Bernardin, through example rather than preachiness, reinvigorated an ancient Christian belief that pain need not be dismissed as of no value but that it can, in a fully lived existence, be mated to meaning.

On a ravishingly beautiful Monday in September, 1996, the kind of day that only comes after wild storms, the Cardinal was in Washington, D.C. He was there for a meeting of bishops and to participate in a protest against partial birth abortions with his fellow Cardinals on the Capitol steps. The first order of business, however, was at the White House where, with a group of honorees that included former Reagan press secretary Jim Brady, Bernardin received the Medal of Freedom, the nation's highest civilian award.

The ceremony had been delayed briefly and Mrs. Clinton, the first lady, had spent time talking to the Cardinal from Chicago. Later, when someone described Bernardin as luminous, she sighed and said, "Yes, yes, that is the word for him: luminous." Yet, in black suit and roman collar that were becoming too big for him, Bernardin looked as pale as the winter moon as he sat on the platform in the East Room as ruffles and flourishes and Hail to the Chief announced the President's arrival.

Clinton turned towards the Cardinal on his right when it came time to read the citation. In a crisp, clear voice, he hailed Bernardin as "one of our nation's most beloved men and one of Catholicism's great leaders.... The value that religious vision and discourse have for the development of a public morality...should be the hallmark of a healthy society." After praising the many causes Bernardin had championed, the President continued, "While others have pulled people apart, Cardinal Bernardin has sought common ground."

The President's voice slowly filled with emotion as he continued, "In a time of transition in his church, his community, his nation and the world, he has held fast to his mission to bring out the best in humanity and to bring people together. Without question, he is both a remarkable man of God and a man of the people."

The President turned toward the frail Bernardin, draped the medal carefully over his head, fastened the clasp, and, seeming to fight off tears, shook his hand. The Cardinal, blending shyness with a sure and unapologetic sense of himself, seemed transparent as, smiling gently, the standing ovation broke on him like a tropical storm, washing over him in ever greater gusts, the richest and most heartfelt applause of the morning. A lavish buffet, enlivened by the music of the Marine Corps band, followed and the Cardinal passed among the guests, including Secretary of State Warren Christopher and other cabinet members, unabashed, smiling gently, a man whose moral authority matched or exceeded the power of all others in the room.

Later that afternoon, after a brief rest, Cardinal Bernardin travelled across the city to Georgetown University. There, in a hall almost as old as the Republic, beneath an array of shields honoring Jesuit saints, Bernardin delivered a major address in which he reiterated the Consistent Ethic of Life. Looking weary, his voice occasionally clouded, he explored the theme of bringing religious values to bear on the nation's problems. He sharply criticized congressional changes in welfare and health care, saying that "the extended policy debates on these issues, in my view, failed to meet basic standards of responsibility" towards the sick and children.

Acknowledging the need for reform in welfare and health care, the Cardinal argued that, evaluated "from the standpoint of those for whom we bear moral responsibility, change does not equal reform, it looks more like abandonment." In a broad survey of American culture, in which 1.5 million abortions are performed annually, which favors capital punishment, and is rapidly moving towards the acceptance of assisted suicide, Bernardin presented the case for an integrated ethic of life in all its stages. Those who argue narrowly for the separation of church and state tend to exclude the voices of the churches on moral issues. A "policy of excluding religious vision, discourse and insights from our search is a price too high to pay. Without vision, people perish."

After this strong presentation and his participation in the protest on the Capitol steps with his brother Cardinals, he returned to Chicago. He had also attended the celebration of James Cardinal Hickey's 50th ordination anniversary. Hickey, a gentle man, remained nervous about the criticism he had leveled at Bernardin's Common Ground project. He approached Monsignor Velo and asked how Bernardin had reacted. Velo, also a gentle man, gave a straight Chicago answer. "He said 'I'd never do that to Jim.'"

Bernardin, however, had other matters to resolve. His mind, that of a Churchman, an individual who believes in and dedicates himself to the Church both as Mystery and as an organization, turned to the future of the Church in Chicago. He would like Rome to appoint a co-adjutor archbishop as soon as possible so that Bernardin could acquaint him with the archdiocese and the city. He did not want an awkward interim, or a break in the administrative side of the Church, for that would create a vacuum in which no decisions would be made and the work of the Church impeded.

On the rainy afternoon of September 19, he held a brief press conference under the residence's port cochere. He had asked the media not to track him to Rome, as they had hoped to do, and they reluctantly cooperated. How could they turn him down when he cooperated so freely with them? He could not visit Pope John Paul II or the offices of the Congregation that advised on naming bishops with reporters and cameras following him. He wanted to follow Roman protocol for this was serious business and, although he planned to return to the Vatican in November to celebrate the Pope's 50th anniversary of ordination to the priesthood, he wanted to lay the groundwork of his mission now.

On September 27, at Castel Gandolfo, Bernardin and Velo did see the Pope, stooped and ailing himself. The Holy Father embraced and thanked Bernardin for all that he had done for the Church. He discussed the importance of Chicago as a source of leadership in the American Church in their half-hour talk.

Bernardin also visited the offices and talked with the officials in their red piped cassocks who vetted the nominations for the bishopric that came in from all parts of the world. Bernardin felt the disease's presence, although he had skipped the chemotherapy for the sake of the trip and was given a steroid injection before he left. But, for the most part, he felt good and even made a pilgrimage with Monsignor Velo to Assisi.

They returned to Chicago on September 30. Bernardin had taken the first steps in trying to assure that all would run without interruption despite his illness. High above Greenland, he also finished some other preparation. On his hallmark yellow pad, he wrote down the arrangements for his own funeral. Father Donahue was to speak to the priests and Monsignor Velo was to preach at his funeral Mass. Velo, his staunch and able companion on a thousand large and small journeys, felt tears coming in his eyes. "Don't worry, Ken," the Cardinal said, "I have cried, too."

Slowly but methodically, the Cardinal, far from denying illness and death, was preparing and strengthening himself and the archdiocese to endure them realistically and to benefit from them spiritually. He resumed his chemotherapy, kept up his civic and liturgical ceremonial obligations as well as his ministry to the sick. He participated in several mass anointings of the sick, receiving the sacrament publicly from his vicar general, Bishop Raymond Goedert, on October 3.

Bernardin now concentrated on two new projects, the convening of the Common Ground Project on October 24, at which he would formally relinquish the chairmanship of the initiative to Archbishop Oscar Lipscomb of Mobile, Alabama. He would meet all afternoon with the board and deliver a major address that evening. A week before that taxing day, however, he made another decision in public.

On October 17, after attending a Catholic Charities luncheon at a downtown hotel, Cardinal Bernardin held an impromptu news conference. His cancer, he announced, had not been checked by the experimental chemotherapy and he had decided, after his last treatment on October 4, to discontinue it. He thought that he might have six months, rather than a year, to live.

"But," he said brightly, "I'm here today. I've got plans for tomorrow and the weekend." His face broke into the smile of a man better reconciled to his journey than his hearers. "It's not over yet." No, he said, answering a question, he did not want the doctors to use any extraordinary means to prolong his life. "I don't have any intention of getting into a frenzy about how I might lengthen my life a few weeks or months." The decision to halt chemotherapy had given him a new sense of peace.

All Chicago realized that they were watching a beloved man taking the last steps in his pilgrimage, unafraid, not sorry for himself, and working as much as he could to the end. Like the shadows that lengthen on the baseball fields in the autumnal World Series, so the shadows were lengthening, gently but progressively, on a man that many Chicagoans now recognized as he truly was. More than a great leader or a man who had risen to become a prince of the Church and might, save for his illness, one day have become Pope, the Cardinal was a good man, a holy man, a saint.

In the October 24 address to the Common Ground meeting, he stressed the positive character of the initiative. Common Ground is, he said softly, "a space of trust set within boundaries. It is a place of respect where we can explore our differences, assured in the understanding that neither is everything 'cut and dried' nor is everything 'up for grabs.'" If arguments arise, "all the better" for the goal is "the fullest possible understanding of and internalization of the truth."

This draining day was the last public appearance Bernardin was to make, save one. On the rainy evening of October 29, he attended the dedication of the Loyola Cancer Center, now renamed after him. Looking very weak, and leaning on his cane for support, he thanked the group for the honor and accepted the prayerful blessing as, led by Loyola President, Father John Piderit, S.J., the crowd of hundreds raised their right hands and prayed over him. Afterwards, he spoke briefly to reporters of the weight of the fatigue that was setting in. He had been told that this engulfing fatigue would be a signal of death's approach.

The Cardinal visited his mother one last time with Monsignor Velo and remained in his residence for the two weeks he had to live. Yet he filled these with as much work as possible, especially on the small book he was writing. He turned over authority to manage the archdiocese to Bishop Goedert. He hosted his nephew and nieces for a weekend, sitting at meals with them and trying, as best he could, to entertain them.

But the people of Chicago knew that their Cardinal — for everyone, and every faith seemed now to claim him — was, like a slender white Easter candle, burning down before them. The media respected Monsignor Velo's wishes not to mount a death watch, to grant this good man the space he needed to live his life out to the full. But Velo began inviting close friends to come to the house in order to bid their friend goodbye.

On November 13, after Roger Cardinal Mahony left the Bishops' Meeting in Washington, D.C., to visit Bernardin, the media could hold off no longer and the red brick residence topped by 19 chimneys was ringed with vans, satellite towers, and illuminated by flood lights. Monsignor Velo brought him the completed manuscript of his book in the morning. "You've done it, Eminence," he said, placing it into his hands. The President and the Pope telephoned the weakening Cardinal during the day.

At 1:33 a.m. on the dark, cold morning of November 14, 1996, surrounded by his sister Elaine as well as, among others, Monsignor Velo, Dr. Gaynor, Father Donahue, Sister Lucia, the housekeeper, close friend Kevin Dowdle and Cardinal Mahony, Cardinal Bernardin peacefully completed the pilgrimage he had begun 68 years before. It was his mother's 92nd birthday. It was also the anniversary of his father's death when the Cardinal was a dutiful six-year-old boy. "He knows his father at last," a friend observed, "and everything else, too."

3. Resurrection

By Monday morning, November 18, 1996, the Church of Chicago was ready to bury its shepherd. At the North State Parkway residence Cardinal Bernardin's own family — his sister, her husband and their children and spouses — was surrounded, at Monsignor Velo's invitation, by a larger family of people who had known the Cardinal well.

Present, too, was the Archdiocesan Administrator, Bishop Raymond Goedert, and a number of priests. But it was mostly laypeople, called by the Cardinal not only friends but, along with the rest of his flock, to a clear awareness that together they constituted the Church as a Mystery. The Church envisioned by Vatican II, to the flowering of which Bernardin had given his life, was in his home, waiting for the return of his remains for one last stop at the house, darkened under his predecessor, that the Cardinal had set alight and made alive with his personality.

Outside, under a bleached-out sky, hundreds of people had gathered behind police barricades and the television reporters stood, like planes being refueled in flight, tethered to the clustered trucks and towers. On the State Street side stairs, ordinary people had celebrated a liturgy of their hearts, heaping up flowers and placing on the steps and lawn lighted candles, cards, and messages for their brother Joseph.

A mood of serenity filled the Cardinal's residence, that mood that struck so many reporters when they discovered it in interviewing Catholics at random around the city. You Catholics, they would say to friends they knew of that faith, seem sad but not depressed, you Catholics seem as at peace with the Cardinal's death as he was in dying.

The house was not crowded with politicians or only the well-to-do, for there were none of the former and only a handful of the latter. Some were surprised to discover the wide range of friends that Cardinal Bernardin had made during his 14 years in Chicago. There were people from every stratum and station, at ease with each other because they had all been at ease with the Cardinal.

At 11 a.m., the hearse from the Lamb Funeral Home pulled into the curved driveway and the pallbearers, among whose number were a millionaire lawyer and a houseman from the residence, descended the front steps and, in the utter silence broken only by the flap of the papal flag above them, removed the casket and carried it into the Cardinal's private chapel. There the casket was opened, the undertakers adjusted the Cardinal's robes, and his sister's family members were ushered in and the doors were closed on their private visit.

A quarter of an hour later, the extended family began to enter, to pray, to remember, and to remind each other of everything he and the faith he preached and exemplified meant to them. It was a sweet but solemn interlude, broken occasionally by the melodic sound of the side door chimes, the ring of a distant phone, and the delivery, around noon, of advance copies of *Newsweek*. Cardinal Bernardin smiled from the cover above the legend, "Teaching Us How To Die." From the kitchen area, the nuns sang, as pure as a children's choir, the moving hymn, "Jesus, remember me when you come into your kingdom."

An hour later, his sister, her husband and their family made one final private visit in the chapel. His sister Elaine had visited their mother who had been in the care of the Little Sisters of the Poor for many years. Nobody thought that she would understand that her son was dead. But Elaine told her as only a daughter could. Did she understand? Elaine asked her, "Do you know where Joseph is?" "In paradiso," the aged lady replied. In paradise.

The casket was returned solemnly to the hearse, the door was latched as quietly as a confessional. Family and friends climbed into the cars that would follow the hearse out of the grounds and down State Street for about a mile to Holy Name Cathedral. Just as the hearse's engine began its restrained throb, a group of parishioners from St. Juliana's on the Southwest Side began, from their places on either side of State Street, to ring handbells.

The hearse and the following cars entered State Street not in silence but to the joyful peals of celebration, to every promise of the Catholic faith suddenly affirmed by the bellringers, some of them children, some of them adults, who stretched along the sidewalks on either side of the cortege. Joseph Cardinal Bernardin was being ushered to his cathedral not in the stark sadness of irredeemable loss but on the updrafts of jubilant faith, on the air made sacred by the sound of bells.

Day and night they came, for 41 hours, often four abreast in lines as long as a mile — the good people of Chicago entering Holy Name Cathedral to bid their Cardinal farewell. Their visitation was interrupted by a special hour for priests on Tuesday night on which Father Donahue spoke of the light and life the Cardinal had brought to the Archdiocese. Another hour had been given that morning to those who had worked with him in the archdiocesan administration. On Tuesday, an ecumenical service was held by non-Catholic clergy complemented by a rabbinical service. Finally, on a cold iron gray day, the doors had been closed to prepare for the funeral Mass of the resurrection on Wednesday at twelve noon.

Guests had gathered in the courtyard of the Cathedral, stamping their feet against the cold as Secret Service dogs swept the church in preparation for the arrival of Vice President and Mrs. Gore along with a delegation of Catholics from the Clinton administration, including retiring White House Chief of Staff Leon Panetta. Governor Edgar and his wife came as did Mayor and Mrs. Richard Daley and other city officials. The largest section of the reserved seats was marked by placards that read simply "Friends."

Knights of Columbus, their hats sprouting plumes of many colors, began the procession into the Cathedral. Eight American Cardinals followed, along with the Pope's representative, the Vatican Pro-Nuncio, Archbishop Agostino Cacciavillan, from Washington, D.C. They were followed by a hundred and more archbishops and bishops, their white miters bobbing above the heads of the people standing in the pews. Representatives from the other great faiths also took places of honor at the right of the sanctuary. So, too, 500 priests came and took their pews as music chosen by the Cardinal seemed to purify the great church as celebrants did their chalices after the Eucharist.

In the front pew, at the right of the casket draped in the white funeral veil, sat Bernardin's sister and her husband. Also there was Octavie Mosimann, the secretary who had started working with Bernardin when he was a young priest in Charleston, South

Carolina, over forty years before and had moved from assignment to assignment with him. There, too, was Sister Lucia who had run the Cardinal's residence, cooked his meals, and cared for him tenderly in his last days. In the next row were the Cardinal's nephew, nieces, and their spouses as well as some cousins from Italy.

It was hard not to be drawn by the energy that played like polar magnetism around the empty red cushioned chair on which Cardinal Bernardin had presided at ceremonies. Next to it stood his crozier, the symbol he carried as a shepherd. On the chair sat the crimson biretta, the square headpiece, that he had received from the Pope when he was invested as a Cardinal in 1983.

Finally, the music paused but the familiar rustle and coughs of people settling down was absent. Everyone, from the loftiest dignitary to the least of Joseph's brethren, were already lost in a ritual that abolished the distinctions of rank among the believers. Neither the government leaders nor the red-capped Cardinals stood out. The rite had constituted a community of the faithful, an evocation of what Joseph Cardinal Bernardin understood when he spoke of the Church.

Roger Cardinal Mahony, the tall, youthful-looking archbishop of Los Angeles, began the Mass with a greeting to all those present. The solemn liturgy began with the ancient Kyrie interwoven with intercessions in Greek, Polish and Spanish. First came a greeting on behalf of the Pope from William Cardinal Baum, the former archbishop of Washington now stationed in Rome. The scriptural excerpts were read by archdiocesan officials Sister Mary Brian Costello and Brother Dennis Dunne. Everyone then sat as Monsignor Kenneth Velo walked towards the pulpit.

The mood in the vast church was transformed almost immediately from one of engrossed mourning of the Cardinal to one of contagious celebration of his life and triumph over death. Speaking directly and confidently, Monsignor Velo introduced himself as the man the Cardinal's aged mother called "the regular driver." He then set the scene, speaking not only to the 1200 in the Church but to people watching on television and radio, painting a picture of the great city sharing in the service for the Cardinal.

He then told of his many drives with Cardinal Bernardin to ceremonies all over the vast archdiocese. The Cardinal sometimes fell asleep as they neared their destination and Velo would say, "Cardinal, we're here. We've arrived." The Cardinal would then take out his comb and ready himself. Offering a perfect imitation of Bernardin's voice, Velo invoked the Cardinal's final urging before entering, "Our objective is to get out of here as quickly as possible."

The Cardinal was now alive, bringing the congregation to life as well. Velo went on to the story that would provide the framework for his reconstruction of Bernardin's life. The Lord's followers had gathered, after His crucifixion, in the Upper Room out of fear. What would happen to them now, they wondered. "Then Jesus came. He showed them His hands and His side. He stood in their midst and said, 'Peace be with you, my peace I give you.'" You can imagine what it must have been like for them, Monsignor Velo continued about these first missionaries of the Church. "They must have been nudging themselves, saying, "Didn't He teach us? Didn't He show us the way?"

Monsignor Velo then alluded to the Cardinal's favorite prayer from St. Francis, "Lord, make me an instrument of your peace." Using these elements, Velo, without theatrics, transformed Holy Name Cathedral into the Upper Room in which the mourners huddled together after the loss of their shepherd. He then reflected on Bernardin's career to people, priests and prelates, identified now with the first disciples.

In these few moments, Monsignor Velo created an environment of spiritual intimacy in which rank and position again fell away. At one moment the listeners were utterly absorbed in the mystery of Joseph Bernardin's life, at another, they were laughing freely, as only a gathered family can, at anecdotes that made the Cardinal they loved appear before them, bearing the healed wounds of his suffering, and bidding them to receive the blessing of his peace.

If, in Shakespeare's famous evocation, "He that outlives this day, and comes safe home, will stand a tip-toe when the day is named," so those who attended Cardinal Bernardin's funeral will find themselves forever moved at its mention. No small thing happened as Monsignor Velo — holding back nothing, risking everything by being real rather than political — visited the great days of Cardinal Bernardin's life, asking, at each, "Didn't he teach us? Didn't he show us the way?"

In an utterly silent cathedral, Velo said of Bernardin, "He made difficult decisions." Velo paused slightly, "Yes, I was with him when he was snubbed by some.... But, hopefully, let us never forget his forgiveness, the Cardinal's forgiveness from the very first moment, and that wonderful reconciliation of which he spoke time and time again. For he knew that it is in pardoning that we are pardoned."

"These past three years," he recalled, the cathedral hushed, "we have gathered around television sets and radios, water coolers and family tables. Our hearts were locked up out of fear. We heard about accusations. We heard about his cancer. We heard about how he was going to die. Through press conferences — many of them — through prayer services, through events, ceremonies and gatherings, he came among us as one who served and said, 'Peace be with you. Christ's peace I leave with you.'

"And in the early hours of Thursday morning, November 14, shortly after friends gathered around his deathbed as Cardinal Mahony ministered to us, we viewed his casket being carried from his residence on North State Parkway — our hearts locked in pain. But as we gather this day, he comes to us as God's instrument to say, 'Peace be with you, Christ's peace I leave with you.'"

Monsignor Velo paused, spoke more gently, as a man's first son might in recollection of his father, "I know there are many people watching, standing with us at this hour. But I ask you to allow me just a few words with the Cardinal."

He spoke easily to the family that now circled him in rapt attention, "You see, it has been a long, long and beautiful ride."

Monsignor Velo turned toward the casket, white palled for resurrection. "Cardinal. Eminence. You're home. You're home."

The mourners, this now permanently linked family, surged to their feet spontaneously, sending waves of applause across the sanctuary, the mystery of water that runs through the Scripture — waters that heal at their stirring, waters on which Peter tried so eagerly to walk, waters parting and returning, waters that wash away our sins and give us new life — this tide, bearing every seed of sacred meaning, acclaimed Cardinal Bernardin and what Monsignor Velo had done in memory of him.

The mood of the Cathedral was transformed in that moment from one tinged with hesitant regret to one wholeheartedly joyful. The Mass proceeded, Bishop Goedert's voice cracked as, in a final few words, he said, for everyone present, "we love you…and will miss you very much."

The 100-car cortege took its place behind the hearse as the deep intonations of "Jesus, remember me when you come into your kingdom" were chanted across the State Street crowds. The cars would ride through a picket line of Chicagoans of every age, color and background, holding signs of farewell or cupping candles against the November wind, as they threaded not only down the grandeur of Michigan Avenue but through the ordinariness of everyday neighborhoods until they reached Mt. Carmel Cemetery in Westchester.

The sun was just setting as the thousands of mourners gathered around the slight rise where stood the mausoleum in which Chicago's archbishops were buried. Light snow began to drift down through the floodlights that played on the scene. The mourners, their distinctions now obliterated by the darkness, sang "Amazing Grace" and Bishop Timothy Lyne preached at another brief service.

Crowds would come by the thousands to visit the mausoleum over the next few weeks. But on that evening, as the lights of the cars pooled on the road that led out of the gates, many of the passengers looked back at the tomb, now a blur of light against the blue-black sky. "Cardinal," they remembered, "Eminence. You're home. You're home."

Index